INTERNET EXPLORER 4
JUMPSTART
FOR WINDOWS 95

TOM BADGETT

MIS:
PRESS

A subsidiary of Henry Holt and Co., Inc.
New York

A subsidiary of Henry
Holt and Co., Inc.

MIS:Press
A Subsidiary of Henry Holt and Company, Inc.
115 West 18th Street
New York, New York 10011
http://www.mispress.com

First Edition—1997

Internet Explorer is © by the Microsoft Corporation. The version of Microsoft's Internet Explorer 4.0 represented in this book is its Platform Preview release. Microsoft will not provide the same level of customer support and documentation for this beta version as for the final release of Internet Explorer 4, and reserves the right to change features previous to the final release as well.

MIS:Press and M&T Books are available at special discounts for bulk purchases for sales promotions, premiums, and fundraising. Special editions or book excerpts can also be created to specification.

For details contact: Special Sales Director
                        MIS:Press and M&T Books
                        Subsidiaries of Henry Holt and Company, Inc.
                        115 West 18th Street
                        New York, New York 10011

10 9 8 7 6 5 4 3 2 1

Associate Publisher: *Paul Farrell*

Executive Editor: *Shari Chappell*   **Production Editor:** *Stephanie Doyle*
Editor: *Andy Neusner*   **Technical Editor:** *Niels Jonker*
Copy Edit Manager: *Karen Tongish*   **Copy Editor:** *Winifred Davis*

DEDICATION

To June. Because she understands.

ACKNOWLEDGMENTS

No writer works alone. Casual conversations give you ideas. Companies provide products and support. Your family allows you the freedom to become intensely involved in "The Book" for weeks at a time.

That's true for every book.

This book is a little different. Microsoft Explorer 4.0 is an evolving product. We produced this book using early beta software so we could provide early adopters of this exciting software the documentation you need to get the most out of the product. Documenting software at this stage of development requires intensive research, above-average technical skills, and patience.

I'd like to especially thank the professional team who worked with me to prepare this book.

Special thanks to Niels Jonker, President and Chief Technical Officer at United States Internet for technical consultation. Niels studied every part of this book, checked what I wrote against the software, and wrote many sections where he felt more technical information was required. His deep technical understanding of computer networking, software development, and the Internet are reflected throughout this book.

Thanks, too, to Andy Neusner, MIS:Press editor on this project. Andy knows it is never easy to work with writers, but when the deadlines are tight and the topic a changing, moving target, it is especially difficult. His patience and support were key to the success of this project.

We also received excellent help and support from Paul Balle, Product Manager of the Internet Explorer Team at Microsoft, and Bill Schneider, at Waggoner-Edstrom Public Relations, who represents Microsoft.

For NetMeeting we needed a modern, capable video and audio platform for testing. U.S. Robotics came through with a pair of their Big Picture Video Kits. This consists of a small color camera coupled with a high speed PSI-bus video card, a 33.6 kbps video modem with sound, and a ton of video-related software. After spending hours online with this product, we can recommend it to you as a good technical solution for multimedia communication.

Finally, thanks to MIS:Press for having the insight to publish this book on such a timely schedule. We hope you find it useful.

Tom Badgett

CONTENTS

Chapter One: Introduction 1

What Is Internet Explorer? 1
Who Should Read This Book? 3
What Is in This Book? 3
    Chapter 2—Explorer 4.0 Background 4
    Chapter 3—The World Wide Web GUI: The Wave of the Future 4
    Chapter 4—Installing Microsoft Explorer 4.0 4
    Chapter 5—The Explorer 4.0 Screen 4
    Chapter 6—Using the Browser and Desktop 4
    Chapter 7—Using Outlook Express 4
    Chapter 8—Using NetMeeting 5
    Chapter 9—Using NetShow 5
    Chapter 10—Using FrontPad 5
    Chapter 11—Explorer Menu and Toolbar Reference 5
    Chapter 12—Explorer 4.0 Help 5
    Appendix A—Using Online Certificates 6
    Glossary and Index 6

Chapter Two: Background and Evolution 7

The GUI Evolution 7
Interoperability—the Goal, the Myth 8
Microsoft Operating Environments 8
    DOS 8
    Windows 11
    Windows for Workgroups 11
    Windows 95 and Windows NT 4.0 13

The World Wide Web 14
The World Wide Web "View of the World" 14
Web Browsers—Cross-Platform Reality 17
Microsoft Internet Explorer 19
Versions 19
Features 20

Chapter Three: The World Wide Web GUI 27

What Is HTML 27
What Is JavaScript? 33
Other Web Tools and Objects 34

Chapter Four: Installing Microsoft Explorer 4.0 37

System Requirements 37
Finding Explorer 4.0 38
Installing the Software 38
Explorer and Windows 41
Configuration Options—General 44
Changing Desktop Tab Settings 46
Changing ScreenScan Tab Settings 47
Explorer and Microsoft IntelliMouse 50

Chapter Five: Screens and Configurations 53

Explorer Components 53
World Wide Web Browser 54
Browser Main Features and Settings 55
Outlook Express 61
Initial Configuration 62
Outlook Express Main Features and Settings 71
FrontPad 80
FrontPad Main Features 81
NetMeeting 83
NetMeeting Main Features and Settings 86
NetShow 89
NetShow Main Features 89
Desktop Interface 92
Desktop Main Features 93

Chapter Six: Using the Browser and Desktop 97

When You Boot the Computer 97
  Create an HTML Directory Display 99
  Edit the HTML Document 102
  Insert the HTML Document on Your Desktop 102
Further Customizing the Browser 103
  Custom Background 103
  Subscribe to a Web Site 104
  Setting Browser Options 108
  Modifying the Task Bar 126
Exploring Local and Network Drives 130
Exploring the World Wide Web 136

Chapter Seven: Using Outlook Express 139

Outlook Express Components 139
Using Outlook Express Electronic Mail 140
  E-mail Components 140
  Configuring Outlook Express E-mail 141
  Mail Options 147
  Creating New E-mail Messages 152
  Sending and Receiving E-mail 156
  Reading E-mail 157
Using Outlook Express News Client 162
  News Client Components 162
  Configuring Outlook Express News 162
  Using the Outlook Express News Reader 162
Using Outlook Express Contacts Manager 165
  Address Book Components 166
  Configuring Address Book 166
  Using Address Book 166
  Importing and Exporting Data 170

Chapter Eight: Using NetMeeting 173

NetMeeting Components 173
Configuring NetMeeting 174
  The General Tab 174
  The Protocols Tab 176

The Video Tab 177
The My Info Tab 178
The SpeedDials Tab 178
The Directory Tab 179
Establishing a Connection 180
Accepting a Call 183
Using NetMeeting Components 184
Chat 184
Whiteboard 186
Audio 188
Video 190
Applications and File Sharing 191
Opening a Host Session 193

Chapter Nine: Using NetShow **195**

NetShow Components 195
Configuring NetShow Player 196
Using NetShow Components 199

Chapter Ten: Using FrontPad **203**

FrontPad Components 204
Configuring FrontPad 204
Using FrontPad Components 205
The General Tab 211
The Background Tab 211
The Margins Tab 213
The Custom Tab 213

Chapter Eleven: Menu Reference **225**

Explorer Internet Browser 225
Windows Explorer 229
Outlook Express 232
NetMeeting 237
NetShow 240
FrontPad 241

Chapter Twelve: Getting Help 245

The Explorer Help System 245
Using Standard Windows Explorer Help 245
Using the Internet Tutorial 246
Using Microsoft On the Web 247
Other Help Options 248

Appendix A: E-mail Security: Using Digital
Signatures and Encryption 251

The Certificate: Public and Private Sections 251
How Digitally Signed E-mail Works 252
Obtaining a Digital ID 252
Telling Outlook Express to Use Your Certificate 259
Sending Signed Messages 259
Sending Encrypted Messages 259

Glossary 261

Index 269

CHAPTER ONE

Introduction

Until the Internet started to grow in popularity, the computer industry hadn't seen a period of excitement and growth to match the introduction of the IBM PC. The parallels between the growth of the PC and the growth of the Internet are many. The IBM product kicked off an industry that had been waiting for standards. The graphical World Wide Web opened global communications to virtually every computer user, although the Internet had been available for more than 25 years. Ease of access and the removal of usage restrictions caused an explosion of interest and access.

This book will help you get more out of this exciting communications resource by showing you all about the latest World Wide Web browser and system interface, the Microsoft Internet Explorer.

WHAT IS INTERNET EXPLORER?

Microsoft Internet Explorer is actually many products in one. First and foremost, it is a World Wide Web graphical browser. Second, it is a local computer user interface and file browser that brings many of the new techniques in use on the World Wide Web to your local desktop.

This latest Microsoft entry into the Web software collection gives you an easy to learn, intuitive software interface to all of the components of the Internet. Explorer also provides useful and flexible Internet e-mail and news clients, giving you access to multiple applications from inside this one program. Moreover, Explorer continues the Microsoft tradition of integrated, look-alike, work-alike applications. If you already are familiar with applications in

Microsoft's Office suite and have even a passing familiarity with the Internet, then Explorer will be a natural addition to your software arsenal.

But Explorer is more. This program represents Microsoft's growing belief in a local and wide area network approach to software applications and its dedication to a common user interface for all software. Explorer's enhanced features let you use it as a common, HTML-style (Hypertext Markup Language) interface to virtually everything you do with your computer and other computers on your local network or the Internet. You can use Explorer to launch local programs, to browse a local or network disk drive, to manage other computer resources, and more. In short, Explorer can become your constant user interface, replacing the Desktop motif of Windows 95 or Windows NT with a Web-centered operating environment that integrates seamlessly with your Internet Access. And you can maintain as much of your native operating system as you like by turning off some of Explorer's integrated features. Under Explorer 4.0, disk drives, folders, and files can appear as Web hyperlinks that you can access much like any other Web-based file or resource.

This feature, called *ActiveDesktop*, is new with Explorer 4.0 and portends an interesting development in cross-platform user interfaces. ActiveDesktop turns your desktop, and the disk drives, folders, and files it represents, into an interface that looks and feels very like a World Wide Web browser. There's even an integrated "FrontPad" utility, a subset of the popular Microsoft FrontPage Web development software, that helps you create new views and desktop objects in the HTML formats as well as World Wide Web pages for the Internet.

Less obvious are the subtle user-oriented features that should help all users get along more easily with desktop navigation. Explorer 4.0 fully supports the long file name conventions that are part of Windows 95 and Windows NT. In addition, file manipulation with Explorer has better drag-and-drop behavior than native Windows, whether copying and moving files or printing.

In addition, Explorer works well with other Microsoft and third-party Windows-compliant applications. You can browse the Web, skip to hyperlinks, and launch related applications—even those that require the Explorer interface—from inside programs such as Microsoft Word 97, Excel 97, Access 97 or any of their predecessors with Internet add-ons.

This product also integrates two applications that use the global World Wide Web as a powerful communications medium. NetMeeting lets you share applications, work with someone else on an electronic whiteboard, conduct multipoint chats, and use video conferencing. NetShow is an Internet or intranet broadcast facility that lets you view headlines, slides, and graphics in an automatic, slide-show environment, listen to streaming audio, and view motion video.

WHO SHOULD READ THIS BOOK?

If you are using the Internet and you wish to use Microsoft Internet Explorer to guide you on your tour, then this book is for you. Internet Explorer is easy to use. If you have even a little experience with Internet browsers, you can use Microsoft Internet Explorer right away.

However, this latest release of Microsoft's Explorer goes much deeper than a simple Internet browser. In fact, it is destined to become an integral part of Microsoft's user platforms. So, if you want to go beyond browsing the Web, if you want to configure and use Internet Explorer as part of a total Microsoft software experience—including local and wide area networking, Windows 95 and Windows NT use, Web site design, and more—then this book can help.

This book will introduce you to Microsoft's Internet Explorer and to the potential for expanded applications. Keep the book handy as a continuous desktop reference tool while you explore new features and expand your comfort zone with this exciting software application.

WHAT IS IN THIS BOOK?

This book gives you enough background on the World Wide Web and Microsoft Explorer 4.0 to help you comfortably use the combination on your PC desktop.

This product includes several components and there have been earlier releases of Internet Explorer. Throughout this book I will refer to Explorer 4 as the current product on which this book is based. If I mention earlier versions, I will include the version number. If I say simply Explorer, I mean Explorer 4.

In addition, Explorer 4 is designed to run equally well under Windows 95 and Windows NT. For the most part the user interfaces for the two operating environments are the same and Explorer 4 works the same in either environment. Therefore when I discuss a particular Explorer 4 feature or mention Windows, assume the description applies to Windows 95 and Windows NT unless I mention otherwise.

After this introductory chapter, you will find additional information available.

Chapter 2—Explorer 4.0 Background

The information in this chapter will help you understand the placement of Explorer 4.0 in the overall scheme of Internet interface products. Don't worry. Chapter 2 is a short chapter.

Chapter 3—The World Wide Web GUI: The Wave of the Future

To help you understand the significance of Explorer 4.0 and how the Internet and World Wide Web operate, I'll *briefly* discuss HTML and other important issues.

Chapter 4—Installing Microsoft Explorer 4.0

Explorer 4.0 pretty much installs itself. Once you secure the basic package, getting it up and running is fairly straightforward. However, in this chapter there are a few suggestions and tips to help you take control.

Chapter 5—The Explorer 4.0 Screen

This chapter provides a brief tour of the Explorer screen so that you can quickly learn what each menu and toolbar means. Use this summary information in conjunction with the detailed data on commands and menus contained in Chapter 11 as a useful reference tool.

Chapter 6—Using the Browser and Desktop

This chapter is designed as a quick entry to functioning with the Browser and Desktop Components of Explorer 4.0. I'll show you the basics of using this package and how to configure it for your own computer style.

Chapter 7—Using Outlook Express

By far the most popular application on the Internet is electronic mail. Explorer supports this communications facility with Outlook Express, a user-friendly e-mail and news client. Once you learn its basics, you may be ready to move to the full-featured Outlook package.

Chapter 8—Using NetMeeting

NetMeeting is an ancillary product shipped with Explorer that supports many high-end communications features: video conferencing, online chat, and application and whiteboard sharing. In this chapter, I'll introduce you to the power NetMeeting.

Chapter 9—Using NetShow

NetShow is an online broadcast facility that lets you post information that automatically updates. Use it as a continuous information source on your intranet or on the Internet. Learn the basics of this Explorer feature in this chapter.

Chapter 10—Using FrontPad

Although a complete tutorial on Web site development is beyond the scope of this book, in this chapter I'll introduce you to HTML authoring, using Explorer's built-in FrontPad facility. From this beginning you will be able to strike out on your own to learn more about online authoring.

Chapter 11—Explorer Menu and Toolbar Reference

A graphical user interface such as the one provided for Explorer 4.0 is self-explanatory and easy to learn. However, a product as rich as this one also has many menu, toolbar, and dialog box features that aren't always obvious. This chapter gives you a visual reference to all Explorer menus and toolbars. Use the chapter as you would a tour of the hardware store, to find precisely what you're looking for and to discover features and facilities you didn't know existed.

Chapter 12—Explorer 4.0 Help

Microsoft software products generally do well at providing mouse-click help both context sensitive and supporting topical searching. Explorer 4.0 is no exception. In addition, this product offers Internet-based help and reference. In this chapter, I'll point out the main features of this help facility and show you how to use it to your advantage.

Appendix A—Using Online Certificates

This brief discussion shows you how they work and details one method of getting your own certificate for use with Explorer.

Glossary and Index

A brief glossary provides a quick reference to important Internet, networking, and Explorer terms that will be helpful as you read this book and learn your way around the software. The Index is complete and cross-referenced to help you find precisely what you are looking for. Use the Index in conjunction with the Table of Contents and this chapter make this book a useful and flexible deskside reference.

CHAPTER TWO

Background and Evolution

The online and local computer resources offered through the Explorer 4.0 interface seem perfectly normal to most users of modern computer systems. Programs such as this have been around only a few years and already it is this hyperlinked, point-and-click environment we expect to see when we sit in front of the computer.

It wasn't always this way.

THE GUI EVOLUTION

The first desktop computers mimicked their larger ancestors with arcane operational procedures and command line interfaces. Early PC users accepted such an interface as normal and natural. After all, it was what they had been used to in the world of mainframes and dumb terminals, the predecessor of the PC. And, to make matters worse, nearly every computer brand used a different operating system and every operating system used different commands and procedures. Competence in one operating system did not mean you could accomplish anything with another.

Moreover, there was little hardware compatibility. Rarely could you use an expansion board or accessory designed for one computer on another brand. However, by the early 1980s some minicomputer and mainframe manufacturers began talking about a then-radical concept: interoperability.

INTEROPERABILITY—THE GOAL, THE MYTH

Most major computer manufacturers in the early 1980s supported the idea of interoperability and an open system, as offered by the PC standard from IBM, was supposed to make it possible to run many key applications on any hardware and operating system. In addition, so the theory went, users of disparate computer hardware could connect their computer over a local or wide area network to freely share important corporate data and to connect to mainframes, the large computers used to do all of the serious computer work in those days. By 1990, or so, many industry experts assumed, we would be enjoying a wonderfully homogeneous computer community.

It never happened.

Instead, wrangles over hardware and software standards, disagreements over networking protocols, continued incompatibility among operating systems, and the rise of personal desktop computing all worked together to thwart even the best intentions of the industry designers and prognosticators.

With the popularity of the World Wide Web, however, and its standardized HTML interface, the goals of cross-platform data, application access, and homogeneous networking began to be a reality. Let's see how this evolution happened.

MICROSOFT OPERATING ENVIRONMENTS

Although the history and evolution of mainframe, minicomputer, and desktop computing over the past 20 years or so is extremely interesting, it is probably less interesting to those who didn't experience it directly. Besides, such a discussion is beyond the intended and practical scope of this book.

It might be useful to review what has happened in the Microsoft world over the past few years to give newcomers an appreciation for the almost amazing strides in computer user interfaces represented by Microsoft Explorer 4.0. Besides, this microcosm of computing also reflects the larger view, mirroring what happened across almost the whole of hardware and software development.

DOS

There's a reason for Microsoft's success as a computer software supplier. It is DOS, the first control software for the IBM Personal Computer.

Until the release of the IBM PC, DOS usually meant any Disk Operating System, the internal control software that manages such low-level tasks as accepting and managing input from the keyboard, reading and saving information on disk, displaying data on a screen, and sending output to a printer.

The first really successful DOS for microcomputers was CP/M (Control Program for Microcomputers). The DOS that IBM acquired from Microsoft, MS-DOS, had many elements of CP/M and also UNIX. MS-DOS started life as 86-DOS, a 1979 operating system for the Intel 8086 CPU (central processing unit). Microsoft bought 86-DOS to supply IBM's early needs and as a companion to Microsoft's successful BASIC-86 programming language.

MS-DOS, and versions from IBM and other companies, was the stalwart underpinning of desktop computers for many years. IBM and Microsoft brought out many versions that got more advanced with the years. All, however, were Text Oriented, meaning character based screens and keyboard input were the basic functions, just like people would perform in the old days when they were connected to the Mainframe Computer with their terminal. Even today, in an age of point-and-click graphical interfaces, MS-DOS commands and features underlie the slick Windows interface. For experienced users, there are still features of the command line interface that are appealing. You can enter commands directly and, in many cases, effect the desired result more quickly. File copying, moving, and deleting are, for many experienced users, much easier done in DOS than in Windows. Figure 2.1 shows a typical DOS command line with a file copy command entered.

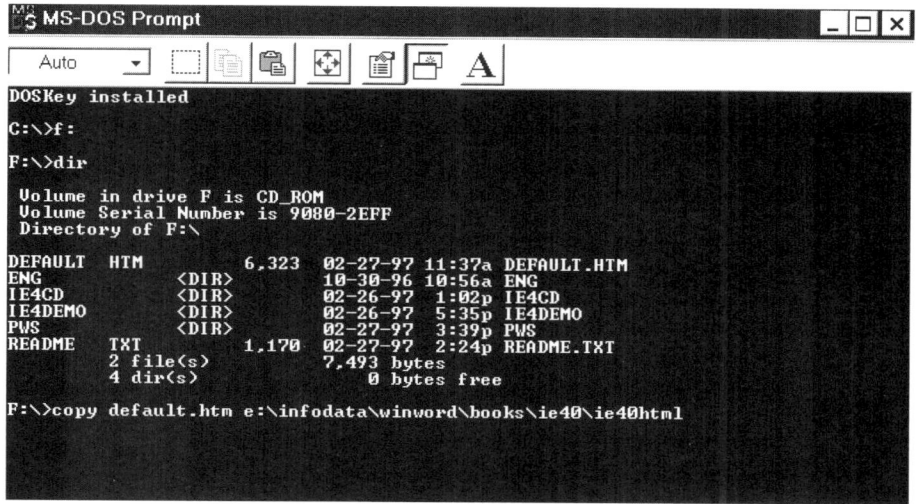

Figure 2.1 DOS command line and Copy command.

DOS is the workhorse, background, backroom manager for low-level functions. To make things happen with DOS, you issue keyboard commands at a simple prompt. Instead of dragging a folder that represents a group of files onto an icon for another folder or disk drive as you would in Windows, you type **copy filename destination** and press **Enter**. In this example, **filename** can be the full name of a single file or a name with variables or wildcard characters that represent a range of file names. The **destination** can be another file name or a directory (folder), and both **filename** and **destination** can include path information such as a disk drive (c:, d:, e:) and/or a directory.

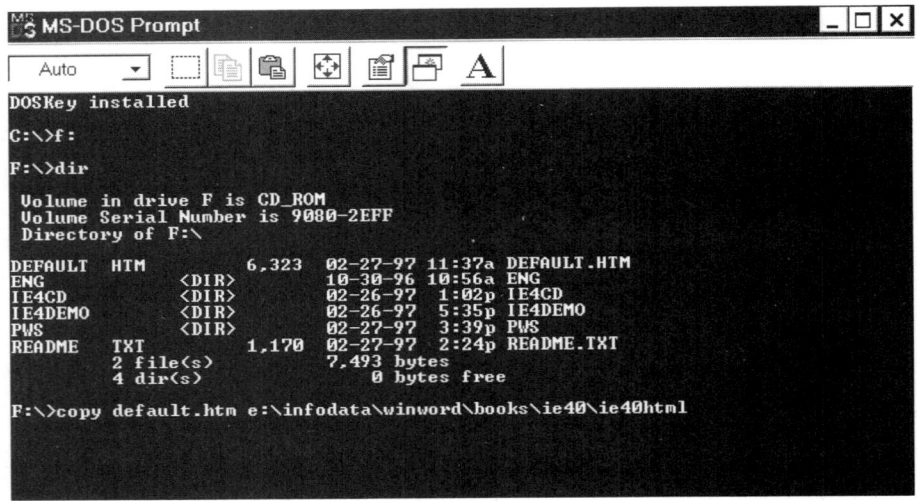

Figure 2.1 DOS command line and Copy command.

Instead of double-clicking on an icon to launch a program, in DOS you type the program name, perhaps with some path information or other data that controls how the program runs. And there is another big difference between the Windows of today and the DOS from then. Filenames used to be no longer then 8 characters and an extension of three characters. After all, IBM engineers reasoned, that is all you need, and why make it more complicated? For computer technicians, this limitation posed no problems; but for normal users, it was desirable to type filenames that were longer to give better descriptions of what certain files contained.

This is the way we interacted with PCs for years. And the programs that ran were mostly black and white and used hierarchical menus or cryptic keyboard commands for navigation.

Every program had different ways to interact with the user, and programs hardly interacted with each other. Nor was it really possible to do a few things at once with your computer. Microsoft thought this had to change, but IBM felt things were going fine. As a result, Microsoft went out on its own and started the 'Windows Revolution' on the PC.

Windows

Then came Windows. The early versions (1.0 and 1.1) were pretty awful and not very reliable, not in the least because the IBM PC and it's successor, the IBM XT (eXtended Technology) did not have the features needed to facilitate Windows, but they set the stage for more powerful and intuitive user interfaces that were made possible by more powerful computers. The AT (Advanced Technology) system was based on an Intel 80286 chip, about 4-10 times as fast as the PC and XT's 8088 and 8086 chips. It could also hold more memory, as much as 16 MegaBytes or roughly 16 million characters. Windows 2 and Windows 286, which had to be run on an AT, were steps in the right direction, but were still quite quirky and unstable. Then came the next generation of computers, based on an Intel 80386 processor. It could run the latest Windows, named 'Windows 386', the first windows that started to become really functional. It provided a consistent user interface across many programs, and it let the user do a few tasks simultaneously. Shortly after Windows 386 came Windows 3.0. By this time most of us were using 80486-based machines, capable of outperforming the 386 machines by a factor of 2-10. The average machine now also had about 4 MegaBytes of memory, a far cry from the 640 KiloBytes the PC had. The Windows interface had become fairly robust and functional and was (mostly) error free. A lot of software vendors were also making programs available for Windows now, and the success of the PC as we know it was underway.

The Windows motif supported a mouse or other pointing device, icons to represent folders and files and later, drag and drop support for many operations. Functions were also added to let a user do a few tasks at once, and to allow programs to share information among each other. Windows 3.1, introduced not long after Windows 3.0, became the most successful Windows platform to date. A typical Windows 3.1 screen is shown in Figure 2.2.

Windows for Workgroups

Windows for Workgroups added a networking component to the familiar Windows graphical user interface (GUI). Two or more computers running Windows for Workgroups (WFW) could communicate over a local area network such as Ethernet or token ring to share disk drives and printers or to send and receive files and electronic mail. By this time, more robust networking schemes, including Novell, were around, but for small workgroups, small businesses, and home and school users, WFW was a giant step in the right direction.

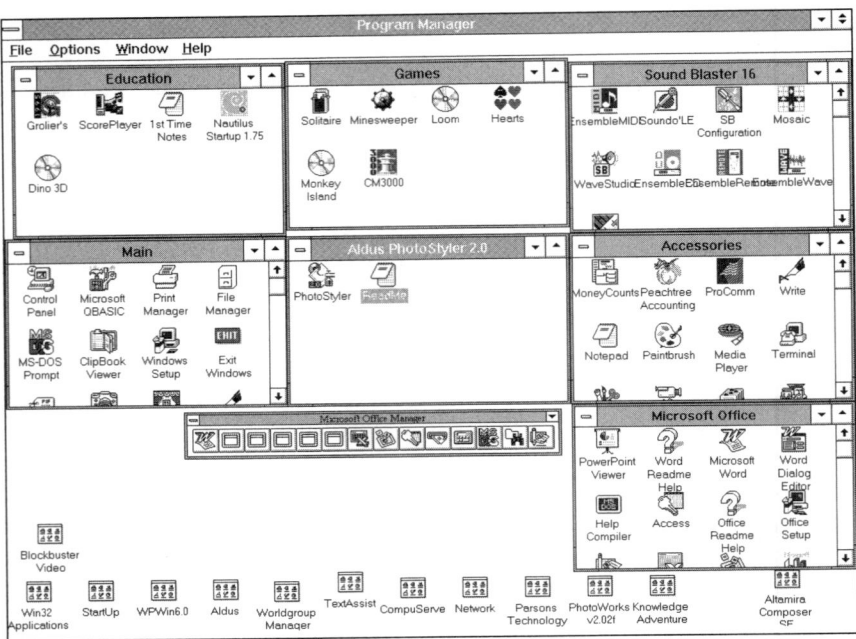

Figure 2.2 Typical Windows 3.1 Desktop.

It was successful because it allowed any computer in the network to make its printer or hard disk available to other computers, whereas almost every other networking scheme required dedicated, expensive and complicated servers to do this. Users didn't have to purchase, install and learn third-party software, which was mostly complex and not GUI driven, just so they could share a printer or a disk drive among a few computers. In parallel with Windows 3 and Windows 3.1, Microsoft started experimenting with new technologies in a separate version of the Windows platform, that was intended to run on more powerful PC computers in more demanding environments. This version of windows was called Windows NT (New Technology). The major new innovation was that this new version of Windows used all the power of the 386 and 486 processors. Initial versions 3.0 and 3.1 were unstable, so version 3.51 was the first truly functional Windows NT for many users. This platform is popular as a network server or a workstation for computer applications that need a lot of horsepower, not the masses. There are two flavors of NT, the server and the workstation version. The first one is meant primarily to serve many PC users for disk storage and printing, the later one is more meant as a workstation Operating System for power users for whom Windows 3.11 just was not cutting it. Where Windows 3.1 users could still make do with a 286 machine with about 2 MegaBytes of Memory, Windows NT users had to have a 386 and 8 MegaBytes.

Windows 95 and Windows NT 4.0

Windows 95 was the next giant step in Microsoft operating system evolution for the masses. It built on the strengths—and learned from the mistakes made—in previous Windows and Windows NT versions. Because much of the technology used in Windows NT would now be usable on people's home computers, and had become easier to use, much of it was included in Windows 95. Windows 95 is much more user-friendly and, in my experience, is much easier for the beginning user to learn than any of the previous versions (though entrenched Windows 3.1 users frequently rail at the changes). Figure 2.3 shows a typical Windows 95 desktop.

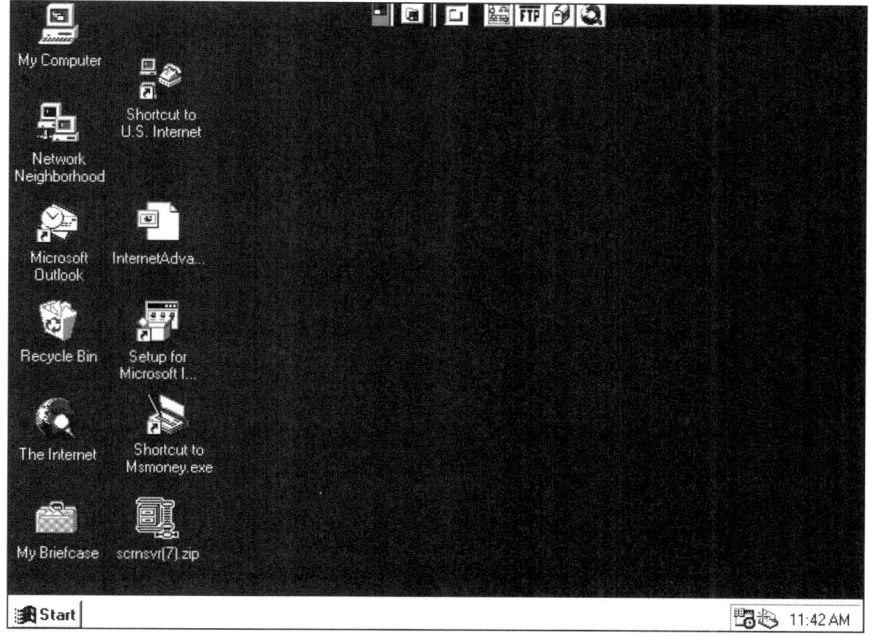

Figure 2.3 Typical Windows 95 Desktop.

A new more user-oriented graphical user interface (GUI) was invented. The minimum system requirements were starting to look much like those of NT in earlier days: An 80386 computer with 8 megabytes of RAM. Windows 95 also strengthened the intrinsic networking components of the Microsoft operating system to support dial-up networking and more networking protocols including TCP/IP (Transfer Control Protocol/Internet Protocol), which opens the door to easy Internet access.

The latest windows NT version is 4.0. It has many of the improvements found in Windows 95, like the GUI and many of its networking and ease of use capabilities. Still, NT is more complex to operate and more demanding on the machine than 95, but today most desktop machine have a 486 or Pentium processor and more than enough RAM to run either operating system. Microsoft is bringing the two platforms closer and closer together, and Explorer 4 is a perfect example of this evolution: It will work on either Windows 95 or Windows NT 4.0, and will make them look and work identical for as far possible. These days, Pentium powered PC's are more than one-hundred times as powerful as the first PC, and they have on average more than 20 times the amount of memory. As operating systems get more powerful, and hardware gets more affordable, this is a trend we will continue to see. As a rule of thumb, there will always be software that will require faster hardware as features continue to be added.

The World Wide Web

Against this increasingly graphics background, the exploding Internet began offering users an intuitive, graphical front end for online data. As with Windows, the World Wide Web interface evolved over several iterations, through several software technologies, to today's state that includes local and remote *object* access, sound, graphics, animation, full-motion video, application and data linking, and more.

The evolution is not complete, by any means, but the capabilities offered by Microsoft Explorer 4.0, IMHO are what we've all been waiting for—longing for—for many years. Figure 2.4 shows one Explorer 4.0 view.

The World Wide Web "View of the World"

In the beginning, the World Wide Web was just a better way of viewing online information. Instead of all-text menus, the Web provided graphics and color, similar to what users of Windows and Macintosh computers expected. This first effort was a great improvement over the text menus, but there wasn't much material available for this environment, nor was there much variety.

The Web browser software was being developed mainly by universities and government-funded organizations to support their research.

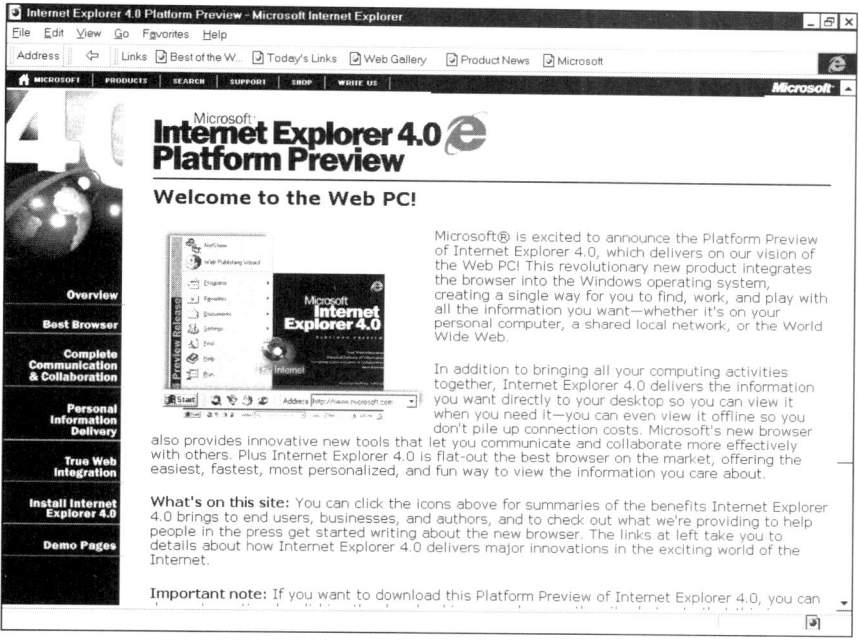

Figure 2.4 Typical Explorer 4.0 Screen.

Today, that has changed. The World Wide Web has added true multimedia access to information stored on one or more remote computers. By *multimedia* I mean graphics images, animation, motion video, sound, and audio. Many of these interactive features have only been added in the last few years, after commercial companies such as Netscape Communications and Microsoft spent large amounts of research money on developing them. All of these objects on your computer screen through Internet Explorer are connected by *hyperlinks*, logical associations that connect everything together and let you jump easily from file to file and host to host to access the data you need. With this object-oriented desktop, you rarely need to concern yourself with where specific pieces of data reside or even in what format they are stored. The server and your client software work together to find and present the data you choose with the click of your mouse. An object in this sense can be a picture, an icon, a button or a block of text. To Internet Explorer, everything is an object.

This automatic navigation across multiple servers to a variety of files and other objects is done with a feature called *Hyperlinks*. A Hyperlink is simply a bit of software instruction attached to an object that tells the software where to go for the next object. Consider the typical World Wide Web page shown in Figure 2.5.

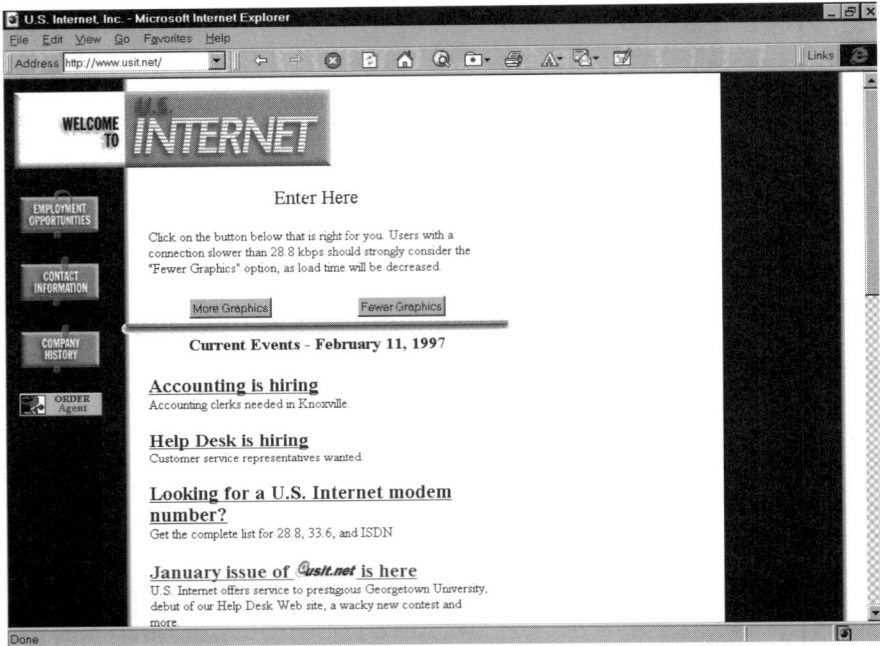

Figure 2.5 A Typical World Wide Web page with Hyperlinks.

The underlined text on this screen represents Hyperlinks to other portions of this same World Wide Web site. Other Hyperlinks can point to pages on other hosts and these hosts can be separated by cities, states, or countries. The interactive nature of these links minimizes concern over where the information actually resides. In the old DOS environment, users had to constantly remember something about the directory tree, which directories (folders) were subordinate to others, and where individual files had been placed.

In the Hyperlinked, online world, you can track this information in your mind if you want to, but the good news is: you don't have to. And, instead of pointing just to files and folders, Hyperlinks can present remote locations, sounds, motion video, animation--any object the computer can process. Consider the site diagram shown in Figure 2.6. This shows how various pages within a Web site might map together.

As you, the user, move down a path of Hyperlinks, you see new information, usually based on the previous display. And you can back up, move forward, and jump ahead in about any order whenever you like. Whether or not you are familiar with earlier computer display methods, I think you can see the value of the World Wide Web motif.

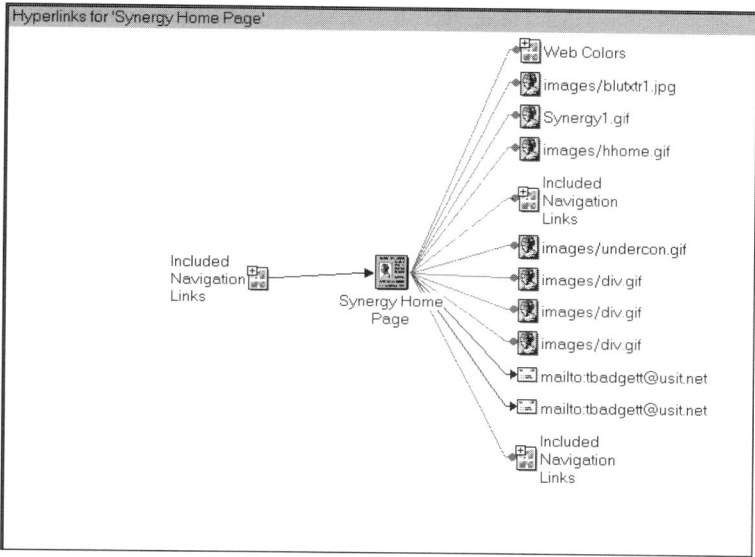

Figure 2.6 World Wide Web site diagram.

Objects that have a Hyperlink attached are easily recognizable; your pointer will change from an Arrow to a Hand with a Pointing Finger when it hovers over them. Making the computer 'fetch' what the Hyperlink is pointing to is as simple as clicking the left mouse button. You are probably familiar with this concept from the Windows Help File, where clicking on an underlined piece of text will let you navigate. Hyperlinks enable you to navigate in the context of the World Wide Web.

Information gathering in this environment is more productive and more interesting, but because of the universal interest in the World Wide Web, an even more important benefit has been provided: almost complete cross-platform software support.

Web Browsers—Cross-Platform Reality

Because the World Wide Web is a client-server environment in which the user interface is displayed and managed on the user desktop and the data is managed and maintained on remote hosts, this is a true cross-platform environment.

Moreover, most of the informational and programmatic data associated with the Web is interpretive, meaning it is stored as plain text on a host (server) that is processed on the client (a local PC, Macintosh, etc.) as it is displayed. That further enables the processing of this information on a variety of hardware and software platforms.

World Wide Web client software exists for Intel-based PCs, for the Macintosh, for the PowerPC platforms, for Digital and other RISC workstations, and for hardware running almost any kind of UNIX, and even some other software platforms. Now users need not be particularly concerned as to their brand or type of hardware. They can still access most sites on the World Wide Web, navigate the Web, and manipulate the software running there.

This hardware-independent environment opens some exciting possibilities for companies and individuals. In the past, if a company wanted to implement a corporate-wide application such as a client database or a knowledge base, a decision first had to be made about the hardware platform. In some companies, particularly those that dealt in publishing, video, or other graphics-based computer jobs, this was a difficult decision, because multiple platforms were already in heavy use. Accounting and engineering people generally used Intel-based or RISC based platforms and the graphics people used Macintosh machines.

I know from personal experience that such situations caused a lot of headache and heartache, and they also cost thousands of dollars in custom programming or multiple software purchases. Today, the HTML environment, coupled with compliant World Wide Web browsers that run on virtually any hardware platform, is changing this situation. Companies can now choose computer hardware for the right reasons, including user preference, performance, and software support, yet still install corporate-wide applications that don't isolate or discriminate against any user.

For example, a company might decide to install a Windows NT server on a Pentium Pro box to serve as the intranet or Internet server for a corporate-wide database. With an HTML-compliant World Wide Web server and an SQL-based (Structured Query Language) database that is accessible through this net server, users anywhere in the enterprise using about any type of computer hardware can read the data, enter new records, edit records, and write reports. Moreover, training time is greatly reduced because users are accessing the information through a familiar interface. Also, new computer users are able to learn data acquisition over the Internet or an intranet, or learn to use e-mail and other computer skills quickly and easily, no matter what platform they learn first. Since this world wide web-based solution is Internet ready, it also facilitates growth and future expansion.

MICROSOFT INTERNET EXPLORER

Microsoft Internet Explorer is one of the many popular World Wide Web browsers. In reality, Internet Explorer is one of two top Web products, the other being Netscape Navigator. While there are a number of browser products in the marketplace, most are either an adaptation of Netscape Navigator or the earlier Mosaic program, on which Netscape Navigator was based. In effect, Navigator and Explorer together account for the vast majority of Web browsers in use today.

Versions

Internet Explorer has been through many revisions, as has any dynamic, growing application. As this book is written, there are only three versions of Microsoft Internet Explorer that have any real relevance for most of us: versions 2, 3, and 4. Within each of these versions there are two or more releases, each adding one or more features. Mostly these revisions reflect support for additional HTML features, adding power and capability to the program, or, particularly in the early releases, adding compatibility with Netscape Navigator.

In addition, there are versions of Internet Explorer designed for different hardware and software platforms. You can get a version for the Macintosh or one to run under Windows NT, Windows 95, or Windows 3.1. However, with Explorer 4.0, Microsoft has taken a leap forward in the browser wars and in their own philosophy about what a browser is and what it does.

Microsoft has stated that Internet Explorer 4.0:

> ...is all about integrating the PC and the Internet, which is Microsoft's overall concept known as the Web PC. This concept embraces the importance of integrating Web tasks into a proven and popular user interface design that leverages current investments in training and solves key customer problems that exist today. The Web PC is the next-step delivery vehicle in Microsoft's overall vision of Information at Your Fingertips (IAYF), which is Microsoft's goal of making and finding information easy and painless, regardless of where it is stored.

As you work with Explorer 4.0 you soon will see this Microsoft vision. The desire is to provide a single, seamless desktop environment that allows users to access simultaneously, through a single interface, information stored on an individual PC, on a local area network, or anywhere in the world on the Internet.

This integration of a Web browser into the operating system interface "leverages the existing investment in training," according to Microsoft. The vision of lowering the barrier between the local computer and the global network is shared by many companies. Sun Microsystems for example, reflects it in its creed, "the computer is the network."

Features

Microsoft has an advantage over the early entrants into the Web browser arena, not only because of its size and broad product base, but because the company can benefit from the experience of those who went before. Explorer 2.0 was a natural-build on the first Explorer release and Explorer 3.0 offered new features and enhancements over Explorer 2.0. Now, according to Microsoft, Explorer 4.0 is designed to provide the compatibility required to fit into the industry, but it also adds features and facilities most requested by users of earlier versions.

Specifically, Microsoft promoted four major goals for Explorer 4.0 while the product was still under development: to make the best browser possible, to provide complete communication and collaboration, to support personalized information delivery, and to provide true Web integration. Tables 2.1–2.3 reflect Microsoft's opinion of how Explorer 4.0 meets these goals. Throughout this book we will look at these specific Explorer 4.0 features and capabilities.

Best Browser

Many users, according to Microsoft, say that finding useful information on the Internet is difficult. Explorer 4.0 is based on "user-focused improvements" to the popular Explorer 3.0 to offer "the easiest, most personalized, and fun way to view the information you care about," according to Microsoft.

Browser features that Microsoft feels are important enough to set off Explorer 4.0 from the competition are listed in Table 2.1.

Table 2.1 Explorer 4.0's User-Focused Improvements

Best Browser Feature	Description
AutoComplete	Recalls Internet addresses so you don't have to retype them completely as you type.
Security	Increased security features help keep conversations and commercial transactions private

Best Browser Feature	Description
Search Pane	View search engine results and World Wide Web pages at the same time
Internet Connection Wizard	Automates Internet connections
HTML Help	Help is built into Web pages, keeping help information up to date and readily available
Pics	Rating services to help you manage access to avoid certain content if you wish
Documentation	Centralized documentation helps you find information about any component from one place
Offline Reading	Reduce online time by viewing selected sites offline
Smart Favorites	Tells you automatically when one of your favorite Web pages has been updated
Custom Home Page	You can customize the Internet Start page to display selected news, sports, weather, and other information
Drag and Drop Favorites	Lets you rearrange your favorites files by dragging and dropping, regardless of alphabetical order
Drag and Drop QuickLinks	Lets you drag-and-drop a cool site onto the Links bar
ActiveX	Provides software components for Web pages
Java	Rising Web programming language support to enhance Web site display
Dynamic HTML	Adds new features to Web pages and Web page development, including the ability to dynamically change text and to call up information linked to specific text on a page
ActiveX Scripting	Allows ActiveX controls to interact with each other and with other applets
Multimedia	State of the art video, sound and animation support for Web pages
VBScript and JavaScript	Two flexible scripting tools that can be used to make Web pages do simple programmed tasks and interact better with the user

Complete Communication and Collaboration

Another user complaint, according to Microsoft, is that present Internet bandwidth limits the productivity and enjoyment of browsing the Web, and communications capabilities "are sorely lacking." Explorer 4.0 is more than just a Web browser; it includes "a complete and integrated set of tools for every type of user." For example, integrated with Explorer 4.0 is an e-mail client that will handle local and remote mail. It also includes support for conferencing, broadcasting and some Web authoring capabilities.

Table 2.2 Explorer 4.0's Communication Features

Communication Feature	Description
Messaging	Use Outlook Express to exchange e-mail and newsgroup messages. Also supports HTML features.
Authoring	Use FrontPad to create and edit Web pages and post them on the Internet or an Intranet.
Conferencing	The NetMeeting conference client is part of Explorer 4.0. This software lets you hold video and voice conversations, share software applications, participate in chat sessions, and share a whiteboard for drawing with other people.
Publishing	The integral Web Publishing Wizard steps you through the process of posting your Web site to a server. The included Personal Web Server turns any computer into a Web Server, making it easy to publish your own Web pages on a local area network.
Broadcasting	NetShow broadcasts high-impact, low-bandwidth streaming video and more to computer desktops for entertainment, training, sales, event coverage, and more.

Explorer 4.0 ships with Outlook Express, a subset of Microsoft's groupware tool Outlook that ships with Office 97 or can be purchased as a standalone product. A Microsoft upgrade path lets you move up to the full Outlook 97 if you need additional features. The FrontPad Web authoring tools built into Explorer 4.0 are probably all that most casual users need. If you want more power, you can upgrade

to Front Page, Microsoft's full-featured Web authoring tool. This is a familiar scenario for Microsoft. Word is a premier word-processing package, but WordPad is included with Windows to provide editing capabilities beyond Notepad. Word will read WordPad documents and you can then upgrade to the full-featured Word at your convenience. The FrontPad to Front Page path is a similar design.

Some communications features Microsoft promotes for Explorer 4.0 are listed in Table 2.2.

Personalized Information Delivery

Users have told Microsoft they find that Web content rarely lives up to expectations. In an attempt to answer these complaints, Microsoft has designed into Explorer 4.0 the ability to have specified information delivered directly to the user desktop. In addition, Explorer 4.0 can notify users when a favorite Web site changes, and lets you read Web sites offline to help reduce expense when you pay per-minute usage charges for Internet connectivity.

Personalized information delivery makes use of the so-called "push and pull" technology. Microsoft calls the push-and-pull technology included with Explorer 4.0 "an open, standard solution that allows Web authors to send information to users either on Web pages, via software components, in e-mail messages, or through broadcast content."

Microsoft summarizes personal information delivery features in Table 2.3.

Table 2.3 Explorer 4.0's Information Delivery Features

Information Delivery Feature	Description
Take the Web with You	Offline Web site viewing, supported in Explorer 4.0, stores favorite sites on your local machine, reducing viewing time, eliminating the need to log on to the Internet each time you want to view a page and potentially saves connection time fees.
Site Subscriptions	An automated feature in Explorer 4.0 lets you pull Web site content to your desktop periodically, by subscribing to sites through Explorer. A visual flag in the Favorites display shows when a page has been updated.

Information Delivery Feature	Description
Premium Channels	Microsoft is working with a number of entertainment and information companies to combine Internet delivery with "studio-quality production values into a breakthrough new experience for users."

True Web Integration

This area is where Explorer 4.0, coupled with other Microsoft products such as Office 97, really begins to change the way we work with our computers and how we use the World Wide Web and other Internet facilities. One of the problems in using any new software and especially a completely new facility such as the Internet, is learning the new techniques required for each one. Although Microsoft Windows has become a standard in user interfaces for Intel-based machines, when you use an Internet browser, the situation is very different. In addition, if you are a Macintosh user your desktop doesn't work as it does for Windows users.

Web browsers provide a degree of commonality across hardware platforms, but a difference still exists between how you manipulate data on your desktop and how you browse the World Wide Web. With Explorer 4.0, Microsoft is attempting to minimize this difference. True Web Integration, according to Microsoft, means two things:

1. The Internet now becomes a seamless part of your desktop operating system, with the browser and browser like navigation available in every Windows view. Microsoft describes this as an update to the Windows user interface to make it "Web savvy."

2. Internet Explorer 4.0 delivers tight integration across its suite of products, which means consistency—including a common toolbar—across all the applications and an easy way to switch among tools.

With Explorer 4.0 you use the familiar World Wide Web interface to browse the Internet, a local or regional intranet, or the facilities of your own desktop machine. Microsoft describes this feature the following way:

> *Rather than layer an additional operating system and user interface over the user's existing computer software, True Web Integration provides users a single easy way to access information—whether it's on the local machine, a local area network, or the Internet. Integrating the Internet into the operating system also turns the computer desktop into a "canvas" that users can customize to create a personalized workspace.*

This additional level of functionality is an installation option, since some users won't have the computer resources to support these added features. If you don't install True Web Integration initially, you can add it later. Explorer 4.0 in the True Web Integration mode combines features of Internet Explorer and Windows Explorer. For example, the familiar Start menu from Windows is combined with a list of Internet Favorites, history lists, and a new Internet find capability. In addition, the new Active Desktop lets you put Web pages, Desktop Components, and Internet news on your desktop screen right beside your familiar shortcuts.

In essence, True Web Integration enables a full-blown World Wide Web interface that replaces most functions on the desktop as we know it. Especially for those who do a lot of work over networks, including the Internet, this will be a welcome upgrade.

As we work through installing, configuring, and using Explorer 4.0 throughout the rest of this book, how these features relate to your real world will become more evident.

CHAPTER THREE

The World Wide Web GUI

Graphical User Interfaces (GUIs) have become increasingly important as the computer industry has matured. More users required computers and computer software that was easier to use. It took longer than most of us thought it would, but as hardware capabilities improved and prices came down, developers finally had a platform that would support the kind of intelligent user interface we needed.

Now, with the rise in popularity of the World Wide Web and associated browser software, a universal interface has evolved that makes computers easy—even fun—to use and most information easy to acquire. Microsoft Internet Explorer is a powerful application that helps you unleash the power of this operating environment.

In this chapter, I want to discuss the World Wide Web environment and the server and client software that makes possible the global sharing of information in a user-friendly interface. Don't worry. This won't be a highly technical discussion, but I want to provide enough information so that those of you who have not worked directly with HTML (Hypertext Markup Language), Java, and other Internet tools will have a better understanding of what Explorer is doing and will be better equipped to use some of the Web development features built into Explorer 4.0.

WHAT IS HTML

HTML is a computer programming language. There have been many such languages over the years. A computer language is simply a tool that lets applications developers easily write instructions for computers. The computer is basically a pretty stupid device. All it understands is whether specific memory locations have their voltage on or off. The first computer programmers worked with the hardware at this level, flipping switches or moving cables to make these minute, individual location changes.

Obviously that was inefficient and limited computer programming to a relatively elite corps of dedicated, highly technical individuals. For this reason, higher level languages were developed to make it easier to interact with the machine. Over time, languages have gotten more sophisticated. As a result, the language does more of the work and the programmer can concentrate on designing the application rather than on computer function.

Although it is still possible to program the computer at the lowest level of ones and zeroes, the specialized functions built in to modern languages make development of specific programs faster and easier. Many languages do this by including standard functionality needed to perform functions that many people will want to perform using the language.

HTML is one of the latest in this evolution of highly specialized computer languages. At first it was fairly limited, providing only the most basic user interface functions, but even in the beginning HTML was a breakthrough development. Not only did it provide a user-friendly environment for accessing information, but it functioned as a platform-independent client-server program. making possible an almost unbelievable range of online information stored on computers all over the world. And because the data resides on a remote host but the user interface information is handled at the local computer, all such use could happen reasonably fast.

In short, the specialty of HTML is two-fold. It was designed to provide the functionality needed to present to a user formatted multimedia information such as text, pictures, sound and many other kinds in a uniform way, and it was designed to do so no matter where or how this information was stored, no matter what kind of computer was being used to view it.

You don't need to program in HTML to fully benefit from the features of Explorer 4.0, but a little insight into this fascinating language can't hurt. Consider the Web page shown in Figure 3.1. You can display this page yourself by typing **www.microsoft.com** on the location line of Internet Explorer. (However, be aware that the Web is a dynamic medium, so what you see on this site today is probably very different from the screen I'm showing here.)

I've labeled some of the major components of this screen. You can see Hyperlinks, graphics images, text, and so on. This is the user side of an HTML page. Behind each of these objects are computer instructions—part of the HTML program—that tell your computer how to display each object and what to do if, for example, you click on a HyperLink. Figures 3.2 and 3.3 show a portion of the HTML instructions behind this screen.

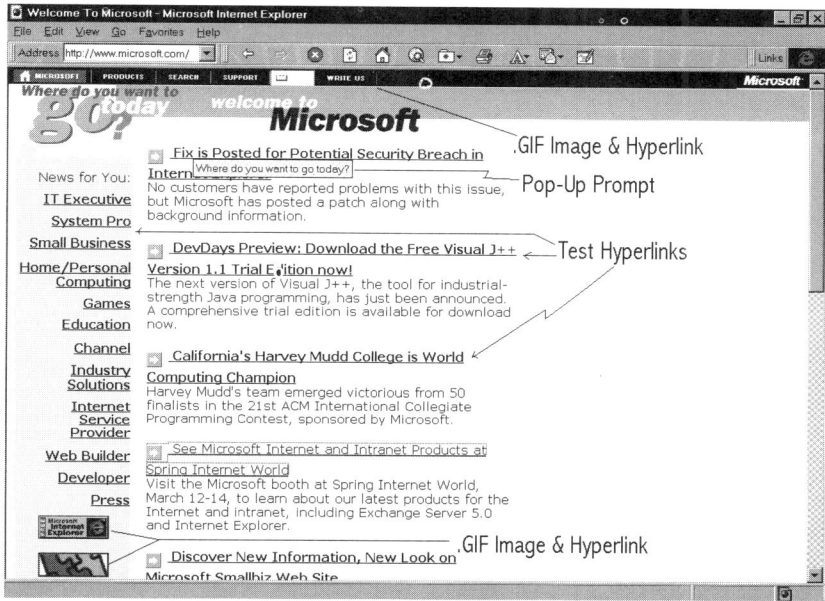

Figure 3.1 www.microsoft.com Web site.

Figure 3.2 Source code for www.microsoft.com.

You can view the source for any HTML page. Click on **View** on the main Explorer menu and choose **Source**.

```
microsoft - Notepad                                                    _ 🗗 ✕
File  Edit  Search  Help
</TABLE>
<!--TOOLBAR_END--><!--HEADER_START-->
<TABLE WIDTH=100% CELLPADDING=0 CELLSPACING=0 BORDER=0>
        <TR>
                <TD WIDTH=251 ROWSPAN=2 VALIGN=TOP>
                <FONT FACE="Verdana, Arial, Helvetica" SIZE=2>
                <IMG SRC="/library/images/gifs/homepage/tagline.gif" WIDTH=251 HEIGHT=76 ALT="Where
                </FONT>
                </TD>

                <TD WIDTH=349 ROWSPAN=2 VALIGN=TOP>
                <FONT FACE="Verdana, Arial, Helvetica" SIZE=2>
                <IMG SRC="/library/images/gifs/homepage/h_microsoft.gif" WIDTH=349 HEIGHT=76 ALT="We
                </FONT>
                </TD>

                <TD WIDTH=100% BGCOLOR="#FFCC00" HEIGHT=40 VALIGN=TOP>
                <IMG SRC="/library/images/gifs/homepage/1ptrans.gif" WIDTH=1 HEIGHT=40 ALT="" ALIGN=
                </TD>
        </TR>
        <TR>
                <TD WIDTH=100% HEIGHT=36 VALIGN=TOP>
                <IMG SRC="/library/images/gifs/homepage/1ptrans.gif" WIDTH=1 HEIGHT=36 ALT="">
                </TD>
        </TR>
</TABLE>
<!--HEADER_END--><!--##### CONTENT_START #####-->
<TABLE WIDTH=600 CELLPADDING=0 CELLSPACING=0 BORDER=0>

<TR>
        <TD WIDTH=10 VALIGN=TOP ROWSPAN=3>
                <IMG SRC="/library/images/gifs/homepage/1ptrans.gif" WIDTH=10 HEIGHT=1 ALT="">
        </TD>
```

Figure 3.3 Second page of source code for www.microsoft.com.

HTML is an interpreted language. That means when you download a Web page, your desktop software client—Internet Explorer 4.0, in this case—interprets each instruction as it is encountered on the page. HTML is similar to early page layout languages or early word processors such as Xywrite where instructions for typeface, text attributes, and other features surround the text you are formatting. In programs such as Xywrite, and in HTML, for example, you specify boldface text with a <B> </B> command pair, like this:

```
The second word bold is in <B>bold</B>.
```

A simplistic example, but if you understand this concept, then many of the other command codes in Figures 3.2 and 3.3 will make some sense. These commands are called 'tags' in HTML. HTML tags have a standard format that makes them easy to recognize: they start with a 'Less than' sign <, and end with a 'Greater than' sign, >. The code in Figure 3.2 provides set up instructions. Notice how the first two lines establish the type of document this is with the <!DOCTYPE> and <HTML> tag. The next line tells the computer this is the start of the 'Document Header' with the <HEAD> tag. The <TITLE> tag tells the computer to display a title section and the contents of the title section, followed by <STYLE> tags to set up the available fonts for the document.

You may have noticed that most tags come in pairs. Look, for example, at the <TITLE> tag. Two lines down, there is another, slightly different tag, namely </TITLE>. The '/' in this context should be read as 'end'. The first TITLE tag can be seen as "Begin". So the pair of Tags signifies: "Begin Title, End Title". The text in between the "Begin" and "End" is the contents of the title. Notice that the STYLE tag works the same: there is a <STYLE> for "Begin Style Definition" and a </STYLE> for "End Style Definition".

In Figure 3.3, which shows code further down the page, you can see how some of the specific features of the page are programmed. For example, the first lines in this figure format a table.

Inside the <TABLE> tag, you can see parameters that format the table, such as table width, cell spacing, and so on. These parameters are another example of the standard HTML format. Parameters are generally included in a "Begin Tag". They consist of a Parameter name, an equal sign, and a value. In some cases, there will only be a parameter name. The parameters for Tags are defined in the HTML standard, not all tags have parameters, and not all parameters are always required. You will for example see TABLE tags at other places that have different parameters than the ones you see here. Some parameters can only have predefined values such as LEFT or RIGHT, others can only have a range of values such as 0 to 100, while yet others can be assigned any value or no value at all. These issues are again all specified by the HTML standard. Notice the IMG tags on several of the lines in Figure 3.3. These specify a picture that is loaded off of the disk on the Web server as the page is displayed. Like the <TABLE> tag, they have parameter / value pairs. A required parameter for the <IMG> tag, SRC, tells the computer the source location of the image. Note that where the tags we looked at so far came in pairs (Begin and End tags), the <IMG> tag only has a Begin.

Because HTML is a text-based, interpreted language, you can create HTML pages easily with Notepad or any text editor. You type in the text, insert the proper commands or tags to manipulate and format the text, include commands to display images, and so on. Many experienced developers create World Wide Web sites in just this way, because it provides total control over formatting and content. Of course, you need a graphics editor or drawing program to create the images, if any, that you'll include on a page, but the simple text editor is all you really need if you want to work at the HTML code level. Obviously you will need an extensive amount of knowledge about the tags and their parameters to succeed.

Once you have the HTML instructions entered for a page, you can view the results in any Web browser. Notice that there are two views of your HTML document, the *source* view, which shows you the HTML instructions, and the *Web* view, which displays the results of these commands. Load an HTML document in a text editor or word processor, and you see the commands. Load it in Explorer (or any Web browser) and the software interprets the commands to display the resulting Web page.

Fortunately, the Web industry has evolved to the point that there are many graphics- or object-oriented editors that work more like a sophisticated word processor, displaying the Web page in its final format as you edit it. You can type text, use menus or toolbars to format it, insert images and move them around the screen, even automatically format a response form and configure it to send the contents as e-mail to yourself or someone else.

The underlying tags and parameters are generated automatically by the computer; in general you do not have to worry about them.

This is a much higher level operating environment than writing HTML code in a text editor. It is this level of Web page development that is included with Explorer 4.0. This interactive way of creating HTML provides excellent results without a lot of hassle. FrontPad doesn't have all the features of Front Page or other full-featured Web development tools, but it is sufficient if you want to develop basic Web pages for your intranet or Internet host.

Figure 3.4 shows a simple Web page under development in FrontPad. You don't see the HTML code in the background. In fact, you never have to look at the code unless you want to. The WYSIWYG (what you see is what you get) editor in FrontPad lets you work with objects and text instead of program code. Most developers, including professionals, start using tools such as FrontPad and FrontPage because of their ease of use and the decrease of tedious coding work.

HTML is just one of many tools used to develop Web pages. From the user's perspective, you won't normally be aware of precisely what instructions are being used, but there may be many types of code embedded within a sophisticated Web page, including VBScript, JavaScript and Java.

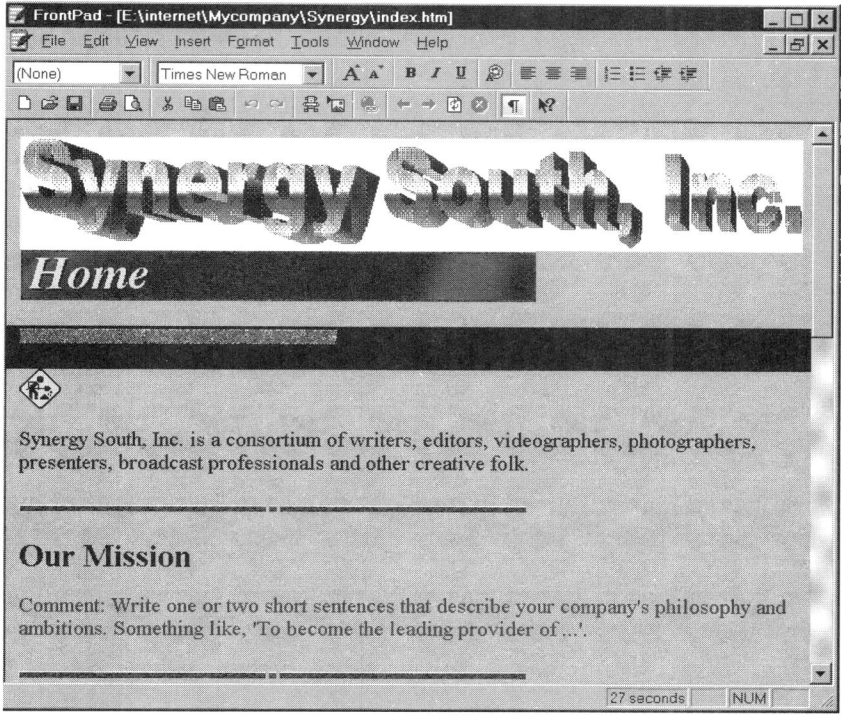

Figure 3.4 Web page in development in FrontPad.

WHAT IS JAVASCRIPT?

Like HTML, JavaScript is an interpretive, object-oriented programming language. JavaScript offers some enhancements to HTML and is being used increasingly for high-end Web page development. Even with its robustness, JavaScript also is cross-platform compatible. JavaScript is visible as instruction in plain text in the HTML sources.

JavaScript code runs in any browser that supports it, including Explorer 4.0. JavaScript was derived from Java, a language developed by Sun Microsystems for making small, powerful applications or Applets. These small programs are compiled by the developer in a form that will allow them to run on a Java computer. The Java computer today consists of a piece of software that runs on your desktop computer, called a Virtual Machine or VM. Object-Oriented Programming (OOP) forms the base concept of Java. Because Java can be run on many machines, and because of its client/server support some industry experts predict that Java may form the basis of networked, intelligent clients. Such a network could deal not only with computers that require a minimal operating system but with intelligent communications devices such as Java-based telephones, promotional and educational kiosks, and so on.

Java is being adopted by most major Web development companies and providers of software for use on the World Wide Web and corporate intranets. By most accounts, Java contains the power of a complete programming language such as C++ but is easier to use and portable. Many companies now build Java development environments that integrate with C++.

Java is based on *applets*, relatively short, self-contained programs that perform specific functions. As you browse the World Wide Web you may see such notices as "Java Applet loading" or "Java Applet Enabled."

While Java can perform many of the same functions as HTML, a Java Web site can include more interactive objects, is strong in animation and other object manipulation, and, in general, enables developers to create more eye-catching, user-oriented pages that can better interact with the user. Java is an addition to HTML that provides greater flexibility.

OTHER WEB TOOLS AND OBJECTS

In addition to these very popular Web development languages, you will come across other tools and utilities as you use Explorer to browse the World Wide Web. There is increasing use of *streaming audio* on the Internet, for example. That means you can choose a sound object and almost immediately start listening to sound, music, or narration without having to wait for the entire audio sequence to download first. Motion video is already being used heavily, especially in news-oriented sites such as CNN Interactive, but look for increasing use of Internet movies as bandwidth increases and compression techniques improve.

Many of these new features are provided by adding little programs to your browser. Internet Explorer 4 has a framework that allows other products to work together with the browser in providing such functions as streaming audio or video. The two most important types of extensions available now are ActiveX from Microsoft and PlugIns from Netscape.

And, as with HTML and Java code, the end user rarely has to be concerned with the behind-the-scenes aspects of using any of these features. That's because Explorer supports most of them and, when a new utility or protocol is encountered, you can usually download an ActiveX or plug-in client that integrates into Explorer automatically.

You don't have to be a computer programmer to delve into the features and capabilities of Explorer 4.0. However, satisfy your curiosity about what drives a favorite Web site by viewing the source code, perhaps even printing it and spending a little time studying the commands as you interact with the page. You'll probably feel better just knowing a little about what is going on. The exact format of all tags and parameters can be found on the Internet, for free.

Enough background and theory. Let's get right to using Explorer 4.0 on your computer. The rest of this book is a series of practical, hands-on sections designed to help you understand how Explorer 4.0 works so that you can use as much as you want of its many powerful features.

CHAPTER FOUR

Installing Microsoft Explorer 4.0

As you would expect, Internet Explorer 4.0 installs much like any other Windows-compliant software. The setup program will handle the physical installation for you, and then you can choose personal options and operational configurations. In this chapter I'll discuss hardware and software requirements for Internet Explorer 4.0, the basic process for installing the software, and some custom options you may choose to enable.

SYSTEM REQUIREMENTS

Explorer 4.0 is a powerful, graphics-oriented application, but it is designed to be functional with minimal hardware. Microsoft recommends at least a 486DX/66 computer with 8 MB of RAM to run Explorer under Windows 95, and a 486DX/66 processor and 16 MB of RAM to run Explorer under Windows NT 4.0.

Consider these the minimum settings to use the features of Explorer. An 8 MB machine is quite limited—running Windows 95 with 8MB or Windows NT with 16 MB computer is practically dysfunctional. However, if you are running Windows 95 or Windows NT, and you are content with the performance of the operating system and your applications, then your machine has all the power it needs to run Microsoft Internet Explorer 4.0.

FINDING EXPLORER 4.0

You probably already have Explorer 4.0. It is widely distributed via Microsoft's Web site (*www.microsoft.com*). As the software becomes more stable and more widely distributed, you will be able to purchase it and it will be distributed as part of the operating system on a new computers. In the latter case, Explorer will be preinstalled and preconfigured. If Explorer is already installed on your machine, move on to the configuration section of this chapter if you want to make changes.

INSTALLING THE SOFTWARE

If you downloaded the software from an online source you have a single file stored somewhere on your hard drive that contains all of the Explorer files in an archived format. To expand the archive and install the software, double-click on the downloaded file name in the Windows Explorer.

If you have Explorer on a CD or other distribution medium, you will find the same file in the root directory of the distribution disk or within an IE4CD or other subdirectory. Double-click **IE4WEB** or other distribution file in Windows Explorer to begin the setup process. The distribution CD-ROM has this file in the \ie4cd\en subdirectory. The precise file name depends on the source of your distribution software and the version you are installing.

You have two options. You can install Explorer so that it becomes part of your Windows operating system (that's the With Shell Integration option), or as an Internet tool (Without Integration). Whether you download the software or install it from a CD-ROM, you should have these file options:

With Shell Integration—\ie4cd\en\ie4web.exe
Without Shell Integration—\ie4cd\en\ie4xr.exe

In this book I will assume you have installed Explorer With Shell Integration.

Regardless of which option you choose, eventually you will see the opening setup screen shown in Figure 4.1 from the ie4web.exe source file.

The installer will warn that you are about to install Explorer 4.0, and you must accept the displayed terms and conditions before you can see the Installation Option screen shown in Figure 4.1. Use the pull-down list in the Installation Option field to specify a Full, Typical, or Minimal installation. Full installation, the default, is the best choice. The Full installation includes Explorer 4.0, Outlook Express, NetMeeting, FrontPad, and multimedia enhancements.

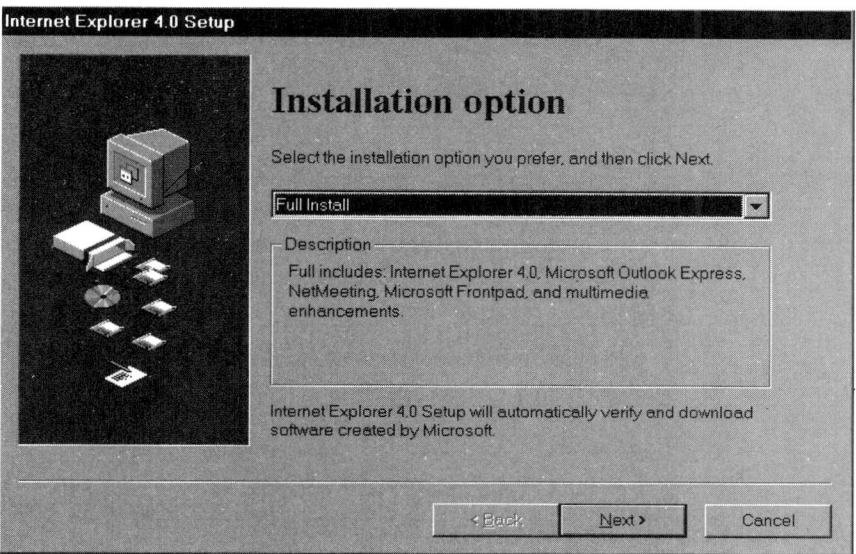

Figure 4.1 Initial Explorer Setup screen.

The Typical installation removes NetMeeting and the multimedia enhancements from the installation, and the Minimal installation includes only Explorer 4.0 and Outlook Express. You can choose to install only some components now, then add more later if you wish.

Once you have chosen the type of installation you want to make, click **Next** to move to the next dialog box, shown in Figure 4.2.

Use this dialog box to select the location for the install. By default, the installer will place Explorer files in the C:\Program Files\Plus!\Microsoft Internet folder if Microsoft Plus is installed. Otherwise, the installer will create a folder for you in the Program Files folder.

Click **Next** after you have chosen the installation location. Using the Microsoft default is probably the best choice. You will see a progress screen that shows you which programs are being installed and how much has been done on each (Figure 4.3).

During the rest of the installation process, you may see several additional dialog boxes that show you what is happening or instruct you to take specific actions. You will be instructed to close all open programs, for example, if the Install Wizard is unable to close them for you automatically. You will see another progress screen that indicates that Explorer is optimizing your system for better performance. Finally, the system will reboot. You will see another dialog box, indicating that the Explorer installer is setting up all programs, and you will see a list of the programs it is working on.

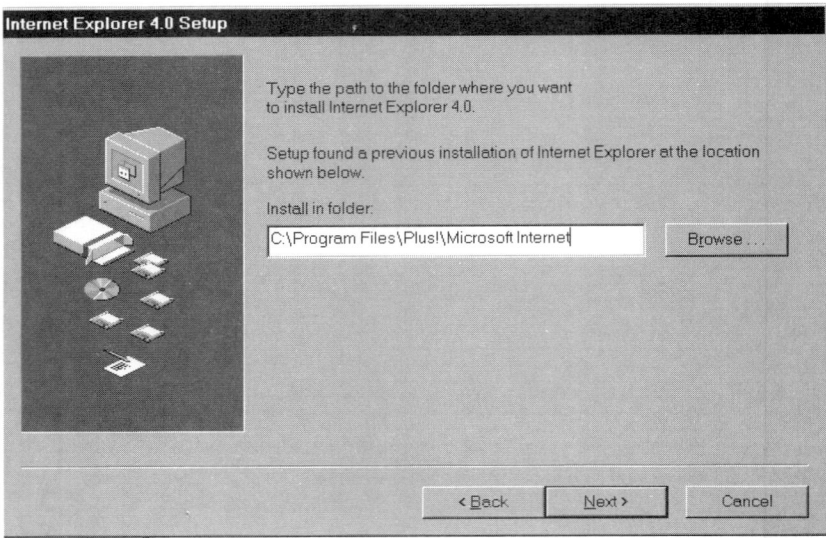

Figure 4.2 Second Explorer Install Wizard screen.

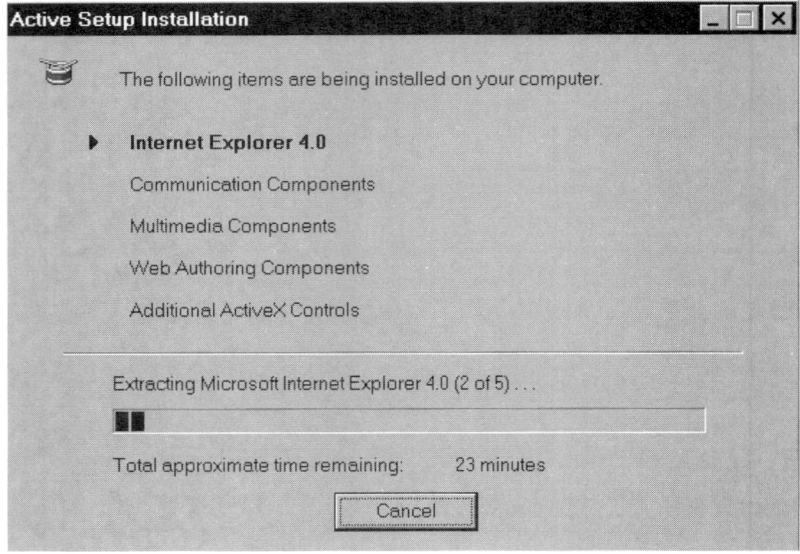

Figure 4.3 Progress dialog box from installation wizard.

EXPLORER AND WINDOWS

When the installation process is complete, you may see a desktop screen that is much different from the one you were using prior to installing Explorer 4.0.

NOTE You can click on **Restore Desktop** to remove the on-screen Explorer symbol and welcoming message and to reset your desktop display, including background color, to the settings that were current before you installed Explorer. Restore the Explorer Welcome and color scheme from the Display Properties dialog box.

If you display the task bar, you'll also notice a change. The Internet Explorer icon is one of the choices. Click on this icon to display the main Internet Explorer screen, shown in Figure 4.4.

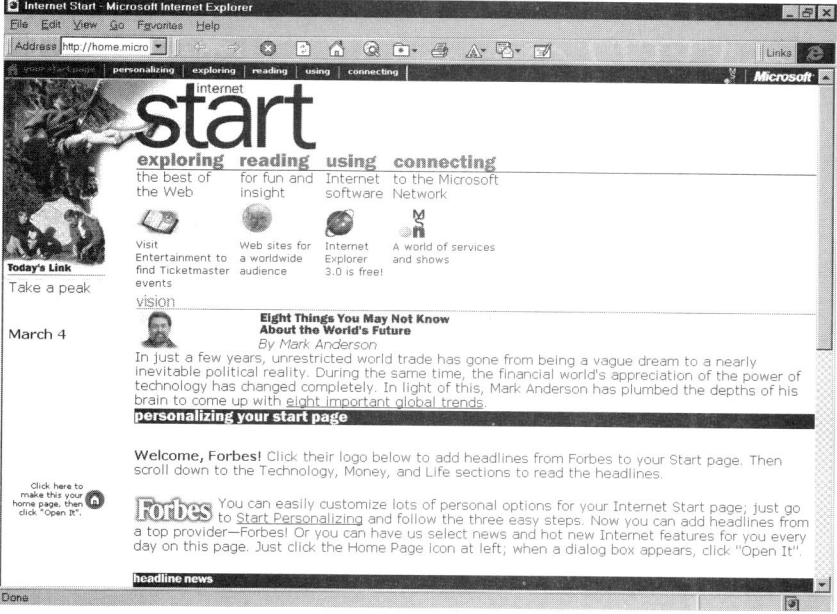

Figure 4.4 Internet Explorer 4.0 main screen.

You'll see other changes as you browse around your desktop. Try clicking on **My Computer**, for example. You'll soon see that Explorer has changed the color scheme and added some features (see Figure 4.5). And you don't have to double-click a shortcut to launch it.

Notice that the background color scheme is new, and Explorer has added a pie chart to show how much disk space is being used. You can move the mouse pointer over any of the objects in the My Computer window (this is called *hovering* in Explorer terminology) and the available space/used space display is updated in the associated graph.

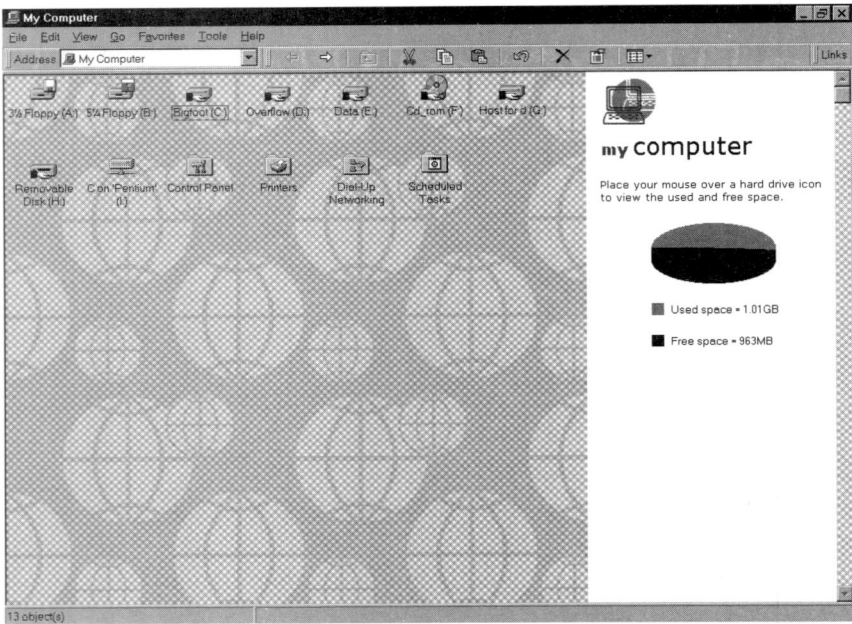

Figure 4.5 New My Computer display.

You will notice that there is a new pointer on the desktop: A hand with a pointing finger. If you have used a Web browser before, you will recognize this hand as the pointer you use to follow a Hyperlink. When you hover over the icons on your desktop, you will see the regular Arrow change to a hand. You'll also see the colors of the underlying Icon change, as your Icon has become 'selected'. Internet Explorer 4 treats your icons and disks as Hyperlinks. As a result, you only have to click the left button once to open a folder or start a program. In short: you previously had to click the left button once to select an icon, this is now done by simply hovering over it.

In the previous desktop, you would hold down the Control key, and click on several icons to select a number of icons. Now, you hold down Ctrl while you hover to select several Icons. Selecting an Area with the use of the Shift key and dragging (Moving the mouse while holding down the left button) has not changed.

You can remove the Explorer color scheme by right-clicking anywhere on the desktop and unchecking Active Desktop. Restore the Explorer display at any time by right-clicking anywhere on the desktop and checking Active Desktop. Even if you remove the Active Desktop color scheme, the other Explorer features are still available.

Notice also an addition to the Display menu: Show Icons. This is a toggle that lets you remove all of the Desktop shortcuts, cleaning up your Desktop display and making room for other objects. You can restore the icon display at any time by reversing the process.

You can see other evidence of Explorer on your desktop. Display the task bar, if it isn't already on the screen, and click on **Start**. You will see Explorer and the version displayed vertically to the left of the pop-up Start menu. If you have been using an earlier version of Internet Explorer, your existing Favorites entries will be added to the Start menu pop-up. You can jump directly to these sites by choosing them from the Start menu, rather than launching Explorer and then selecting the location you want to visit.

The Find options on the Start Menu have been expanded as well. Now you can look for objects over the Internet, and you can search for people from the Start-Find menu. In addition, you can drag and drop Start Menu items to rearrange the order (I'll discuss all of these expanded features later in this book).

Finally, right-click anywhere on the desktop and choose **Properties** to display the dialog box shown in Figure 4.6.

The Properties dialog box in Figure 4.6 shows a Plus! tab. Microsoft Plus! is an optional add-on to Windows 95. If you have not installed this optional software, this tab will be absent from the Properties dialog box.

NOTE

Notice that this tabbed dialog box is different from the standard Windows Properties dialog box. You can see that Explorer has taken an active role in your computer's operating environment.

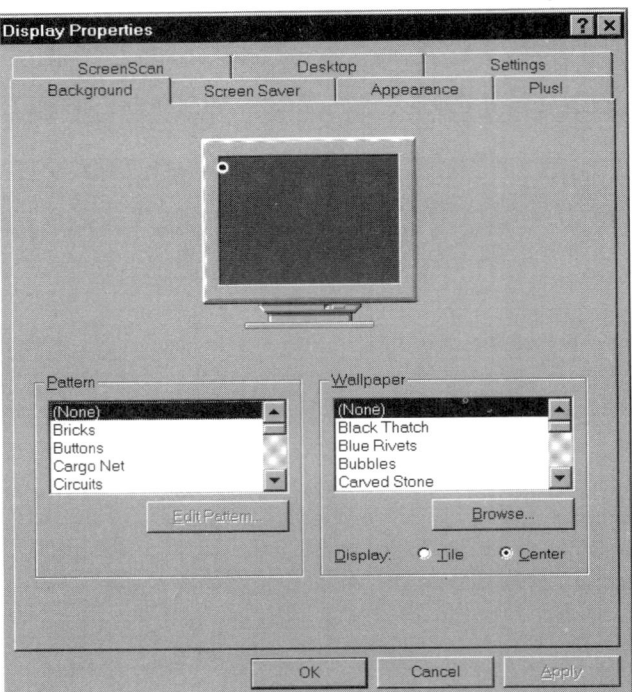

Figure 4.6 Desktop Properties dialog box.

CONFIGURATION OPTIONS—GENERAL

The tabbed dialog box in Figure 4.6 shows two new tabs, Desktop and ScreenScan. You can use these tabs to set some of the configuration options for Explorer 4.0. The Desktop tab lets you set certain display options for your Explorer desktop, whereas the ScreenScan tab demonstrates an interesting feature of Explorer, the ability to find previously installed, running applications and provide a configuration tab for them. ScreenScan is continuously running virus scanning software from McAfee. It was installed and running when I installed Explorer. The setup routine for Explorer detected the running program and created a configuration tab for it. You may see different results on this configuration dialog box, depending on what software you have installed and running.

If you open the Desktop tab, you will see the screen in Figure 4.7.

Use this dialog box to change the Desktop background and to toggle off or on the Explorer Welcome message. By default, Explorer displays a small HTML document as part of the desktop. This is stored in the c:\windows\web subdirectory in Windows 95 and in the C:winnt\system32\web subdirectory in Windows NT and displays the square "hey! I'm a Desktop component" image among your desktop icons. If you uncheck this document in the Active Desktop window (Show these objects on my desktop background), this image is removed. It is also removed if you choose **Use Standard Windows Desktop** or if you specify a local HTML document as the background instead of the Explorer default.

If you uncheck the **Show Internet Explorer 4.0 Welcome Message on my desktop** box, the right-screen Explorer logo and welcome text is removed. This has the same effect as clicking on the **Restore Desktop Settings** hyperlink on your Explorer desktop.

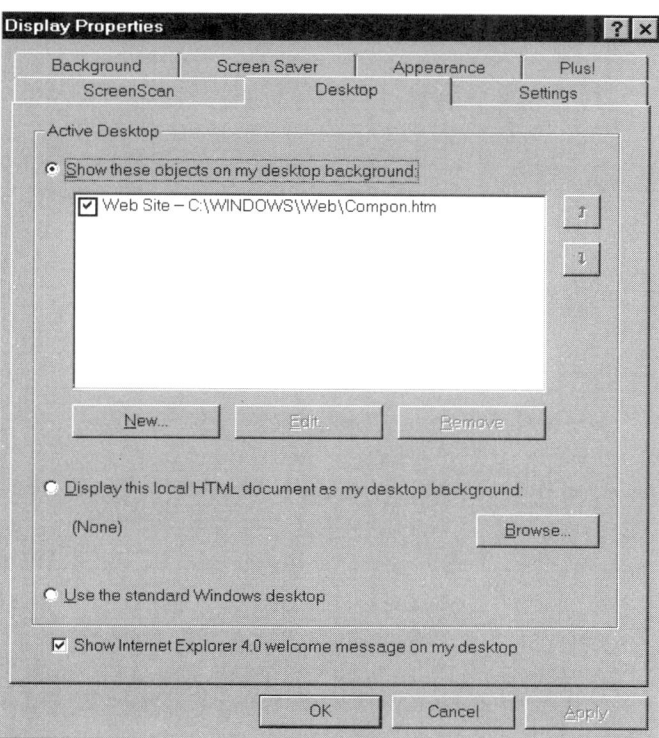

Figure 4.7 Properties Desktop tab.

CHANGING DESKTOP TAB SETTINGS

Suppose you want to replace the desktop-component image with one of your own, or add your own images files to the Explorer/Windows desktop via HTML documents or graphics. To remove the sample Explorer image, simply uncheck it in the Show these objects... window. Here are the steps, from the Desktop tab of the Display Properties dialog box (see Figure 4.7), for adding a new image to your desktop:

1. Click on the **New...** button to display the New dialog box, shown in Figure 4.8. Choose whether you want to use a picture or a Web document as the source of your new image.

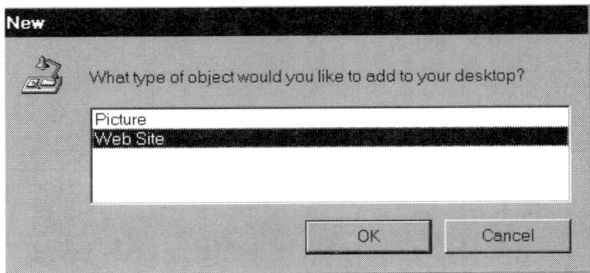

Figure 4.8 New dialog box from Desktop tab of Display Properties dialog box.

2. In the New Picture or New Web Site dialog box, type a path and file name or URL to the image you want to add to your desktop. Use the Browse button, if you wish, to locate the proper document.

3. Click on **OK** to close the file selection dialog box and return to the Desktop tab in the Display Properties dialog box. The new document or file is added to the display list.

4. To view the new image on your desktop, click on **OK** to close the Display Properties dialog box.

Whether you have chosen a Web document or an image (clip art, photograph, graphic), the selected file will be displayed on your desktop as a background image. One of the really interesting aspects of these desktop images is that you can move them (not too surprising) and you can size them (surprising). Try this with the default HTML image that installs with Explorer.

Hover over the image and notice that a rectangular handle appears in the upper-left corner and a triangular handle appears in the lower right corner. If you hover over the rectangle, the mouse cursor changes to a set of crossed arrows. If you hold the left mouse button, you can drag the image anywhere on your desktop. Use the triangular handle to expand or compress the image by holding the left mouse button and dragging the image to the new size. You would expect to be able to resize a graphics image in this way. It is interesting that you can resize an HTML display that is part of your desktop as well, and the next time you load Windows, the new size will be maintained.

CHANGING SCREENSCAN TAB SETTINGS

If you are running ScreenScan, as many users are (it is one of the most popular shareware applications downloaded from a number of online sources), you will see the configuration tab shown in Figure 4.9 on your Desktop Properties dialog box. Even if you are not running this application, the discussion in this section shows the level at which Explorer can integrate your existing applications.

You can change the range of disk drives scanned by the ScreenScan utility with the ScreenScan tab on the Display Properties dialog box. Click on the **ScreenScan** tab to display the dialog box shown in Figure 4.9.

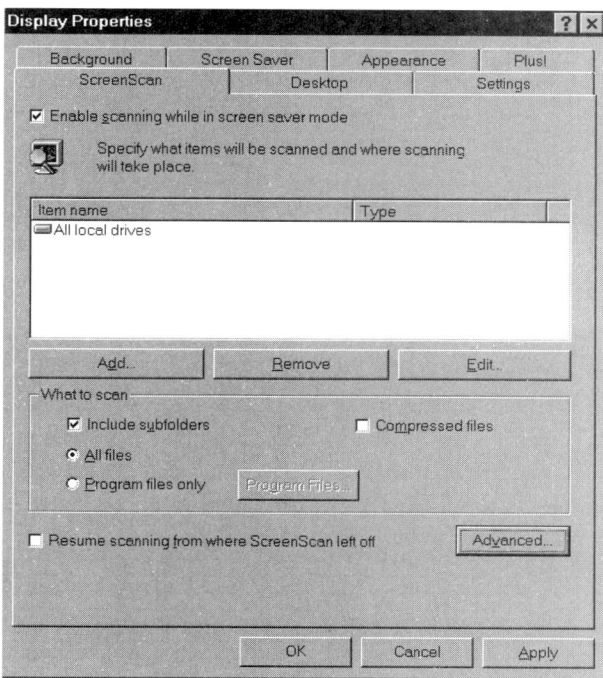

Figure 4.9 Display Properties ScreenScan tab.

To add new drives to be scanned, display the ScreenScan tab and do the following:

1.   Click **Add…** to display the Add dialog box shown in Figure 4.10.

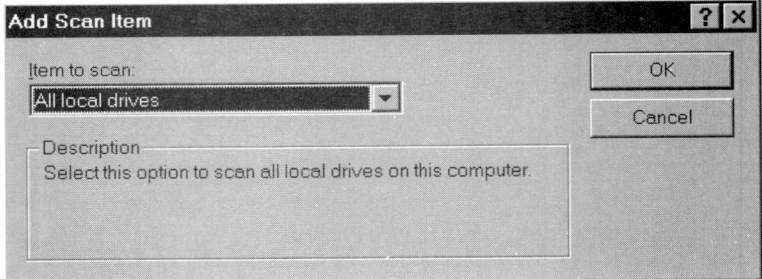

Figure 4.10 Add dialog box from ScreenScan tab of Display Properties dialog box.

2.   Pull down the list from the Item to scan: field and choose **Drive** or **Folder**.

3.   Enter a path to the drive or folder you want to scan in the Description field of this dialog box or click on **Browse** to display the file manager dialog box shown in Figure 4.11.

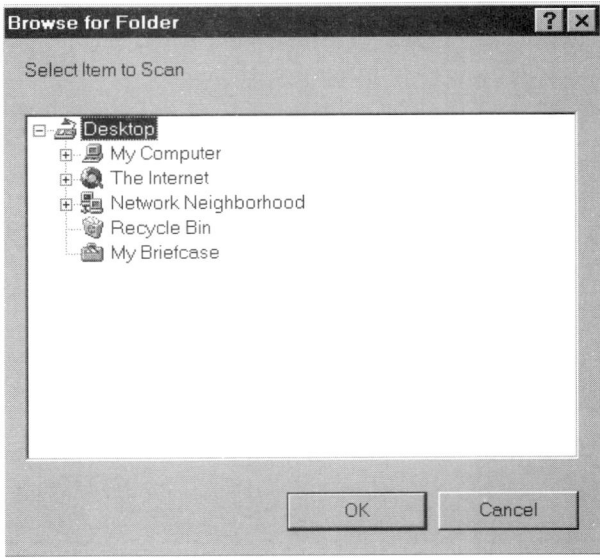

Figure 4.11 Browse for dialog box from Add Scan Item browse selection.

4. Double-click on **My Computer** to display a list of available disk drives on your local machine, or choose **Network Neighborhood** to select, for example, a network drive.

5. Once you have chosen the drive or folder you want to add to the scan list, click on **OK** to close the Browse dialog box and return to the Add Scan Items dialog box.

6. Click on **OK** again to close the Add Scan Items dialog box and return to the ScreenScan tab of the Display Properties dialog box. The new drive or folder you specified will appear in the Item Name window.

NOTE

By default, ScreenScan looks at all local drives, that is, those connected directly to your computer and not over a network. You can specify a subset of local drives by removing the All Local Drives designation, and then adding individual drives as described earlier.

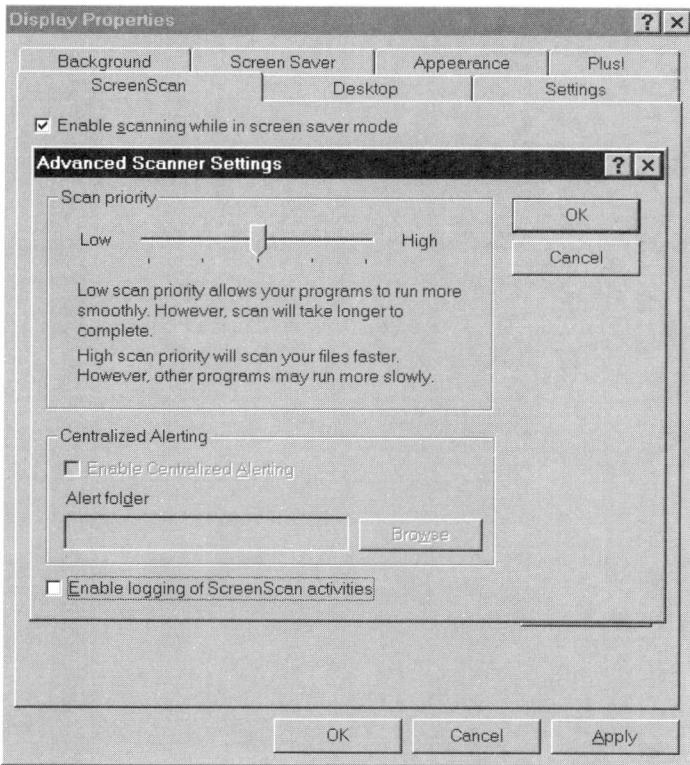

Figure 4.12 Advanced dialog box from ScreenScan tab of Display Properties dialog box

To further customize the Scan behavior, select or deselect items in the What to scan group beneath the Item name window of this dialog box. You can limit the scan to the root directory of specified drives, for example, by unchecking **Include subfolders** in this group, and you can limit the scan to Programs by clicking **Program files only**. You can also shorten some scan times by checking **Resume scanning from where ScreenScan left off**, but you will reduce the security of the current scan as well.

To specify how much of your computer's CPU power is dedicated to the scanning feature, click on **Advanced** to display the dialog box shown in Figure 4.12.

Make any changes you want on the Advanced dialog box (the items are well-documented right on the dialog box), then click on **OK** to return to the Display Properties dialog box.

To close the ScreenScan tab, click on **OK** to return to your Windows desktop or choose another tab from this dialog box.

EXPLORER AND MICROSOFT INTELLIMOUSE

The IntelliMouse, a new mouse design from Microsoft, includes a small wheel and pushbutton switch combined and located between the left and right buttons. The wheel functions aren't supported by all applications yet, but Explorer 4.0 supports most of the wheel's features. This new mouse requires a special mouse driver, which comes with the mouse hardware. It also has spawned some new screen navigation terms, which are defined in Table 4.1.

Table 4.1 IntelliMouse Terminology

Action	Description
Wheel Up	Press the wheel forward, away from you. This scrolls the on-screen display up, revealing parts of a document that are below the current display position
Wheel Down	Move the wheel back, toward you, to scroll down and reveal portions of the current document above the current display position.

Wheel up is the same as clicking on the up arrow at the top of a vertical scroll bar; *wheel down* is the same as clicking on the down arrow at the bottom of a vertical scroll bar.

The IntelliMouse wheel moves in clicks rather than with a smooth, continuous movement. Each click of the wheel moves the screen display approximately three lines, more or less, depending on the type of document displayed.

In addition to moving the wheel up and back, you can press it just as you would the left or right buttons. Under the wheel is a small switch (the *microswitch*), which controls other mouse functions. For example, If you quickly click the wheel while moving it forward, you turn on a slow, automatic scroll in some applications. You can watch the screen click upwards one line at a time until you click the wheel again. If you press down on the wheel and move the mouse across your desk or mouse pad, you will pan the display left and right. This is useful when your screen resolution is set for the minimum (640 x 480 pixels) and you want to view portions of a document that aren't visible to the right or left of the current cursor position. This operation is usually called *dragging the wheel* (i.e., press and hold the wheel button, then move the mouse).

You can use the **Ctrl** (**Control**) and **Shift** keys in combination with wheel movements as well. To *zoom* the display (enlarge or reduce the size of on-screen objects), hold down the control key while you move the wheel (**Ctrl+Roll**). You can control positioning of text in some applications with a **Shift+Roll** operation, moving a selected topic up or back in the outline hierarchy, for example. This operation is called a *DataZoom.*

If you don't have an IntelliMouse, you can use conventional mouse navigation and objection selection techniques. Also, be aware that not all programs respond to new IntelliMouse commands yet.

Now you have the basic understanding of how Explorer 4.0 installs, how to change some of the configuration settings, and a little about how it works. You'll use this background information as you work through the more detailed information in the rest of this book.

CHAPTER FIVE

Screens and Configurations

You've seen basic Explorer features during the installation. You've read about its high points in the previous chapter. In this chapter I want to concentrate on other features of the Explorer suite and describe specific objects and how they work. You will then be more familiar with the Explorer product and we will have common ground for the rest of the book. In this chapter we also will finish the configuration and customizing of the Explorer installation to prepare you to use all its features.

I will spend relatively more time and space discussing the Browser and Outlook Express components than I will FrontPad and the other programs included with Explorer 4.0. That's because these two features, in my opinion, form the core of what most of us will do with Explorer 4.0. The other utilities will grow in individual popularity as the Web—and our personal experience—grow. Besides, you'll find more detailed information on all these programs in later chapters. Also, because Explorer and its components interact in so many ways with the other software installed on your computer, you may get some additional configuration dialog boxes. You may also see some additional options in existing dialog boxes.

EXPLORER COMPONENTS

Remember that Explorer is really several products in one. It includes:

1. The Internet Explorer World Wide Web Browser
2. Outlook Express e-mail and news client

3. FrontPad Web page development tool
4. NetMeeting conferencing client
5. NetShow broadcast utility
6. A Desktop front end and enhancements to Windows

Each of these components operates individually—though in an integrated fashion—and each has its own opening display. The precise appearance of the Explorer-enhanced desktop depends to some extent on what applications you are running and how you have configured your Windows environment. Let's look at each of these components individually.

WORLD WIDE WEB BROWSER

Microsoft Internet Explorer has been a popular World Wide Web browser for some time. Now, with release 4.0, it is serving this function as well as the other integrated features that make this product so functional and unique.

Once you have installed Explorer 4.0, it provides an interface for your Windows desktop (see Desktop Interface, below), but it also remains a powerful, easy to use, functional Web browser. To launch the Web Browser, display the Task Bar, if it is not already visible, and click on the Internet Explorer icon on the bar. You should see a screen like the one in Figure 5.1.

Figure 5.1 Internet Explorer browser main screen.

The basic Explorer screen is similar to all Windows applications, as you can see from Figure 5.1. You can get detailed information on each browser menu and tool selection in Chapter 11. In this section I want to point out some of the main features to help you get started with Explorer 4.0's browser.

Browser Main Features and Settings

If you have used Explorer 3.0 or later, you already are familiar with many of the basic features of the 4.0 program.

Notice the Address window on the toolbar. It is narrower than the Address window on earlier releases of Explorer. That's because the address window was then on a line by itself, below the toolbar. The current arrangement leaves more of the screen free for viewing Web pages, but still lets you view the whole Web address if you wish. Here's how:

1. Move the mouse pointer over the Address display and to the right over the bar that separates the Address window from the left-facing arrow that appears next on the toolbar. The pointer will change to a double-ended arrow.

2. Grab the separating bar and drag it to the right. The Address window will widen and the toolbar shrink.

Now you can see more of the current Internet address, but less of the toolbar. You can reverse the process whenever you want by dragging the separating bar back to the left to reduce the Address display but show more of the toolbar.

You can also remove the Address display and toolbar, replacing them with buttons that take you to specific, preprogrammed locations on the Internet. Click on the **Links** button on the far right of the toolbar to display the links buttons, shown in Figure 5.2.

Figure 5.2 Links bar display.

These buttons let you jump directly to Best of the Web, Today's Links, Web Gallery, and Product News, Web pages that keep the same address but change content regularly to reflect new information.

You can customize these buttons to display more text by right-clicking anywhere on the Links bar and choosing Text labels. The bar enlarges and you will see the full text labels for each of these locations. While this makes it easier to determine what site each label represents, it takes up more of your screen display.

Use ToolTips to tell you what each Explorer icon does by hovering the mouse pointer above any icon. A small pop-up box displays a title for the selected icon.

N O T E

Restore your toolbar by clicking on the **Address** button on the left of the Links bar. If you have enabled Text Labels, you will see text descriptors for each of the toolbar buttons beneath each toolbar icon. Note also that when you display Links and then return to the Address display, the Address field may be wider than before, obscuring some of the toolbars. You can restore the toolbar display by dragging the Address field to the left, shrinking the display field and showing more tool icons.

The Text Labels menu choice is a toggle. Click it once to turn on labels and a check mark is displayed beside the menu selection. Click it a second time to remove the Text Label display and the check mark beside the menu item.

N O T E

There are some other changes from previous versions of Explorer. For example, display a Web site, pull down the Favorites menu and choose Add to Favorites. You will see the dialog box shown in Figure 5.3.

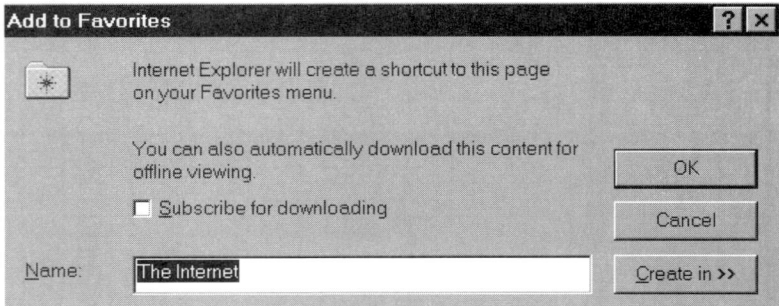

Figure 5.3 Add to Favorites dialog box.

This is very like the Add to Favorites dialog box of previous versions of Explorer, except for the Subscribe for downloading checkbox in the middle of the dialog box. This checkbox is a new feature of Explorer 4.0 that lets you specify certain Web sites for automatic downloading.

NOTE You can view which sites are subscribed and change the settings for them by choosing Subscriptions from the Favorites menu.

The site will be copied to your hard disk and updated periodically. When you choose Subscribe… and click on **OK**, you will see the dialog box shown in Figure 5.4.

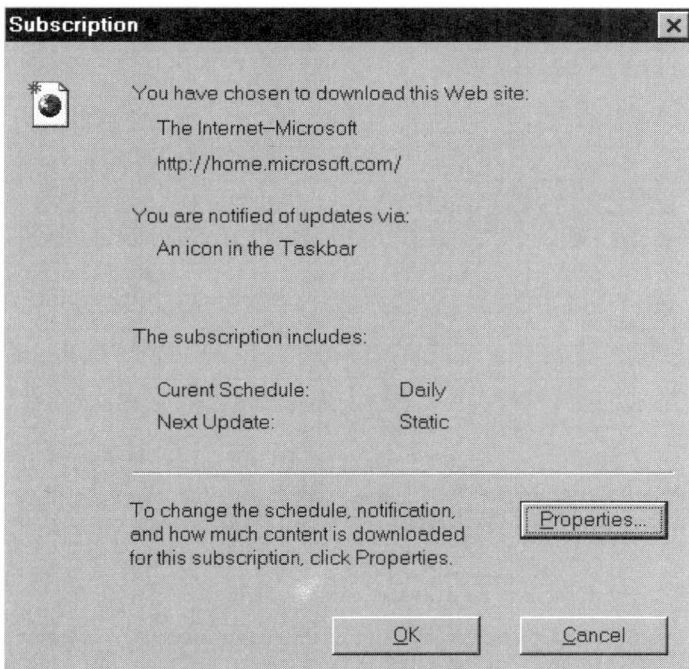

Figure 5.4 Subscription Configuration dialog box.

This dialog box summarizes the current settings for this subscription. You can make changes in the default settings by clicking on **Properties** to display the Site Subscription Properties dialog box, shown in Figure 5.5.

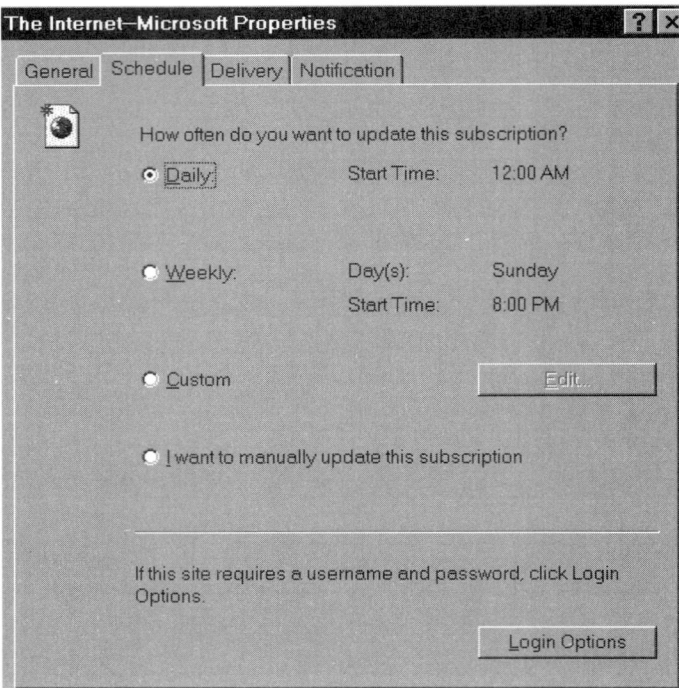

Figure 5.5 Site Subscription Properties dialog box.

This is a tabbed dialog box. Click on any tabs you want to bring to the front of the display and change the items you need to change. You have control over the frequency of the update, how much of the site will be downloaded, and you can tell Explorer to send e-mail when this site has been updated. Web sites are constructed in layers, so to capture more or less of a site, choose how many levels of the site you want to save to disk on the Delivery tab of this dialog box.

Want to see the full-width Address field and all of the Address or Link icons on the screen at once? You can. Simply grab the line that separates the Address/Tool bar or Links bar from the Web site contents and pull it down, making it wider. Explorer separates the Address field from the icons of the Link or Tool bar to produce a display similar to the one shown in Figure 5.6 (you can make similar configuration changes in earlier versions of Explorer, but with fewer options).

Figure 5.6 Expanded Explorer Address and Tool Bar.

Changing the display in this way is like accessing click stops. The various sections are summarized in Table 5.1.

Table 5.1 Explorer Display Configuration Settings

Click Stop Setting	Description
First click	Adds Text Labels to Address or links Bar
Second click	Display the Links bar beneath the combination Address (or Link) and Tool bar (Figure 5.6).
Third click	Removes the Links bar and expands the Tool bar with Text labels below the Address field.
Fourth click	Adds the Links Bar so the Address, Tool, and Link bars are all displayed with Text Labels

You can reverse the display expansion by grabbing the bottom bar and collapsing the display by moving the mouse up the screen.

There are some changes on the File menu, new features you won't find on previous releases of Explorer. The Work Offline menu item, for example, lets you work with Explorer and Web pages without actually being connected to the Internet. In addition, the New menu and the Send To menu choices have been expanded.

As with earlier versions of Explorer, you can use the View Options dialog box (see Figure 5.7) to change the way some Explorer basics work.

You'll see the same tabs on the Explorer 4.0 Options dialog box as appeared on previous versions, but some new items are there, particularly on the Programs tab. This tab gives you access to some new features, including the Payment Manager and Address Manager, facilities included in the new Wallet component of Explorer.

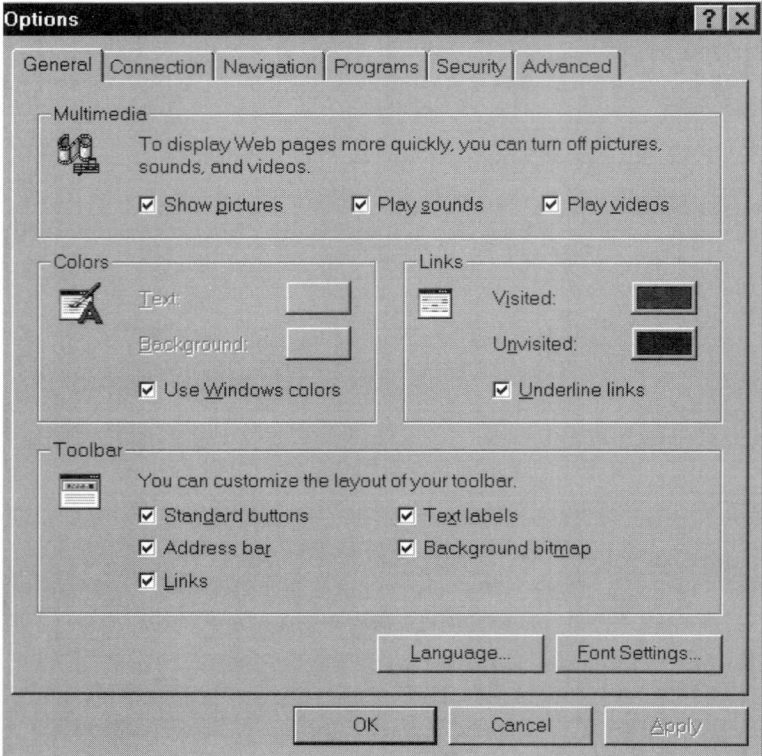

Figure 5.7 Options dialog box.

Also notice the Advanced tab. It has some new features (if you have used an earlier version of Explorer) that let you configure the way this program works (see Figure 5.8).

Use this tab to toggle on and off a variety of display and operational settings. Most of these settings should be self-explanatory. And, for the most part, Explorer's default settings should work fine for you. One setting you might want to change is under the Settings button at the top of the dialog box, where you can change how often your Web cache is updated and how much of your hard disk is used for cache storage.

Also, in the Advanced window of this dialog box, you might want initially to change Print settings—for example, if you want to show the background images of specific pages when you print them. However, this will slow down printing and use more printer resources.

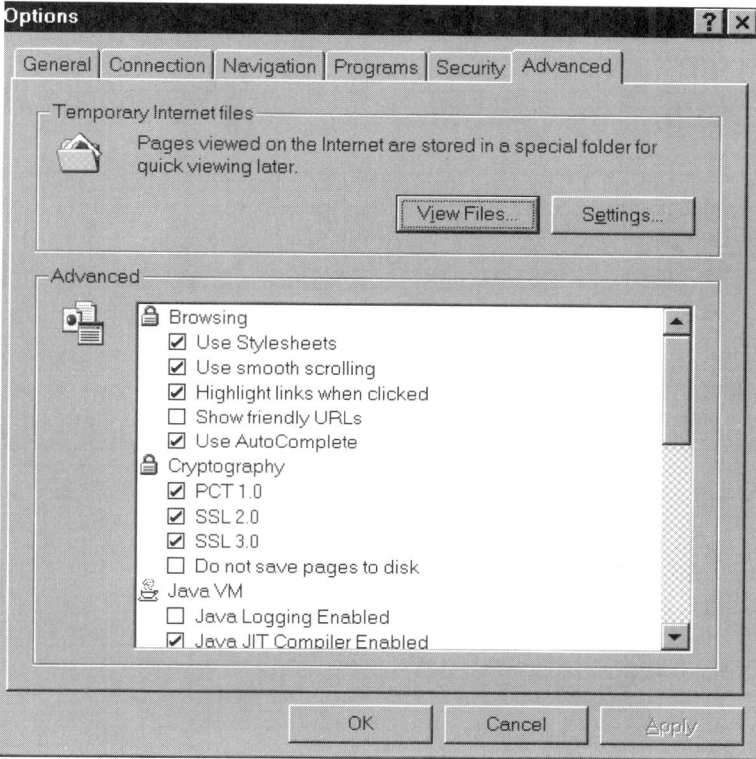

Figure 5.8 Advanced tab from Browser Options dialog box.

Finally, notice the Go menu. This menu includes choices for Mail, News, and Contacts, features contained in Outlook Express, a new addition with Explorer 4.0.

OUTLOOK EXPRESS

Outlook is Microsoft's comprehensive software tool chest client that manages local and Internet electronic mail, a contacts database, faxing, a group calendar, a task list, and more. It is designed as a direct competitor for groupware products such as Lotus Notes. Outlook is included with the Office 97 software suite or can be purchased as a standalone application.

A subset of Outlook, Outlook Express, is included with Explorer 4.0. Outlook Express handles some of the same tasks as its big brother, and offers a natural upgrade path to the more comprehensive product. However, for most of us, Express will provide all of the online messaging support we're likely to need, including the ability to browse USENET newsgroups and post messages to them.

Initial Configuration

Outlook Express installs with the other Explorer files automatically, so you don't have to do anything to get it installed. However, you can't really use it until you have entered some basic information. The first time you use Outlook Express, a Wizard steps you through these configuration issues.

You can start Outlook Express in two ways: from the Start menu and by selecting Send Link To on the Browser File menu and choosing Mail Recipient. Of course you could also use My Computer or the Run menu and navigate to the Outlook Express program file, but that's way too much trouble. To create a shortcut on your desktop, do the following:

1. Open My Computer.
2. Select the disk drive where you installed Explorer.
3. Open the Program Files folder (or the folder where you installed Explorer if you did not accept the defaults).
4. Open the Outlook Express folder.
5. Right drag the msimn program folder to your desktop and choose Create Shortcut from the popup menu. You will see an icon on your desktop that looks like a stack of mail and the title reads "Shortcut to Msimn." If you have trouble remembering what Msimn means, right-click the shortcut name and choose **rename** from the pop-up menu. Name the shortcut simply "Outlook Express" or anything else that makes it easy to remember.

To launch Outlook Express from the Start menu:

1. Display the Task Bar, if it is not already visible.
2. Click on **Start** and point to Programs.
3. Click on **Outlook Express Mail**. Outlook Express is launched and you will see the main screen for a moment, then you should see the dialog box shown in Figure 5.9. This is the Internet Connection Wizard.

NOTE

If you have previously used a product such as Microsoft Internet Mail or the Universal Inbox, some of the configuration questions will not be shown and some dialog boxes will not appear, or will appear in a different form. This is because Outlook Express copies the setup information from the previous Inbox or Microsoft Internet Mail setup.

Figure 5.9 Internet connection Wizard dialog box.

Follow the Wizard's instructions to configure Outlook Express so it can handle your mail for you.

Type a name for your Internet e-mail account. This can be any name up to 255 characters and is used to identify profile information about your e-mail account that is stored on your computer. If you have previously configured an e-mail account under Windows, use the existing e-mail account name, if you wish, or type a completely new name. The Internet e-mail name can be your own name, your Internet account name, the name of your Internet service provider (ISP), and so on.

Click on **Next** to display the Display Name dialog box, shown in Figure 5.10.

Type the name you want mail recipients to see when you send them mail. This usually is your full name, but it could be the name of your business or other identifier. This is not your e-mail address. That comes next.

Click on **Next** to display the e-mail address entry screen, shown in Figure 5.11.

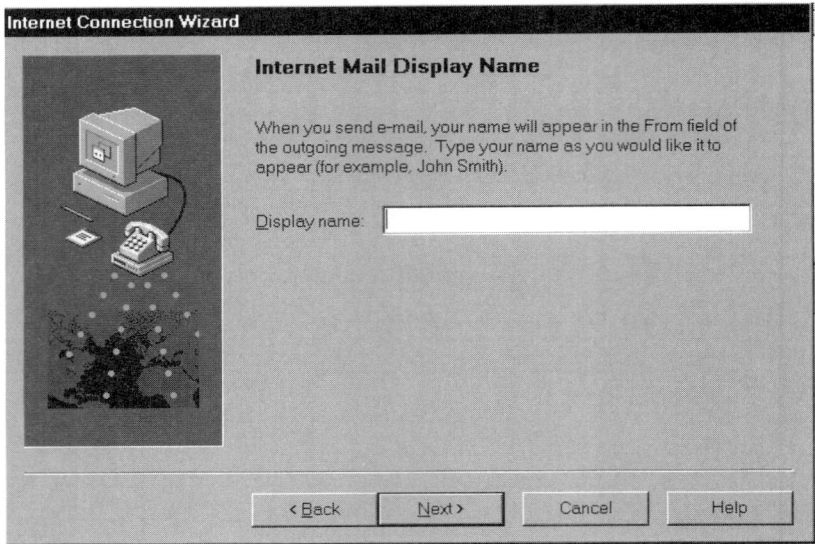

Figure 5.10 Display Name Wizard dialog box.

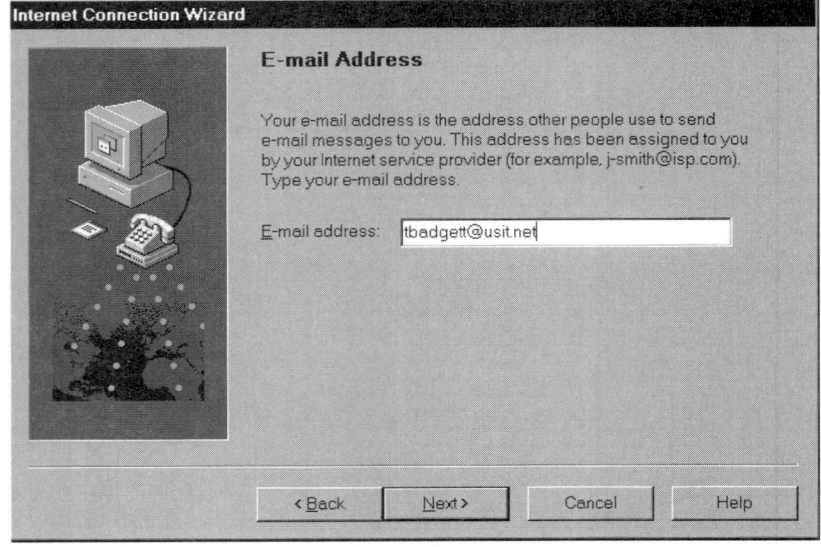

Figure 5.11 E-mail Address Entry screen.

Type your e-mail address. This consists of your account name, an "at" sign (@), and the host and domain name of your e-mail host. I've shown this dialog box with my e-mail address entered. If you need help with this information, contact your ISP, or click on the Help button on this Wizard screen.

Click on **Next** to display the e-mail Server Addresses dialog box, shown in Figure 5.12.

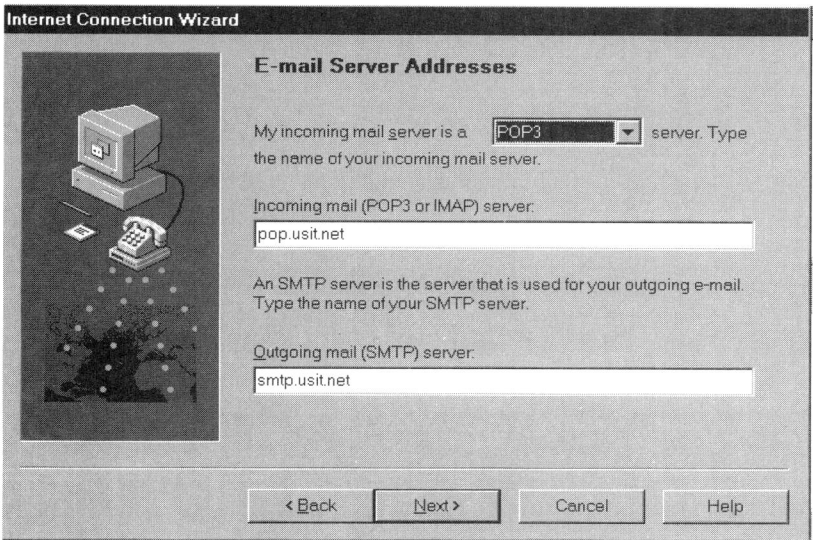

Figure 5.12 E-mail Server Addresses dialog box.

Enter the server identifier for your incoming and outgoing mail servers. These addresses consist of a machine name and a domain name. Depending on your ISP, both addresses may be the same, since some e-mail configurations use the same machine for incoming and outgoing mail, or they may be different. You'll have to get this information from your ISP (Internet service provider) or network administrator if you don't already know it. A POP3 (Post office protocol version 3) e-mail system is assumed. You can specify an IMAP (Internet mail access protocol) server by pulling down the selection list in the server type field at the top of this dialog box.

Click on **Next** to show the Internet Mail Logon dialog box, shown in Figure 5.13.

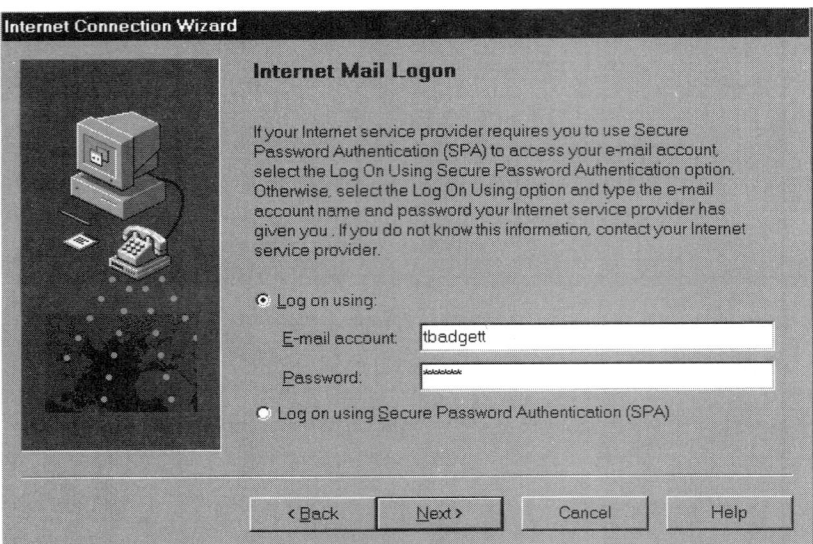

Figure 5.13 Internet Mail Logon dialog box.

Type your e-mail account name and password in the appropriate fields. The e-mail account name is the name you use to log onto your Internet account and usually will be the same as the first part of your e-mail address. The password is your secret code that lets you log onto your account. If your ISP requires you to use Secure Password Authentication (SPA), then click on the SPA button at the bottom of this dialog box instead.

Click on **Next** to display the Choose Connection Type dialog box shown in Figure 5.14.

If you access the Internet through a Local Area Network (LAN) with, say, an ISDN link or dedicated server, then click **Connect using my local area network (LAN)**. If you use a dial-up link to the Internet, click on the **Connect using my phone line** button.

Click on **Next** to display the final Wizard dialog box if you connect using a LAN, or the Dial-Up Connection dialog box (Figure 5.15) if you use a dial-up connection.

If you have an existing dial-up connection profile for Internet access, choose **Use an existing dial-up connection**. You can create a new profile, if you wish, by clicking on **Create a new dial-up connection**.

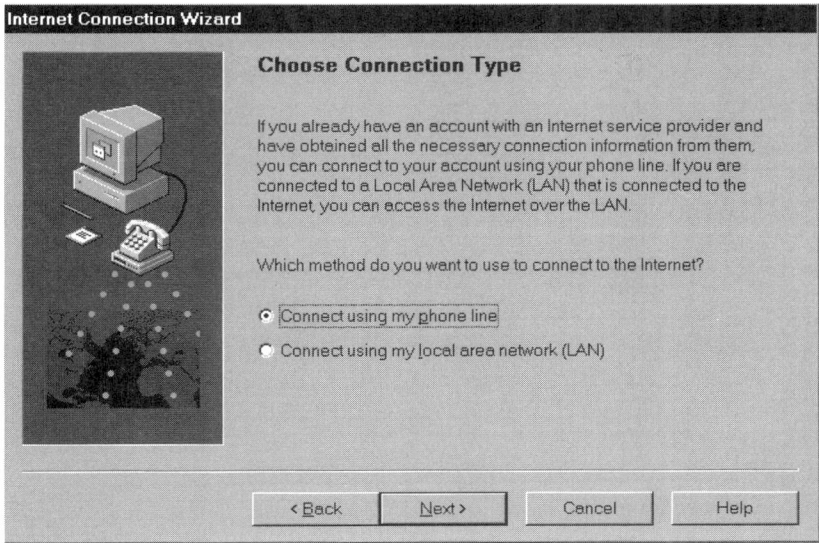

Figure 5.14 Choose Connection Type dialog box.

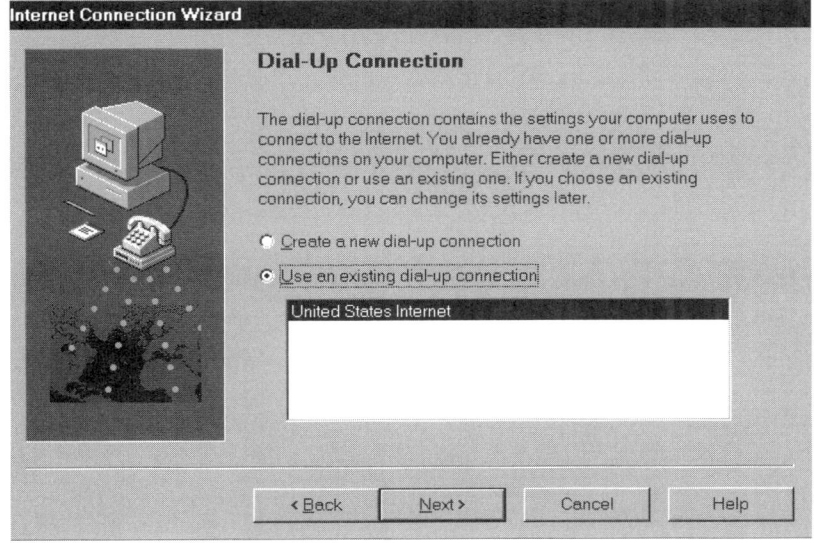

Figure 5.15 Dial-Up Connection dialog box.

Click on **Next** to display the final Wizard dialog box if you are using an existing dial-up profile, or to configure a new profile. If you are creating a new profile, you will see the Wizard dialog box in Figure 5.16.

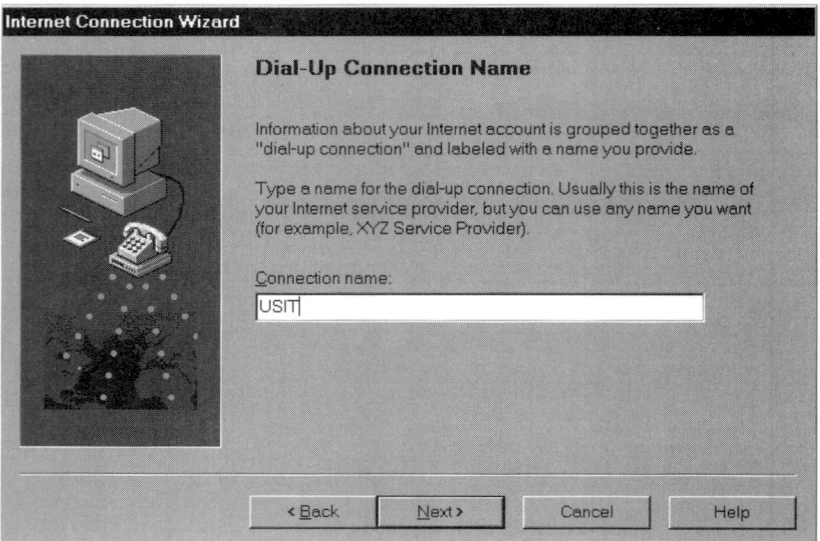

Figure 5.16 Configure New Dial-Up Connection Name Wizard dialog box.

Type a name for the new dial-up profile and click **Next** to display the Wizard dialog box shown in Figure 5.17.

Enter the telephone number for the new connection and click **Next** to show the User Name and Password dialog box, shown in Figure 5.18.

Enter the user name and password you use to log onto your Internet account and click **Next**. You will see the dialog box shown in Figure 5.19.

If your ISP uses PPP (Point to Point Protocol) connections, you can click **No** on the Advanced screen. If you need to specify a SLIP (Serial Line Internet Protocol) connection, click on **Yes**. If you choose **No**, or after you specify SLIP connection on the next dialog box, click **Next** to display the final Wizard dialog box.

Click on **Finish** to complete the Outlook Express configuration. The main Outlook Express screen shown in Figure 5.20 is displayed.

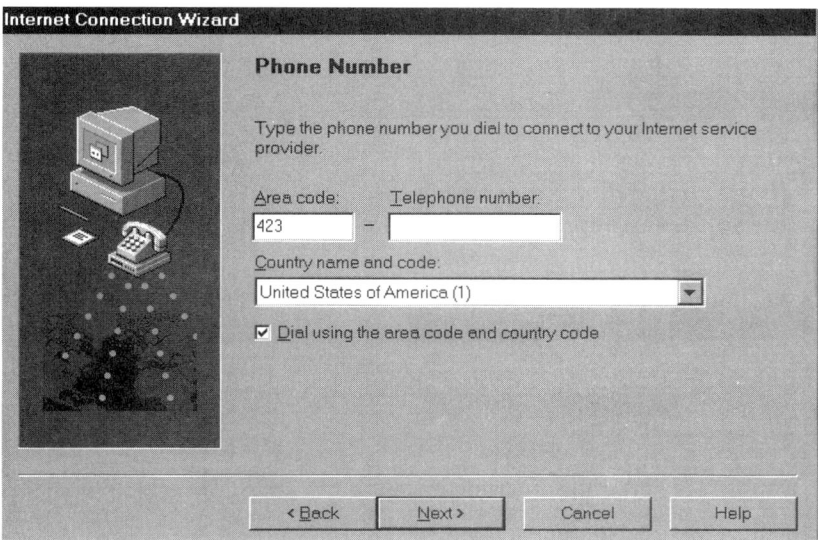

Figure 5.17 Phone Number Wizard dialog box.

Figure 5.18 User Name and Password dialog box.

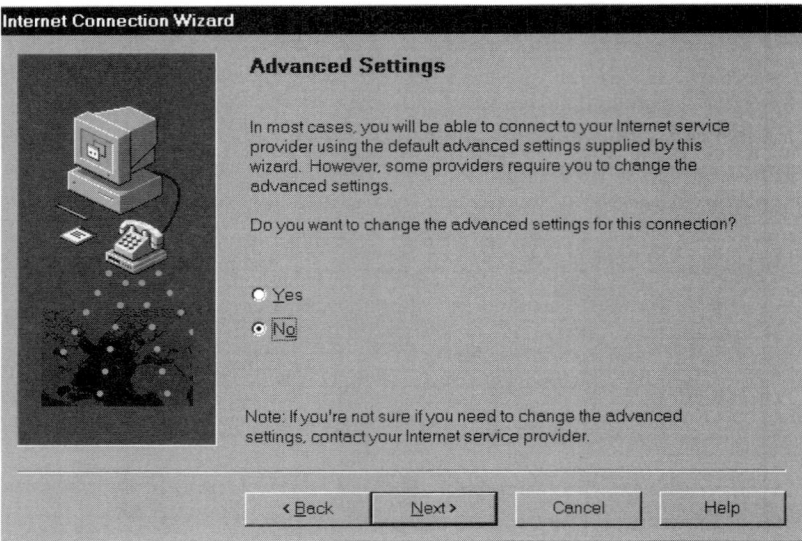

Figure 5.19 Advanced Settings dialog box.

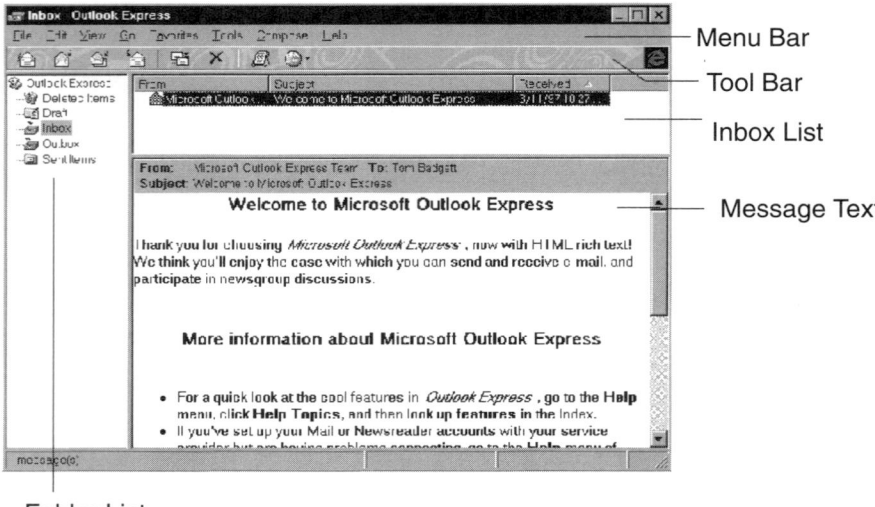

Figure 5.20 Main Outlook Express screen.

N O T E In this example you launched Outlook Express through the e-mail client. This configured your e-mail account and displayed the inbox by default. You must step through similar configuration screens to use USENET News. The first time you use the news component the Wizard will ask you to fill in a name for the profile, your display name, your e-mail address, your NNTP (News) server address, and connection type. The process is virtually identical to that just described for configuring your e-mail profile.

Outlook Express Main Features and Settings

Outlook Express is more than an e-mail client. It also lets you read and post to USENET news groups and maintain a personal address book. From the Address Book you can send e-mail to an individual or a group, print a contacts reference list, and import and export individual records or complete contacts lists.

You can view available Outlook Express services all on the same screen by clicking on **Outlook Express** at the top of the Folder List (on the left side of the main outlook screen) to produce the display in Figure 5.21.

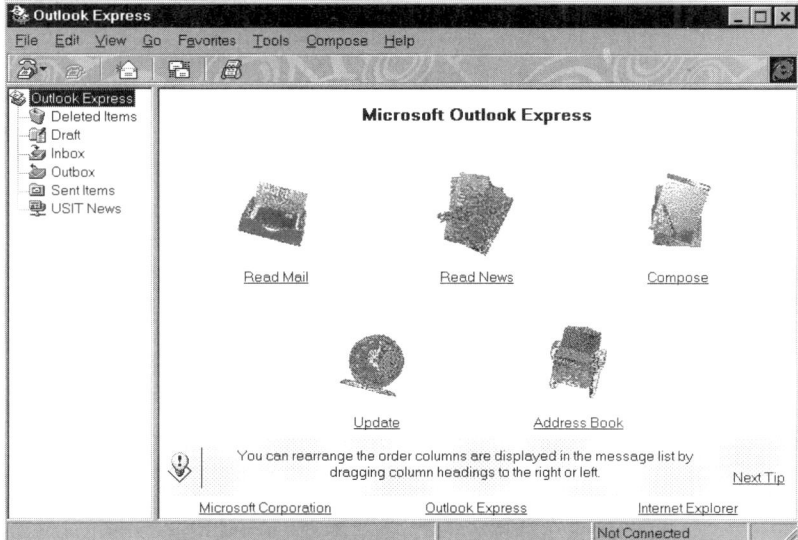

Figure 5.21 Outlook Express Services icons.

Notice the tip at the bottom of the screen. A different tip is displayed each time you open this screen, and you can display new tips by clicking on the Next Tip link beside the tip display.

There are three Hyperlinks at the bottom of this dialog box, beneath the Tip line. These are World Wide Web connections that launch the Explorer browser and take you directly to Microsoft Web sites for corporate information, as well as data on Outlook Express and Internet Explorer in general. These pages are an excellent way to get up-to-the-minute information in these areas. This is just one more example of the integrated nature of Explorer. Web pages such as this become a part of your desktop within many applications, not just the Web browser.

You can choose from these icons to read your mail, read news, compose a new e-mail message, access the address book to look up a name or make changes, or to update selected news groups. Notice how these selections are displayed as icons with associated Hyperlinks. When you hover over one of the choices the pointer changes to a hand, indicating that this is a Hyperlink. A single click opens the selected location. Explore some of these selections to become familiar with how individual screens for these utilities appear.

Changing E-mail Settings

In addition, there are some additional configuration settings you may want to use here. One is with your e-mail. If you're like me, it can sometimes be difficult to keep track of the high volume of mail—remembering to read it all, getting around to answering it, being able to find a previously read message. With Outlook Express, you can automatically store incoming e-mail messages in separate folders according to criteria you specify.

To customize your Outlook Express Inbox, do the following:

1. Click on **Tools** and choose Inbox Assistant… to display the dialog box shown in Figure 5.22.
2. Click on **Add** to display the Properties dialog box shown in Figure 5.23.
3. Fill in appropriate portions of the top and bottom sections of this dialog box.

    At the top specify what message header information the Assistant should filter. For example, if you receive mail addressed to yourself and also to several other groups, you can enter separate properties to direct mail to you into one folder and mail to each group into separate folders.

Similarly you can capture the From field and store all message from a specified sender to a separate folder. Click on the **Folder** icon beside any of the header fields (To:, CC:, From:. Subject:) to access your address book if you wish to select a name. Otherwise, just type the name in the appropriate field.

At the bottom of the dialog box, tell the Assistant where to store the specified messages. For example, you can copy the specified messages to a certain folder, leaving an original in the Inbox, or you can move specified messages to a certain folder. You can automatically forward specified messages to one or more e-mail recipients, and you can tell the Assistant not to download messages.

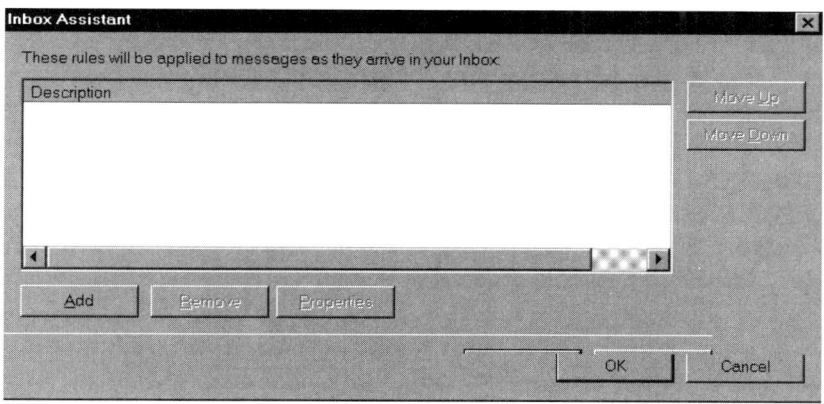

Figure 5.22 Inbox Assistant dialog box.

4. When the configuration settings are complete, click on **OK** to return to the Inbox Assistant dialog box, where the new message properties you just created will appear. (See Figure 5.24.)

There is a checkbox beside each profile in the Inbox Assistant window. You can uncheck any of these boxes to temporarily disable individual filters. If you are moving or copying messages to folders other than the Inbox, you'll need to create these folders from the main Outlook Express screen before you use Inbox Assistant. Use the File New Folder... command sequence from the main menu (of File Folder New Folder...) to create new folders to hold your distributed messages. Then in Inbox Assistant click on the Folder... button to select the folders you want to use.

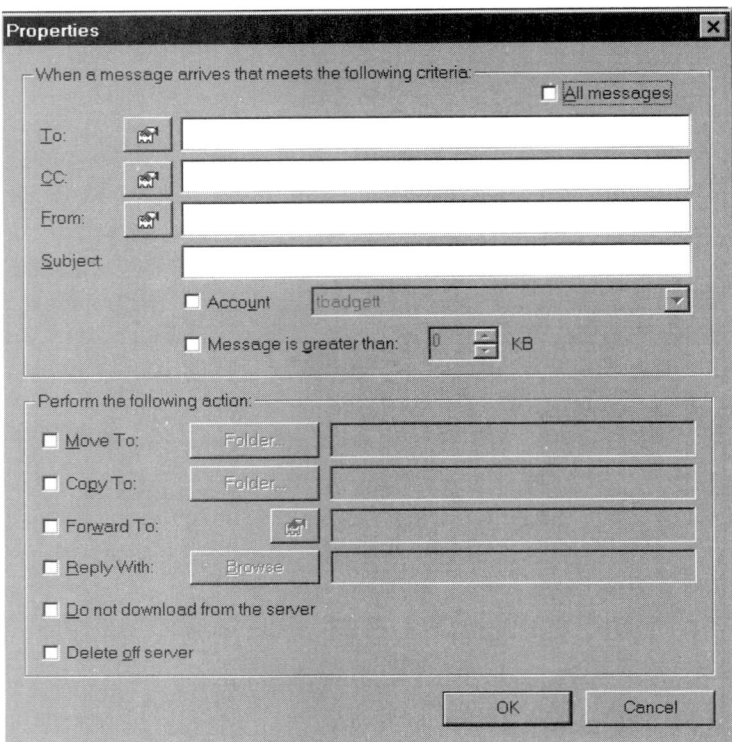

Figure 5.23 Inbox Assistant Properties dialog box.

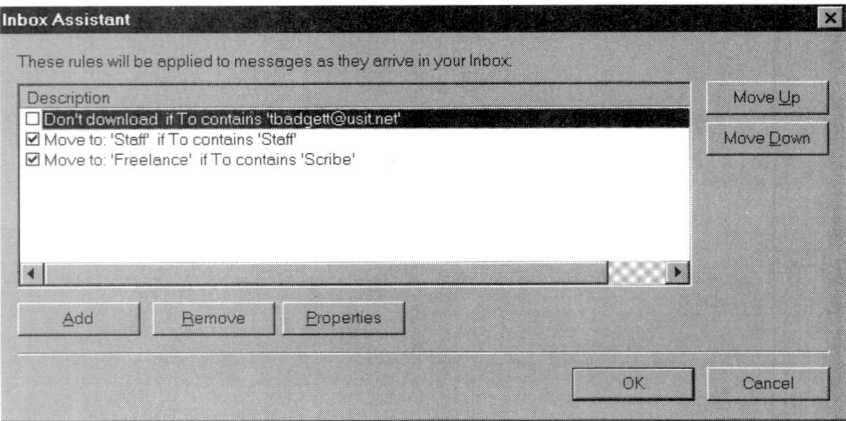

Figure 5.24 Inbox Assistant with completed entries.

N O T E   You must create a separate profile for each different type of message you want to handle specially. Create one profile to store your personal messages to a specific folder, create a second profile to store messages directed to "Staff" to another folder, and so on.

N O T E   Outlook Express downloads your mail messages from the e-mail host and removes the originals from the host. If you read your e-mail from multiple locations, you may want to leave some messages on the host. Create a profile that specifies which messages you want to read from another location and click on Do not download from the server at the bottom of the Inbox Assistant dialog box.

You can change your original Outlook Express configuration with the Tools Accounts... menu sequence, which presents the dialog box shown in Figure 5.25.

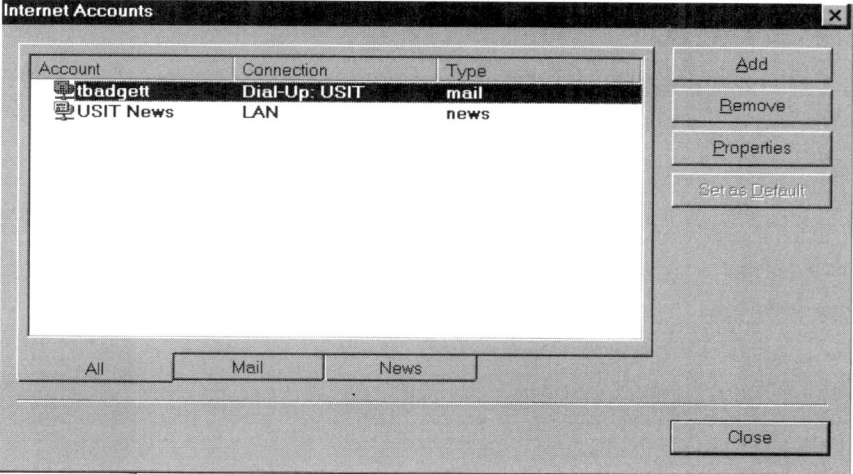

Figure 5.25 Tools Accounts... dialog box.

For example, suppose you installed Outlook to use a modem connection, then you install a local area network or add LAN Internet access to an existing network. Use this dialog box to change how you connect to the Internet. Here's how:

1. Use **Tools Accounts...** to display the Accounts dialog box.
2. Select the account you want to change. You may have only a single entry in this box if you have created only one connection profile.

3. Click on **Properties** to display the Account Properties dialog box.

4. Click on the **Connection** tab to bring it to the front of the display (Figure 5.26).

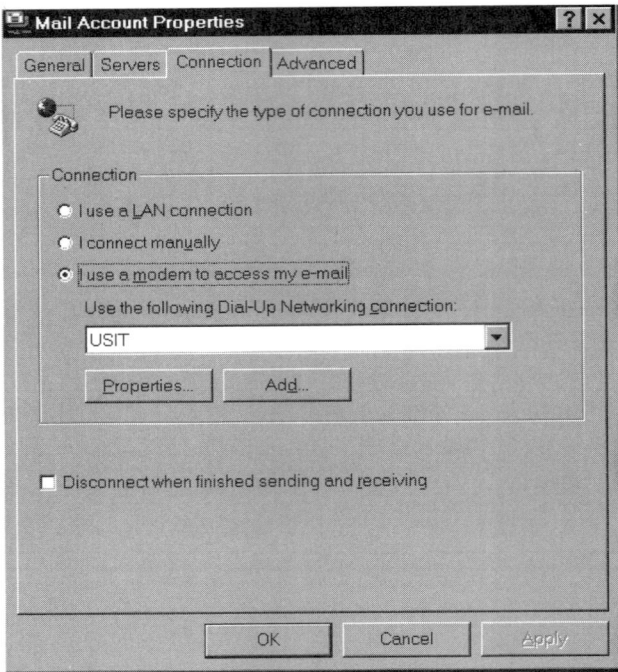

Figure 5.26 Connection tab of Account Properties dialog box.

5. Choose the new connection type you want to use and click on **OK** to return to the Accounts dialog box.

6. Click on **Close** to close the Accounts dialog box and return to the main Outlook Express screen.

As you can see from Figure 5.25, there are other tabs on the Account Properties dialog box. Choose any of these to change other Account settings if you wish. For example, you can change the e-mail account name (and other account information) under the General tab, or change the servers for mail and news on the Servers tab.

In addition, you may want to change some of the general e-mail settings. Use the Tools Mail Options... menu sequence to display the tabbed dialog box shown in Figure 5.27.

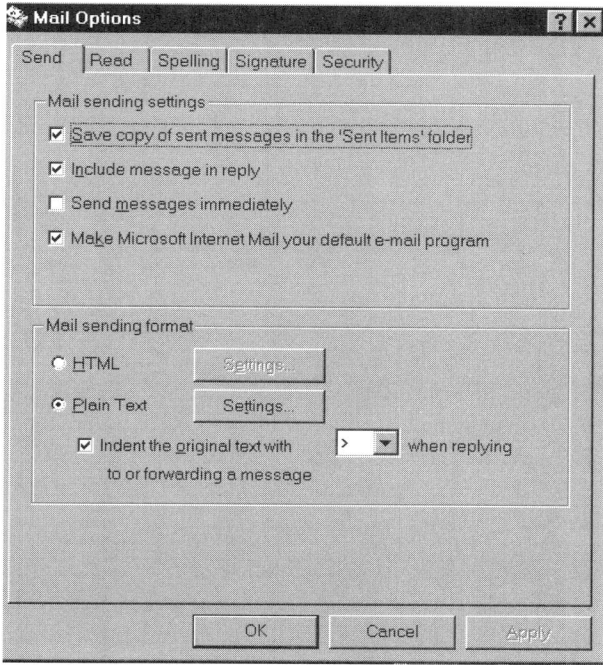

Figure 5.27 Tabbed Mail Options dialog box.

If you haven't used e-mail before, you likely will have to gain some experience before these settings mean very much to you. If you have some e-mail experience, on the other hand, the settings available on this dialog box are fairly straightforward. They simply let you change some of the characteristics and behaviors of your e-mail account. You can experiment with them to derive the settings that are right for you.

Changing News Settings

When you installed Outlook Express, you specified the main settings required for reading USENET news. However, the first time you access the news server you will have to download the list of available news groups. You can change some general news options, and you may also want to set some initial filters.

To specify news options, use the Tools News Options... command sequence to display the dialog box shown in Figure 5.28. This is similar to the mail options discussed earlier.

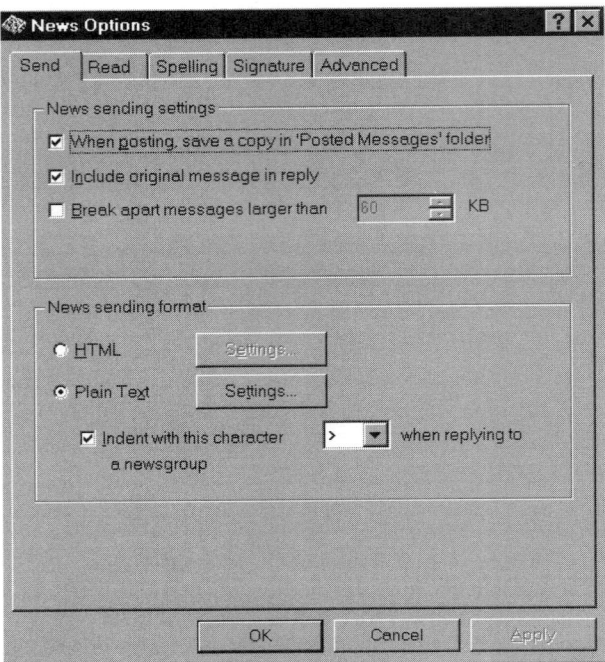

Figure 5.28 Tools News Options... dialog box.

As with the Mail Options dialog box, these settings will only mean something to you after you have some experience with News. For the most part you can use the Outlook Express defaults and return to this screen later when you want to make changes.

To download the first set of available news groups:

■ Click on **Outlook Express** in the Folders list to display the action icons (See Figure 5.21).

■ Click on **Read News** to display the News folder. (You can also use the Go News menu sequence from the main Outlook Express menu, or simply click on the News folder in the Folder list).

■ Use Tools Newsgroups... to display the Newsgroups dialog box. The first time you do this you will see the dialog box shown in Figure 5.29 and Outlook Express will download available news groups.

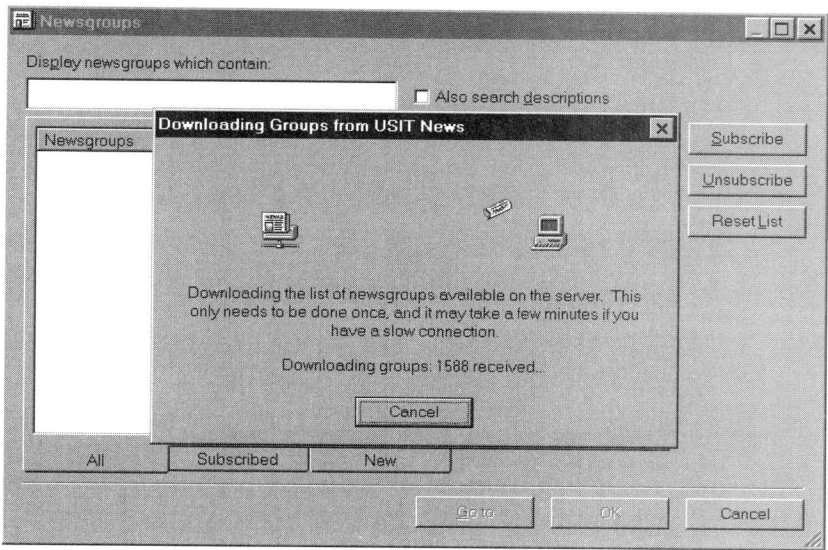

Figure 5.29 Download Newsgroups dialog box.

If you are using a dial-up connection, Outlook Express will have to dial the telephone, establish a News server connection, and begin the download. How long this takes depends on the speed of your connection and the number of News groups maintained by your News provider. For example, at United States Internet, there are over 30,000 news groups. The download over a 28,800 bps connection takes awhile. After the download is complete, you will see a dialog box similar to the one in Figure 5.30.

Remember that your Newsgroup screen may not look exactly like mine, since each ISP supports a slightly different list of news groups.

From this screen you can type in a word and Outlook Express will display only news groups that contain that word. Use the **Subscribe** button to select the groups to which you want to subscribe.

Outlook Express also includes a News filter that can provide additional group selection. Access this dialog box with the Tools Newsgroup Filters... menu sequence. This action displays a dialog box similar to the Mail Inbox Assistant (See Figure 5.22). Click on **Add** and specify how you want Outlook Express to handle specific news articles.

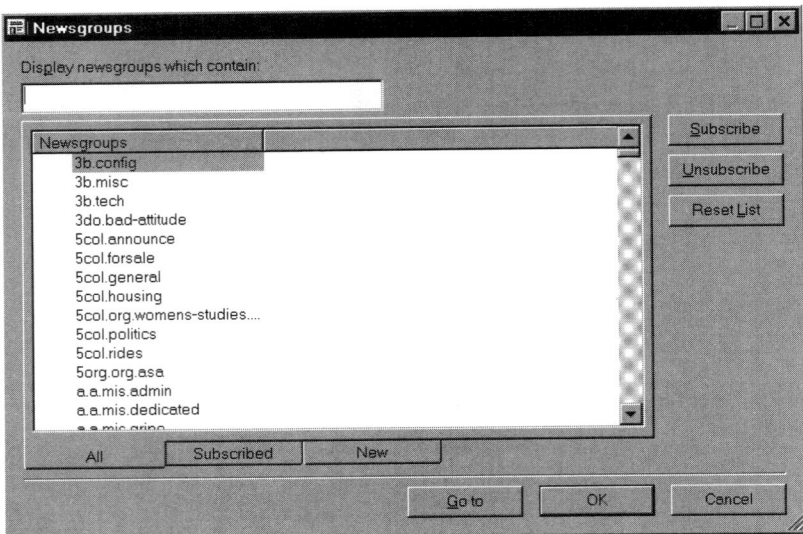

Figure 5.30 Newsgroup dialog box.

FRONTPAD

It wasn't that long ago that developing Web sites was the job of professionals—highly paid professionals. Then only some of the rest of us could even access these sites. Today the Web is the topic of news and feature articles; it is the talk of school, cocktail parties, and bridge clubs. And products such as Explorer 4.0 have put the power of Web development into the hands of anyone interested enough to give it a try.

FrontPad installs with Explorer, but it actually is a separate application. You can't launch FrontPad from inside the Explorer browser. Use the **Start** menu, point to **Programs**, point to **Accessories**, and choose **FrontPad**. You'll see the opening screen shown in Figure 5.31.

Avoid this lengthy navigation to the FrontPad executable by creating a shortcut on your desktop.

N O T E

Menu Bar
Format Bar
Tool Bar

Web Page Editor

Status Bar

Figure 5.31 FrontPad opening screen.

FrontPad is basically an editor and graphics manipulation program that uses HTML code in the background to drive the display and user-initiated actions. You can use it to create basic Web pages to promote yourself, your business, or a product.

FrontPad Main Features

Perhaps the most remarkable feature of FrontPad is how unremarkable it is on the surface. If you are familiar with Microsoft Word or any Windows-compliant editor, then FrontPad should be fairly easy to use. Notice, for example, how similar the FrontPad screen is to the Microsoft Word opening screen, shown in Figure 5.32.

You can see in this figure a menu bar that contains some of the same selections as on the FrontPad screen, a toolbar, and a format bar. You'll be pleased to learn that FrontPad operates in ways that are similar to Word—the same page-oriented editor, the same easy image management, font control, and more.

You'll also find some new features in FrontPad. Pull down the **Insert** menu, for example. Some of the same items that appear on the Word Insert menu are there: Break..., Symbol, Comment, File, and Hyperlink (Word 97). But there also are some Web-specific choices on the FrontPad Insert menu: Webview components, Video, Background sound, and Webbot component.

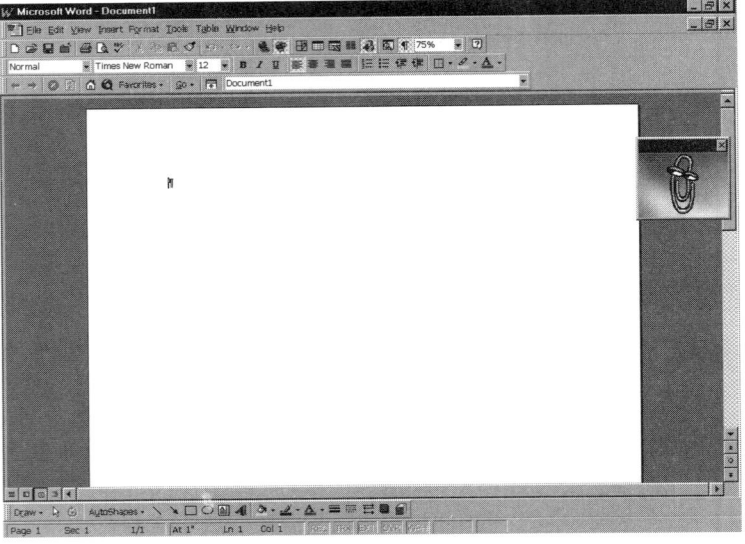

Figure 5.32 Microsoft Word opening screen.

Notice the status bar at the bottom of the FrontPad screen (Figure 5.31). The 2 seconds field indicates that FrontPad estimates that it will take a user who views this page on the Internet only two seconds to load the current page. The 2-second figure is not surprising, since the current page is blank. However, this flag helps you judge how long a page under design will require to load from your local hard disk (or wherever it is stored while under development). This will help you fine-tune a page design for optimum performance, as the number will change while you are building your page. If you add a few large graphics you will see the estimated load time increase substantially.

You can use the File Open... command sequence to load any HTML file to which you have access into the FrontPad editor. FrontPad interprets the HTML code and displays the finished page. If you'd like to see the HTML programming behind a page you've loaded, use View HTML... and FrontPad will open a dialog box like the one in Figure 5.33.

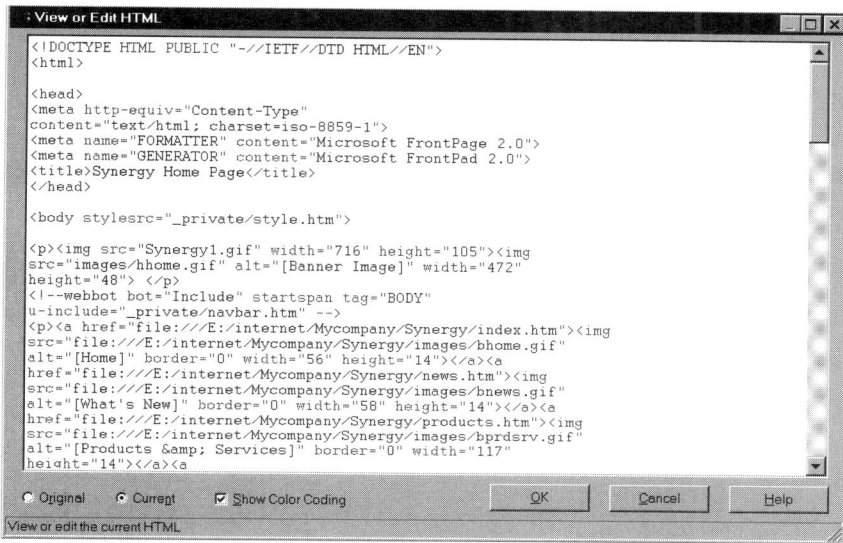

Figure 5.33 View HTML FrontPad dialog box.

As you learn more about Web page development you may want to experiment with editing content and page attributes directly in the HTML editor. By switching back and forth between HTML and Page view you can achieve the precise effect you want. However, FrontPad may change your HTML code automatically as it is saved. Note, also, that there are some things that FrontPad cannot display in the WYSIWIG mode.

NETMEETING

NetMeeting may be a portent of the future of online communications. There have been several similar products available, but NetMeeting puts together in one package several features that formerly were separate. NetMeeting is a powerful communications tool that includes audio, video, text, and shared applications. It uses the power of the Internet's global reach to add to its own functionality.

Launch NetMeeting by clicking on the **NetMeeting** icon in the program tray of the Taskbar, or from the Start menu: Click on **Start**, point to **Programs** and choose **Microsoft NetMeeting**. You will see the opening screen shown in Figure 5.34, an opening configuration Wizard. You'll go thorough this setup sequence only the first time you run NetMeeting.

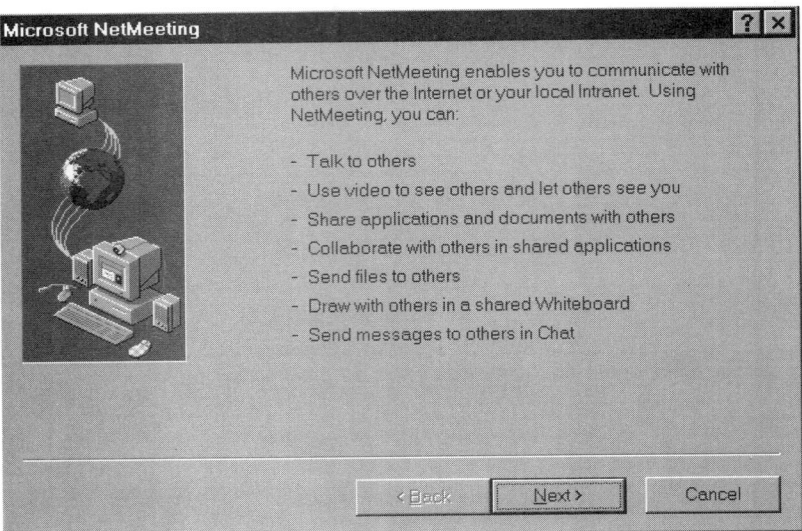

Figure 5.34 NetMeeting Opening Configuration Wizard screen.

To complete the Wizard configuration and present the main NetMeeting screen, do the following:

■ Click **Next** to display the Directory Server Wizard dialog box. A directory server is like a meeting place for people who want to communicate using NetMeeting. Several Microsoft directory servers are available in a pull-down list on this dialog box.

■ Choose a directory server and click on **Next** to display the personal information Wizard dialog box, shown in Figure 5.35.

■ Type information about yourself in the fields of this dialog box. You must supply at least your first and last name and an e-mail address.

■ Click on **Next** to display the next Wizard dialog box. This is an information screen that tells you to close all programs that use audio. The NetMeeting Wizard will next tune your audio for use by NetMeeting.

■ Disable any running audio programs and click on **Next**. The Audio Tuning dialog box will be displayed.

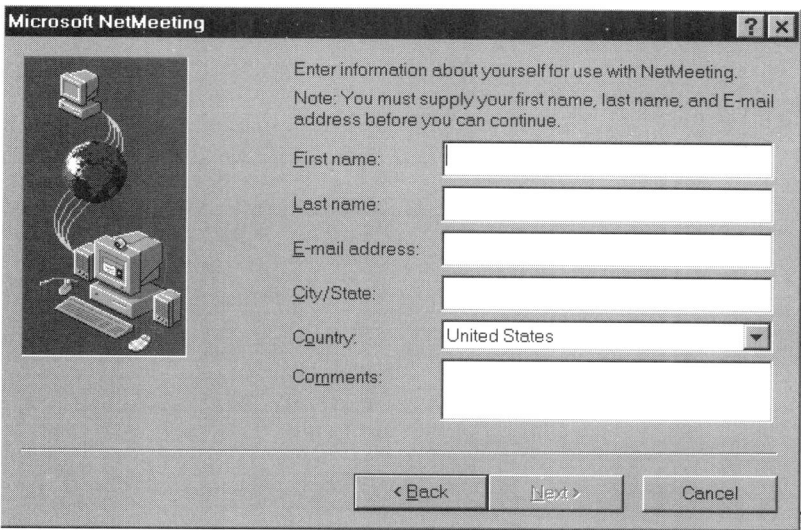

Figure 5.35 NetMeeting Personal Information Wizard dialog box.

■ Choose the speed of your Internet connection and click on **Next**. The Wizard asks you to click on Start Recording and read some text into the microphone attached to your sound card.

■ As requested, click on **Start Recording** and read the text. The Wizard will attempt to configure your sound card. If yours is a card not supported by NetMeeting you will see a warning message. Continue with the Wizard, anyway.

■ Click on **Finish** to complete the audio-tuning Wizard. You will see the main NetMeeting screen. Use **File Logon** to connect to the server you specified during the configuration. You will see the screen in Figure 5.36.

If there are other users logged into the same server, you will see their e-mail addresses, names and locations. You can also tell by the icons that appear in the second and third columns whether their computers are equipped with audio and video. Remember, NetMeeting is strong in audio and video features, but you can also use it for text connections.

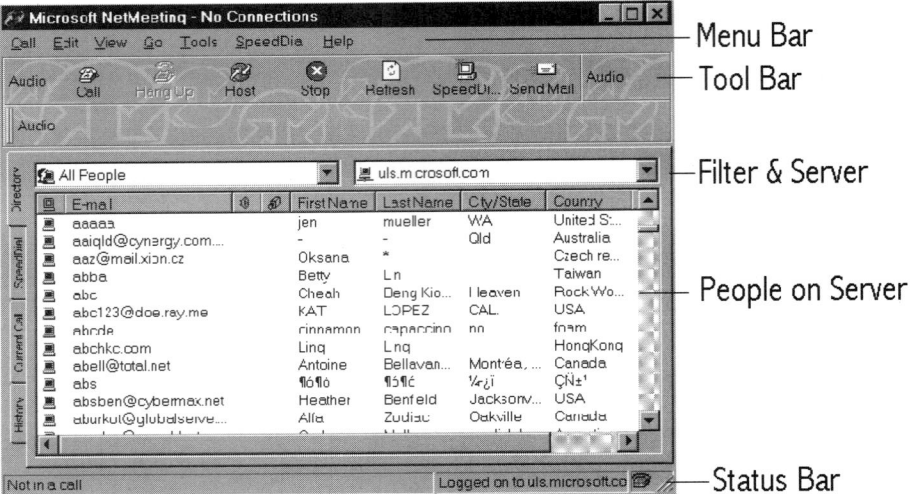

Figure 5.36 Main NetMeeting Screen after Logon.

NetMeeting Main Features and Settings

The NetMeeting screen is fairly straightforward. As a result, it should be comparatively easy for you to learn your way around this interesting program's features. If you don't see any names and e-mail addresses in the middle of the screen when you launch NetMeeting, remember to use the Call Log on... command sequence to connect to the server you specified during configuration.

Notice the vertical tabs on the left side of the NetMeeting dialog box. You can click on these tabs to display different information in the center of the screen. By default the Directory tab is on top, listing the other users connected to the same server you are using. Until you have used NetMeeting awhile, there probably won't be any information on the other tabs.

There are two pull-down lists above the directory display, one that lets you determine the names to appear in the directory display and another to set the NetMeeting server. The default directory display shows everyone on the current server, but you can choose to show only people in a call, only those not in a call, users with audio and video support, users with only audio support, and only people from your own country. As you make selections from this pull-down list, NetMeeting updates the directory display to reflect your changes.

Similarly, you can pull down a list of available servers to choose a different connection. If you change from the current server, NetMeeting automatically disconnects from that server and logs you onto the new one. The names in the directory display will disappear during the transition. Then you will see a new list of users connected to the new server.

When you have such a server connection, you can use NetMeeting like a chat program, with keyboard, audio, and video. You simply browse the list of people connected to the server, select some you'd like to contact, and place a call.

You can also use a direct modem connection to talk with another person. And, of course, you could use your own corporate or personal local area network for computer conferencing. If you install NetMeeting to use a modem connection, then you can easily dial a specific user for a NetMeeting conference. If you configured NetMeeting for a network or ISDN connection, then you may have to add modem support. Here's how:

1. Select **Tools** from the Main menu and choose **Options** to display the tabbed NetMeeting Properties dialog box.
2. Click on the **Protocols** tab to produce the display shown in Figure 5.37.

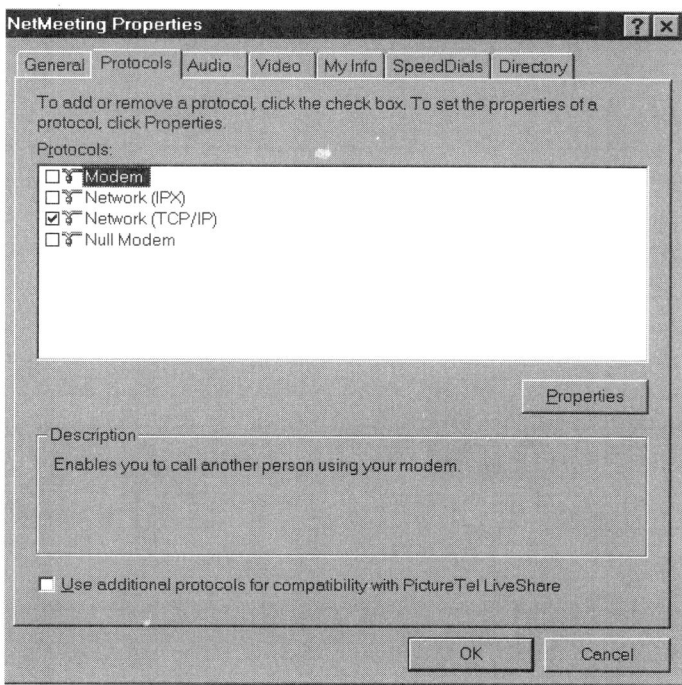

Figure 5.37 Protocols tab of NetMeeting Properties dialog box.

3. Click on the **Modem** protocol to add Modem Connection to the list of protocols available to NetMeeting. If you are using a local area network, choose **Network**. To use a direct cable connection to another computer choose **Null Modem**.

4. Click on **OK** to close the Properties dialog box and effect the changes.

Notice also the other tabs on the Properties dialog box. You can use this dialog box at any time to change your e-mail address and online name (the My Info tab). You'll quickly learn that personal users of the Microsoft NetMeeting servers rarely use their real names, favoring instead descriptive pseudonyms that depict their political or sexual leanings, their professional interests, or their current mood. You can do the same, changing your information as desired. Remember, however, that you need to use your real e-mail address.

Also, consider the power of this NetMeeting program. It can be used by coworkers or collaborators who need to work together on a serious project but who can't get together. It can be used to stay close to family members and friends. While a first look at some server entries may prompt you to turn off NetMeeting, don't, as the old saying goes, throw the baby out with the bath water. This is a serious product that can serve you well in serious business applications. I'll tell you more about this—and discuss security and privacy concerns—in Chapter 8.

Change your connection speed and other settings (including whether to automatically accept incoming calls) on the **General** tab, configure your audio and video hardware with these tabs, tell NetMeeting how to handle SpeedDials with the SpeedDials tab, and set the default server for automatic log-on with the Directory tab.

What is a SpeedDial? This is a separate personal directory that lets you quickly connect to selected users. You can add people to your SpeedDial list by selecting an entry in the Directory display, and clicking the **Add SpeedDial** button on the toolbar. You'll see a dialog box that lets you change the SpeedDial name and make other settings before the entry is saved. Once you have created some SpeedDial entries, you can view them by clicking on the SpeedDial tab beside the Directory display on the main NetMeeting screen.

NetMeeting is a real-time communications tool, but you also may need to access e-mail and news as you work with it. To do so, click on **Go** on the main menu and choose **Read Mail** or **Read News**. Outlook Express will launch so you can review your inbox for late information.

There are other communications tools built into NetMeeting. Pull down the **Tools** menu, for example. There you'll find a selection to transfer a file to another user, to open a whiteboard to share notes or drawings, or to open a Chat window so you can converse with connected users by using the keyboard.

You can also serve as the host for a conference by clicking the **Host** icon on the toolbar and answering some questions. This lets other users connect to your computer as a host. Of course, you must notify other people that you are setting up a host and when to log in for a meeting. Again, see Chapter 8 for more information on the specifics of using NetMeeting.

NETSHOW

Whereas NetMeeting supports interactive, multiuser communications with keyboard, whiteboard, video, and audio, NetShow supports one-way communications over a network. NetShow is a broadcast utility that lets you provide sequential graphics, text, and video information to a broad audience.

Launch NetShow from the Start Menu by pointing to **Programs**, then to **Microsoft NetShow**, and finally choosing **On-Demand Player**. You will see a small application window like the one in Figure 5.38.

Menu Bar

Current & Play Time

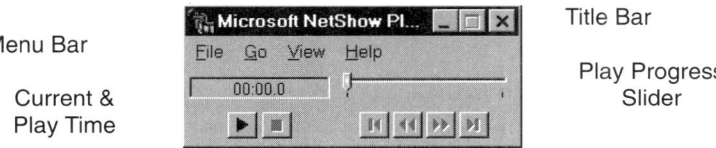

Title Bar

Play Progress Slider

Play Control Buttons

Figure 5.38 Opening NetShow screen.

All you see with this initial display are the play control and timer displays, plus the menu bar.

NetShow Main Features

To see how NetShow looks and works with a file loaded, use File Open Location... to display the Open Location dialog box. Type the location suggested by the prompt above the Open field of this dialog box: **mms://msnetshow.microsoft.com/nsoteach.asf**. Now you'll see the screen shown in Figure 5.39, a streaming animation of the NetShow logo.

Figure 5.39 NetShow Main screen with Tutorial for ASF Editor file loaded.

This process retrieves an .**ASF** file from the Microsoft Web site and provides a good demonstration of what NetShow is all about. When the motion stops, click on the rightmost button in the play control group, the arrow buttons at the very bottom of the NetShow player dialog box. This jumps to the next marker in the file and plays another sequence.

NOTE

To use the NetShow player successfully you need a 486/50-based computer or faster, you should have 16 MB of RAM, and you'll need a 16-bit sound card. An 8-bit sound card will greet you with lots of NetShow silence.

You can learn more about the file you just loaded by viewing the Properties dialog box. Right-click the center of the image and choose Properties, or use File Properties from the main menu. Either way, you will see the dialog box shown in Figure 5.40.

The seven tabs on this dialog box let you browse through the current settings and make some configuration changes. You can view statistics about the current download, for example, showing any errors in reception, and you can see a list of available file markers—and jump directly to one—by displaying the **Markers** tab (see Figure 5.41)

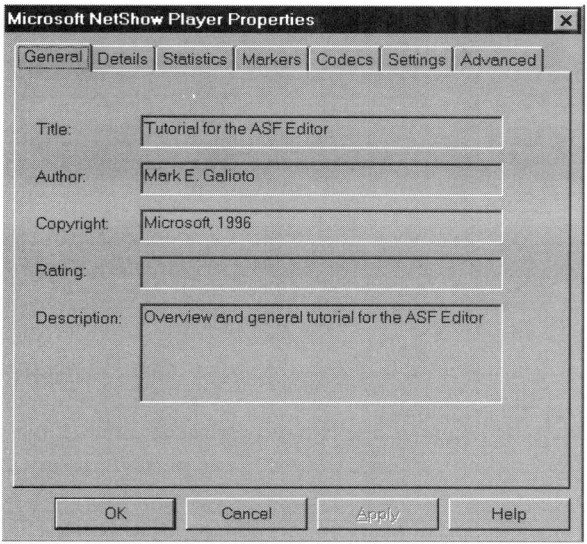

Figure 5.40 NetShow Properties dialog box.

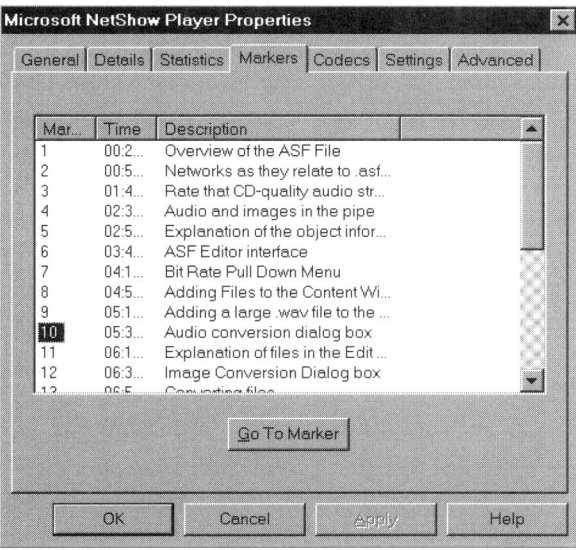

Figure 5.41 Player Properties Markers tab.

To get the latest information about NetShow—and to download the latest release of the software—click on **Go** and choose the NetShow Homepage or NetShow Software updates. This is another example of the tight integration of the Explorer components with the World Wide Web. By the way, on the Software Update Web site you can download more than just the latest version of the NetShow player. There you will find additional documentation, ASF file converter software, NetShow Server, and editor software. If you plan to use NetShow, you should visit both of these Web sites.

DESKTOP INTERFACE

Explorer 4.0's desktop interface is at once its most visible and most obscure feature. On the one hand, Explorer additions to your desktop are everywhere, putting Explorer 4 right before you all the time. On the other hand, you can quickly become accustomed to these changes and soon forget that they are "new" at all. At the same time, the more you use your computer after you install Explorer 4.0, the more you will find its sometimes subtle ways of augmenting your desktop.

After installing Explorer 4.0, you will find a new color scheme on your desktop and the Explorer 4.0 banner in the upper right hand corner of your desktop.

Compare the two desktops shown in Figure 5.42 and 5.43.

Figure 5.42 Standard Windows 95 Desktop.

Figure 5.43 Explorer 4.0 with Active Desktop.

Figure 5.42 shows a standard Windows 95 desktop using the default gray-green background. Figure 5.43 is the same desktop with Explorer 4.0's Active Desktop feature enabled. It is a hard to appreciate the impact of this difference with the gray scale images of these figures, but the Active Desktop has a black background, and the Explorer banner periodically changes to a Web page full of motion and color. The image in the middle of the screen prompting you to add objects to your desk is actually another HTML document stored on your hard drive. The car image at the bottom of the screen is a clip art image I added from the Desktop tab of the Display Properties dialog box.

From this most obvious difference, you can browse your desktop and Windows applications to see the subtle ways Explorer has integrated itself into your operating environment. I'll discuss some of these in the next section, just to get you started. Then we'll spend some more time with this issue in Chapter 6.

DESKTOP MAIN FEATURES

Another difference you will notice immediately between these two 95 desktops is that the shortcuts displayed on the Explorer screen have been changed to hyperlinks. Hover over one of the shortcut icons. Notice how the shortcut name is underlined and the pointer changes to a hand? This is just one of the subtle moves to make your operating system—Windows—operate more like a

World Wide Web site. The idea is to make it easier for users to transition between online and local environments. Indeed, the ultimate goal is to virtually erase the difference between online and local environments.

Just as you can jump to another site or a specific location within the current site on the Web by single-clicking on a Hyperlink, when you single-click on a shortcut icon, the associated application is launched. In conventional Windows, you would have to double-click a shortcut icon to launch its application.

You'll find evidence of Explorer in Windows utilities as well. The backgrounds have changed in programs such as Windows Explorer, and the My Computer display includes a drive space graph and a new background.

Why? Because even though the name Windows Explorer remains on the Programs list of the Start Menu, this utility actually is Internet Explorer formatted as a desktop browser. That fact will help you understand the other changes noted below, and demonstrates the subtle integration of Explorer into your desktop and operating environment.

Files and folders in Windows Explorer display and function as Hyperlinks when you hover over them. Also notice the toolbar displays in Windows Explorer (Figure 5.44). Back and Forward arrows have been added to help you easily navigate a directory tree. The Explorer browser lighting convention—lighting an icon only when you hover over it—is enabled.

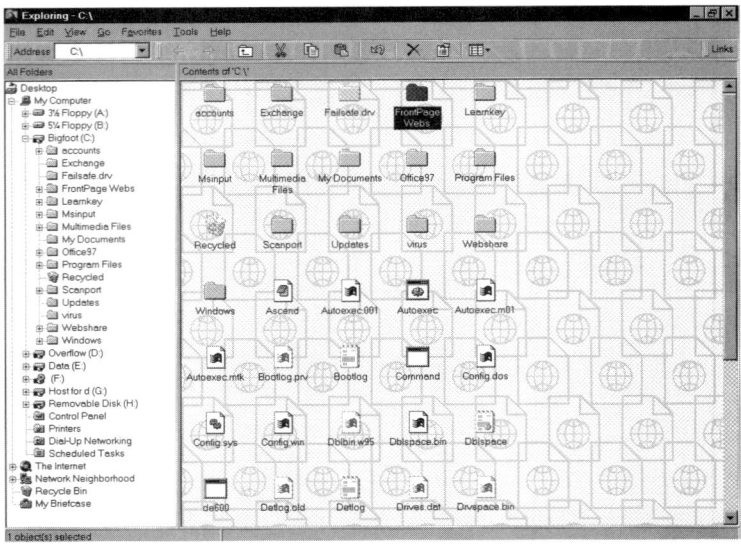

Figure 5.44 Windows Explorer screen.

The Windows Explorer toolbar itself is changed, giving the icons a flatter appearance, and there's a Links button—like the one on the Explorer browser screen—that lets you jump directly to the *Best of the Web, Today's Links,* the *Web Gallery,* and so on. Pull down the list of locations in the Address window and you'll see The Internet as one of the choices. Click here to launch the Explorer browser, displaying your default start location. With Links displayed, you click on **Address** to return to the toolbar and location display. And the individual icons for Large Icons, Small Icons, and Details have been replaced with a single icon that displays a pull-down list for these selections. You can also right-click the Windows Explorer toolbar and add text labels or customize the toolbar.

If you are in a network you have become accustomed to seeing the Map Network Drive and Disconnect Net Drive icons on the Windows Explorer toolbar. They're gone after you install Explorer 4.0, but you'll find these utilities on the Tools menu, as always. The Go menu has been added to let you jump to Web locations or open Outlook Express to check mail or read news. The Favorites menu from the Explorer Browser is there too, so you can open any of your favorite Web or network locations.

Do you want to change the way you explore local and network objects with Windows Explorer? Click on **View** and choose **Options** to display the Options dialog box shown in Figure 5.45.

At the View tab of this dialog box you can specify the files that will appear in a Windows Explorer display. This is similar to the File Types display you may be familiar with in the original Windows Explorer.

The middle group on this dialog box—Web View—lets you configure the background display and how the mouse works. By default, you can single-click on folders or files to open them, just as you would with a Web Hyperlink. You can turn this feature off if you prefer the double-click procedures of standard Windows. At the bottom of this tab you can toggle other features, such as full directory display and whether you show file extensions.

The File Types tab on this dialog box lets you associate file types with specific applications so that you can launch a program and display a file by choosing the file name from the Windows Explorer display.

You'll see some additions to your taskbar on the Windows desktop as well. The Explorer browser and Outlook Express icons are permanently installed to the left of the taskbar, beside the Start button, so you can launch them easily. Also, the tray area on the right side of the taskbar includes an icon for NetMeeting and for Subscriptions, Web sites you tell the Explorer browser to update for you periodically.

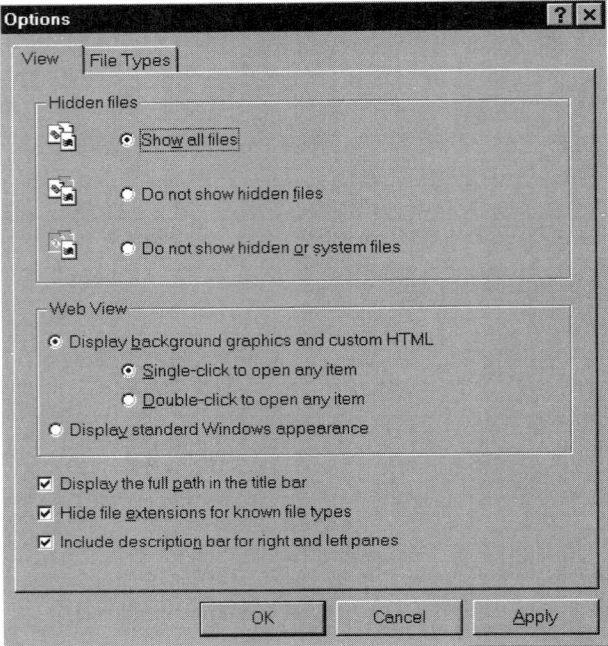

Figure 5.45 Windows Explorer Options dialog box.

The Start menu includes an Explorer 4.0 banner, and after you install Explorer you can drag and drop program names in the Programs list of the Start menu. You can even drag programs off of the Programs list and onto the quick reference list at the top of the Start menu. Again, these are indicators that Microsoft is attempting to merge the Web/online environment with your local desktop.

In the next chapter we'll look at some practical uses, with examples, for the browser features introduced here.

CHAPTER SIX

Using the Browser and Desktop

If you have read the previous chapters in this book you have seen many of Explorer 4.0's features. In this chapter, and the ones that follow, I want to provide some brief hands-on examples for using specific applications and utilities.

WHEN YOU BOOT THE COMPUTER

After you first boot your computer with Explorer 4.0 you probably won't give this new environment a second look. As I showed in Chapter 5, the background color is different from the standard Windows default and, unless you have removed them, you will see an Explorer banner and a prompt for adding objects to your desktop.

I talked about some possible changes to the desktop in previous chapters. However, there still are a few things you can do to customize your Explorer 4.0 desktop. For example, if you're not using desktop shortcuts that much, you may want to remove them to produce a clean, uncluttered desktop.

Do that by right-clicking anywhere on the desktop to display the desktop menu. Click on **Show Icons** to toggle off this option. Your desktop then will be similar to the one in Figure 6.1.

Figure 6.1 Explorer 4.0 Desktop without Shortcut icons.

Now all that's left on the desktop is an advertising promotion for Explorer and an HTML file that tells you how to add objects to the desktop. How can you navigate your programs without the shortcuts? Doing so isn't very different from the standard Windows desktop. After all, you could always just delete the shortcut icons. That would leave the Start Menu and program list, or special toolbars such as the Microsoft Office bar, for starting programs.

With Explorer 4.0, you now have an interesting alternative to these standard navigation tools. You can turn your desktop into one or a series of HTML documents that contain Hyperlinks to folders on your local computer, on your LAN, or on the World Wide Web. There are automatic utilities to help you create these files and, with the included FrontPad HTML editor, if you want to try your hand at Web page development you can completely customize your operating system desktop.

In addition, if you are using Office 97, the HTML Wizards for earlier office software, or any other Web-savvy package, you can probably create Web pages from inside these programs that would serve as a handy desktop navigation aid. For example, you could save a Microsoft Access database with a Switchboard (a database form that serves as a menu) to an HTML format, insert it onto your desktop, and have easy access to the Access data without having to launch Access to get to it. Or use PowerPoint to create a series of slides that include

Hyperlinks to images, sound files, and other system resources. Also, you can display multiple files for different applications, or create one well-integrated Web site stored on your local hard drive that provides access to everything and fills your desktop screen. You could do the same thing by running the Explorer browser and loading a Web page, of course, but the beauty of this capability is that it becomes a part of your desktop, separate from the browser itself.

Also, you can add toolbars to the task bar. For example, you can insert an Address or Links bar like the one on the Browser toolbar, you can drop a set of icons from the desktop onto the task bar, and you can create custom toolbars that reside on the task bar or anywhere else on your desktop (I'll show you how to do this later in this chapter).

This customizing capability can lead to a virtually unlimited variety of Windows desktop schemes. As this book is written you are on your own in developing a custom desktop, but just wait. I predict that Microsoft, shareware producers, corporate developers, and many hardware and software companies soon will produce custom desktop schemes to promote computer lines, to support in-house work groups, to provide easy access to frequently used programs and utilities, and to ease the training task for new computer users.

Until then, how can you customize your own desktop? Here's how:

1. Use a Windows Explorer Customize utility to create an HTML document that displays files and directories.
2. Use FrontPad to edit the automatically-created document, if you want.
3. Use the Desktop tab from the Display Properties dialog box to load this Web page automatically to your desktop when you start your computer.

Of course, you can download one or more Web pages from a corporate site or use FrontPad or FrontPage to create a custom page to provide the user interface you want. I'll show you how to do that in the next section of this chapter. See also Chapter 10 for details on creating a custom desktop webpage using FrontPad.

Now for the details.

Create an HTML Directory Display

Since the Windows Explorer utility is really a specially configured version of Internet Explorer 4.0, you can use it to create a Web page that contains the folders and files you want to access through an HTML file on your desktop. A Wizard associated with the Windows Explorer makes the task easy:

1. Click on **Start** on the task bar and point to **Programs**.
2. Choose **Windows Explorer**.
3. Choose the folder you want to use as the top of your HTML directory tree.
4. Click on **View** on the main menu and choose **Customize This Folder...** to present the dialog box shown in Figure 6.2.

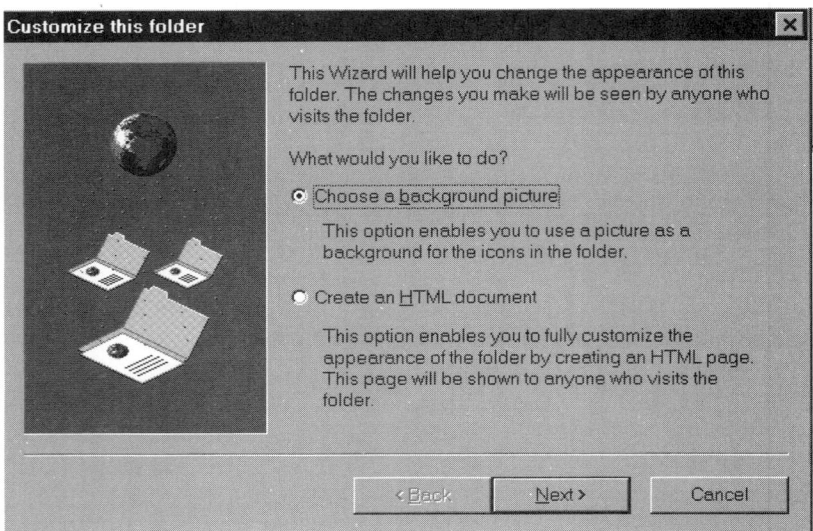

Figure 6.2 The Windows Explorer Customize this folder dialog box.

5. Click on **Create an HTML document** to toggle on that option.
6. Click **Next** to display the next Wizard screen, shown in Figure 6.3.

Click on **Advanced** if you want to change the default folder and file name for this HTML document.

NOTE

7. Review the steps suggested by the Wizard and click **Next** to display the action summary shown in Figure 6.4.
8. Click **Finish** to complete the process.

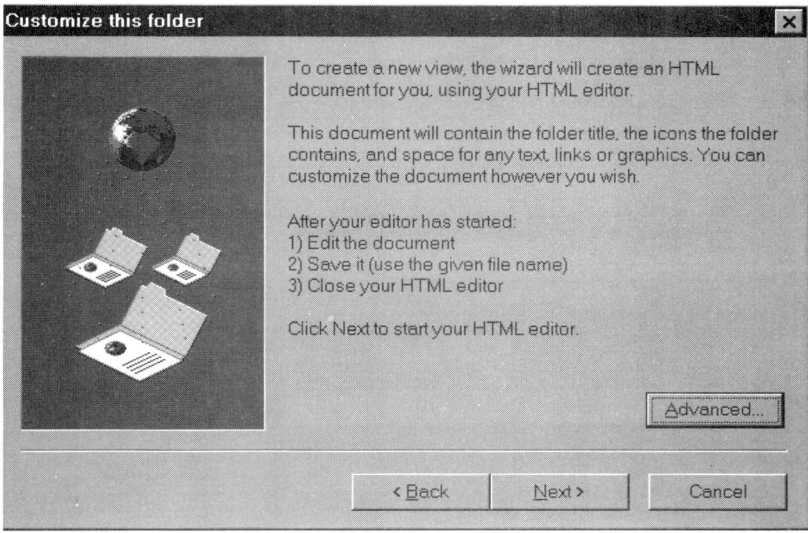

Figure 6.3 A Customize Wizard create HTML view screen .

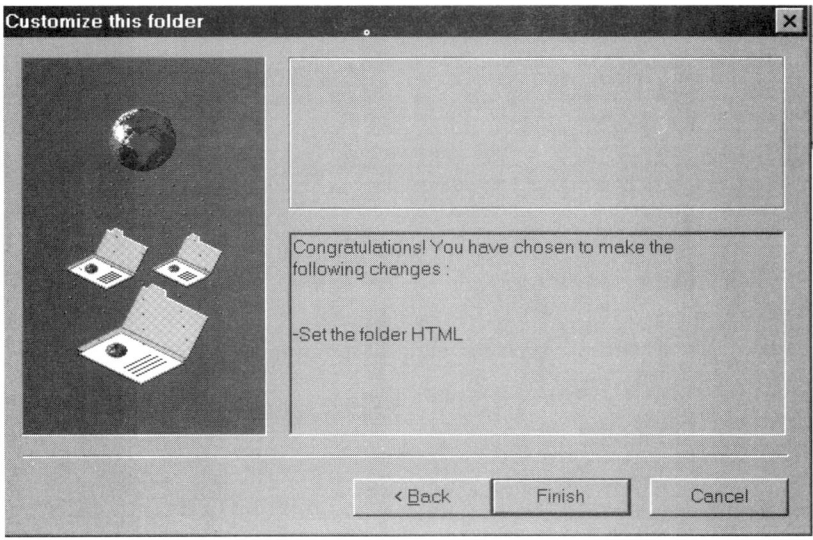

Figure 6.4 Customize Wizard action summary screen.

WARNING

This feature does not work in Windows 95 in early beta versions of Explorer 4.0. A page is created, but with errors. Second use produces a file-not-found error. It does work after a fashion in Windows NT, but only for the root directory of a drive.

Edit the HTML Document

The Wizard creates an HTML file named **Folder.htm** inside the folder you selected before launching the Wizard. This new file is identified by the globe icon that designates a Web page document. You can launch FrontPad to open this new file and make any changes you want before inserting it onto your desktop display. (For more information on using FrontPad, see Chapters 5 and 10.).

Insert the HTML Document on Your Desktop

To display the new file on your Desktop so you can use it as a Web-style navigation tool, do the following:

1. Right-click anywhere on the desktop to display a pop-up menu.
2. Choose **Properties** to show the Display Properties dialog box.
3. Click on the **Desktop** tab to produce the display shown in Figure 6.5.
4. Click **New** and choose **Web Site** from the New dialog box.
5. Click on **OK** to display the New Web Site dialog box.
6. Type the path and filename of the HTML document you just created. For example, **c:\windows\folder.htm**. Click on **Browse** if you need to navigate to the file you want to use on your desktop.
7. Click on **OK** to close the dialog box and return to the Display Properties dialog box.
8. Click on **OK** to close the Display Properties dialog box. The new file will be displayed as part of your Windows Desktop.

If you remove shortcuts from your desktop, pages such as this become your primary method of navigating your local hard drive or local area network.

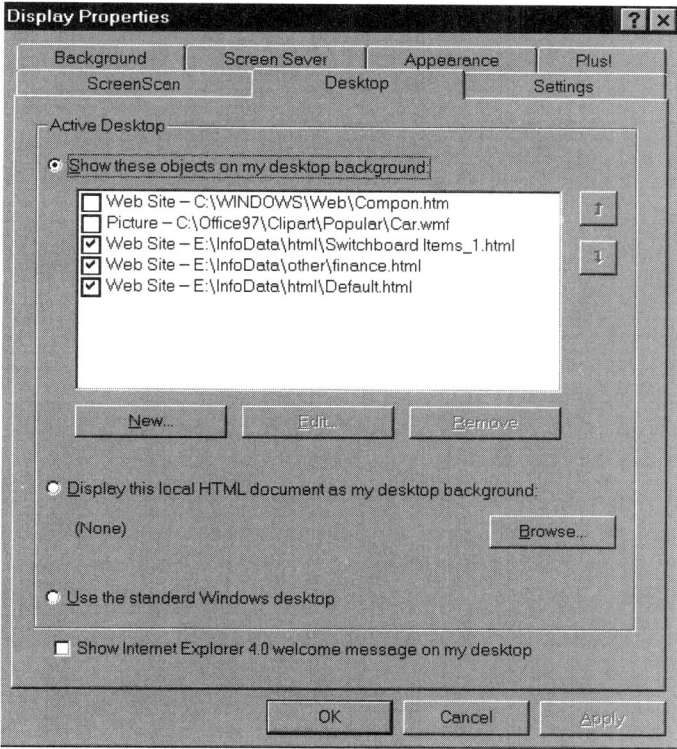

Figure 6.5 The Desktop tab of Display Properties dialog box.

FURTHER CUSTOMIZING THE BROWSER

While you can work successfully with the default Browser settings, there are some things you might want to try. I'll discuss a few of them in this section.

Custom Background

You probably noticed that the first Wizard screen let you choose between creating a custom background for the Windows Explorer or creating an HTML document that contains the files and subfolders in the selected folder.

To create a custom background for the Windows Explorer, use **View Customize This Folder...** and click on **Choose a Background Picture**. Click

Next to continue the Wizard and follow instructions to choose a graphics file that will be used as the background picture. A word of warning: This feature does not function in the platform Preview release.

Subscribe to a Web Site

Another feature that adds strength and versatility to Explorer 4.0 is the ability to download specified Web sites to a local drive and then to tell Explorer how often you want to update the local files. This is particularly useful for sites that rarely change, if you have a slow dial-up link, or for sites that frequently change, if you have an automatic high-speed connection, such as ISDN or a direct network connection. Explorer calls this a *subscription*. Here's how to subscribe to a Web site:

1. Launch the Internet Explorer Browser.
2. Navigate to the Web site to which you want to subscribe.
3. Click on **Favorites** on the main Browser menu, and point to **Subscriptions** and choose **Subscribe**. You will see a dialog box similar to the one in Figure 6.6.

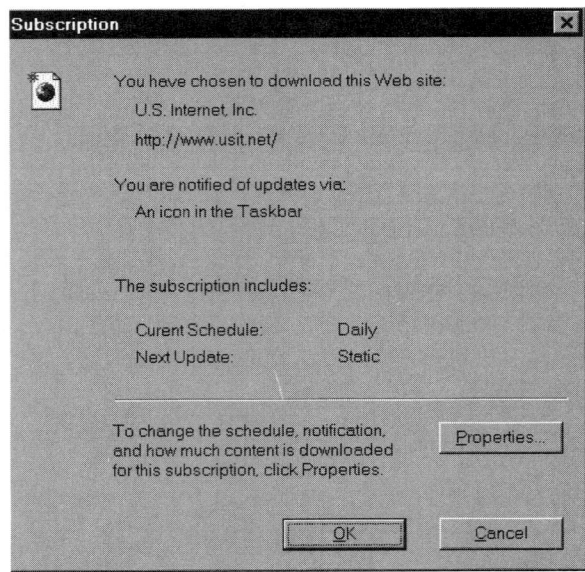

Figure 6.6 The Browser Subscription dialog box.

4. Click **Properties** to display the Properties dialog box, shown in Figure 6.7.

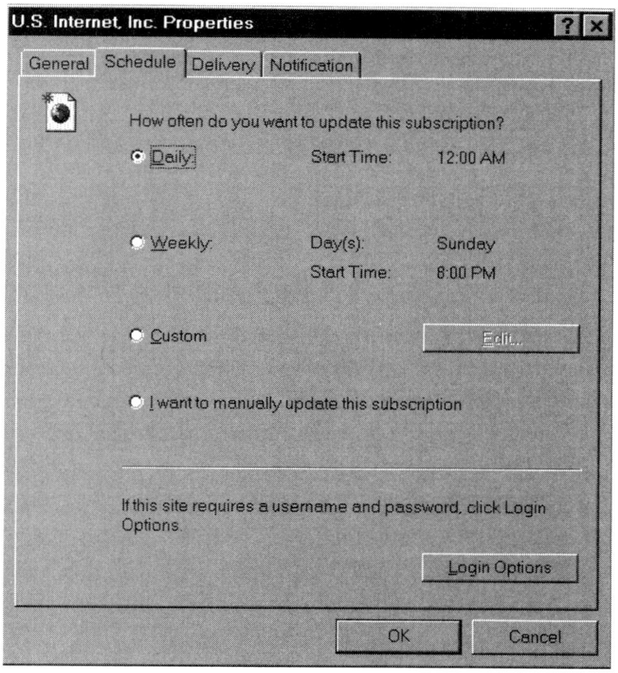

Figure 6.7 Subscription Properties dialog box.

5. Choose the update frequency you want for this site. If you choose **Custom**, you can click **Edit** to specify the frequency. If you choose to manually update, then the files on your local drive won't be updated unless you do it yourself.

6. Click on **Delivery** to bring the Delivery tab forward (see Figure 6.8).

7. Choose how much of the current site you want to download. The default is the selected page only.

    If you click on the **This page and...** button, you can specify the number of pages to download. If you are looking at the home page of a site, for example, you can tell Explorer to download just the next level, the next two levels, and so on. You also have the option of following Hyperlinks from the current page. Use this option carefully. The amount of data downloaded with this option selected can become quite large. If you want, you can tell Explorer to download only a certain number of bytes, so you won't inadvertently capture hundreds of megabytes of Web data.

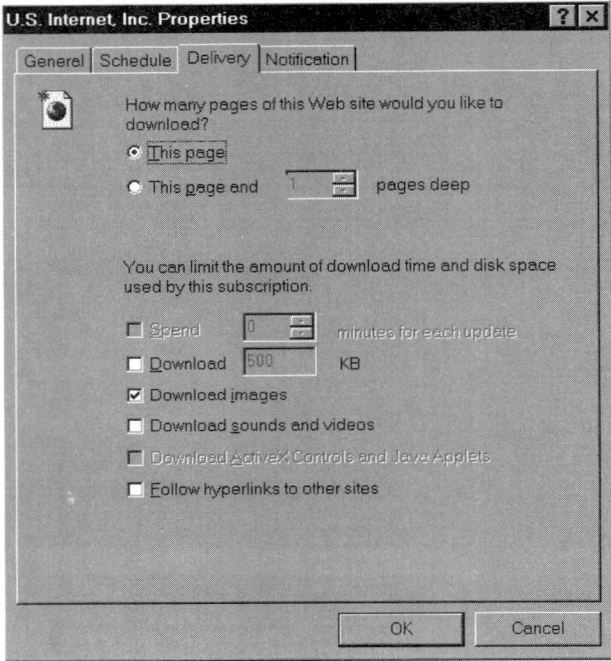

Figure 6.8 Delivery tab of Subscription dialog box.

8. Click on **Notification** to bring that tab forward. This lets you decide the way you want to be notified when your subscribed page changes. Your choices are an icon on the task bar or an e-mail message.

9. Click on **OK** when you have made all of the changes you want. This closes the Properties dialog box and returns you to the Subscription dialog box.

10. Click **OK** again to return to the subscribed Web page in the Browser.

You can review your subscriptions at any time by clicking on the **View** menu, pointing to **Subscribe** and then choosing **View All**. You will see a display similar to the one in Figure 6.9.

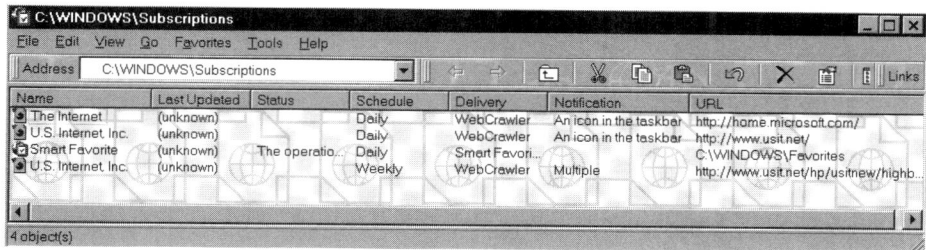

Figure 6.9 View All display from Subscribe menu.

You can right-click any of these subscriptions and choose delete from the pop up menu to remove them (except Smart Favorite. Microsoft retains control to that one). You can also select the entry and click on the X icon on the toolbar.

There also is an Update All choice on this menu. This will override the update settings for each Web page and cause Explorer to update your subscribed pages immediately. Depending on the speed of your computer and Internet connection, and the number and size of the subscriptions, this may take quite a while.

The Options selection on the Subscribe menu lets you set some global options with the dialog box shown in Figure 6.10.

This dialog box has four tabs: General, Dial-Up, Daily Schedule, and Weekly Schedule. You can see from Figure 6.10 that the General tab provides toggles for monitoring changes to Web sites and for displaying a notification icon on the task bar. Click on each of these tabs to reveal other choices:

> *Dial-Up*: You can tell Explorer to automatically dial-up and connect to the Internet on this tab. If you use a network connection, you probably won't need to enable this option.
>
> *Daily Schedule*: Specify the hours you want to conduct a daily update, and tell Explorer how frequently between these hours to update the pages.
>
> *Weekly Schedule*: Specify the day, time, and frequency of Weekly updates on this tab.

Unfortunately, the subscribed sites that Explorer downloads are stored in a hidden directory and are not in standard HTML format (at least they don't have the standard **.htm** or **.html** file extensions), so you can't use them on your desktop. You can, however, use a third-party product, such as Web Whacker, to copy one or more pages off of the Internet and use them directly on your desktop.

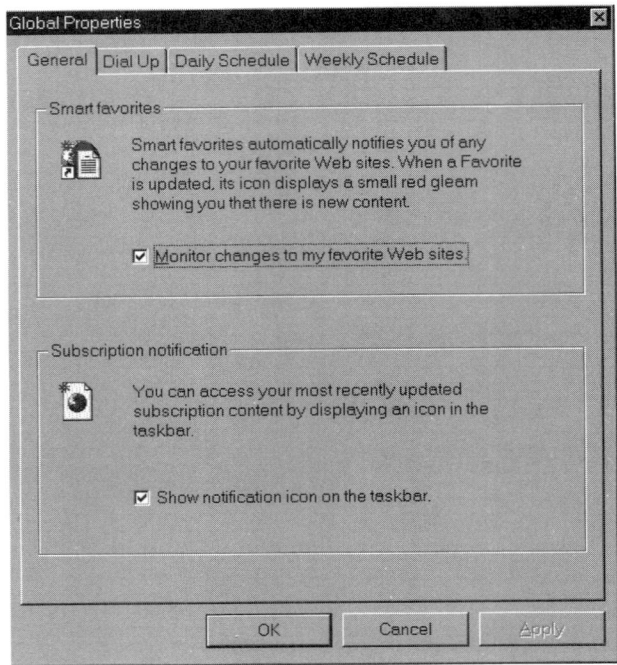

Figure 6.10 Subscribe options (Global Properties) dialog box.

In addition, when you add an HTML object to your desktop that is not located on your local computer using the method described above, the Wizard will bring up a dialog box asking if you would like to update the component on a daily basis. If you answer **Yes**, the component will be added to your automatic subscriptions. Choosing the **Advanced…** tab in this dialog box, will let you adjust the update settings. By returning to the Subscription program, you can modify the settings later.

Setting Browser Options

Finally, check out the tabbed Options dialog box, displayed when you click on **View** and choose **Options** from the main Browser screen (see Figure 6.11).

You must be in Internet Explorer when performing this action. You get there by clicking the **Internet Explorer** icon in your task bar.

N O T E

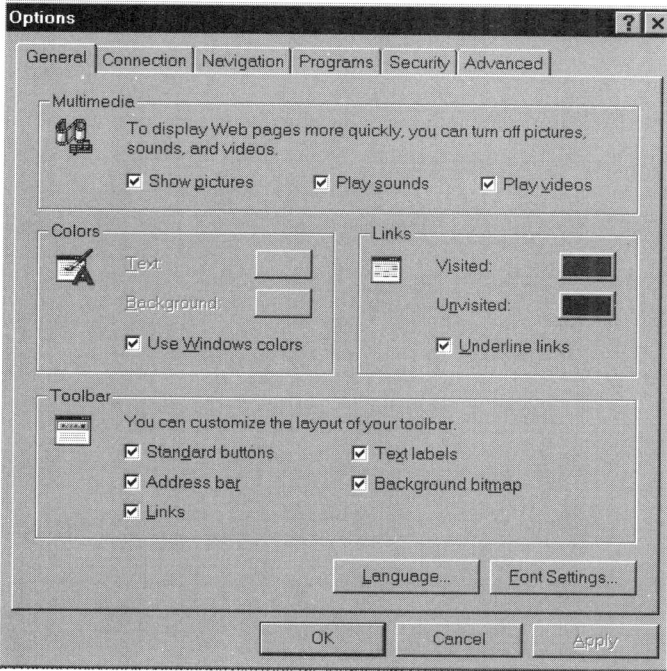

Figure 6.11 Browser Options dialog box.

This dialog box contains six tabs: General, Connection, Navigation, Programs, Security, and Advanced. You can view each of these tabs for yourself. Below, I'll summarize the settings they contain.

The General Tab

You can see from Figure 6.11 that the General tab of this dialog box has four groups, Multimedia, Colors, Links, and Toolbar. The *Multimedia* group lets you specify what multimedia objects you want to download. Explorer will get pictures, sounds, and videos unless you remove the checkmark beside one or more of these choices. If you are on a slow connection, you may want to de-select some or all of these options to increase performance.

By default Explorer uses the Windows color scheme. If you uncheck this box in the *Colors* group, you can choose what colors you want to use for text and backgrounds. Simply click on the color buttons beside the Text or Background labels and you will see a pop-up color selection dialog box.

The *Links* group defines how various on-screen objects will appear, including the look of a Hyperlink that you have visited, versus one that you have not seen. Be aware that these color settings are default values. HTML code in the Web page can change them.

The *Toolbar* group lets you customize the main Browser toolbar. All objects are selected by default, but you can toggle off one or more of the objects in this group, if you wish.

The Connection Tab

The Connection tab contains two groups and an Automatic Configuration button, as you can see in Figure 6.12.

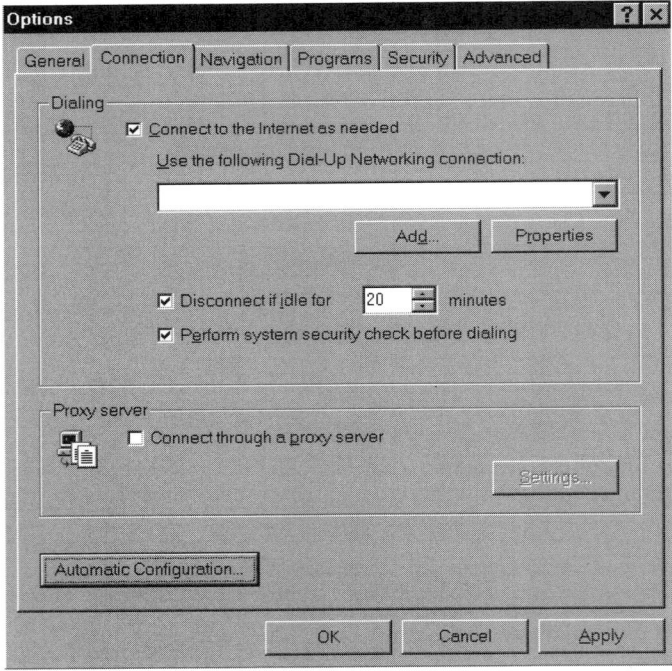

Figure 6.12 The Connection tab of the Browser Options dialog box.

This dialog box specifies how Explorer will connect to the Internet. If you use a network connection, including some types of ISDN connections (which are really network connections that use a router to connect), leave this dialog box alone—leave all the choices disabled. If you are using a dial-up connection, click on the **Connect to the Internet as needed** button. This will enable the **Dial-Up Connections** field so you can specify which dial-up networking profile you want to use. If you haven't created a dial-up networking profile, click on **Add** on this dialog box and follow the Wizard instructions.

To use a Proxy server connection, simply click on the **Connect through a Proxy server** choice at the bottom of this dialog box to enable it. In most cases, you will not need to use a Proxy server. If you do, your Network Access Provider or Network Administrator can tell you what to put in this field.

The Automatic Configuration button at the bottom of this dialog box opens another dialog box where you can enter a URL for a site that contains configuration data. This is a useful feature for corporate sites where all users should have the same Explorer configuration.

The Navigation Tab

Use the Navigation tab to set some of Explorer's defaults, including the start page and what site is used for searching. The Page: field at the top of this tab (see Figure 6.13) is a pull-down list that lets you specify a name and online address for the start page, search page, and up to five quick links. Quick Links are the buttons that appear on your toolbar when you click on Links on the right side of the Browser toolbar.

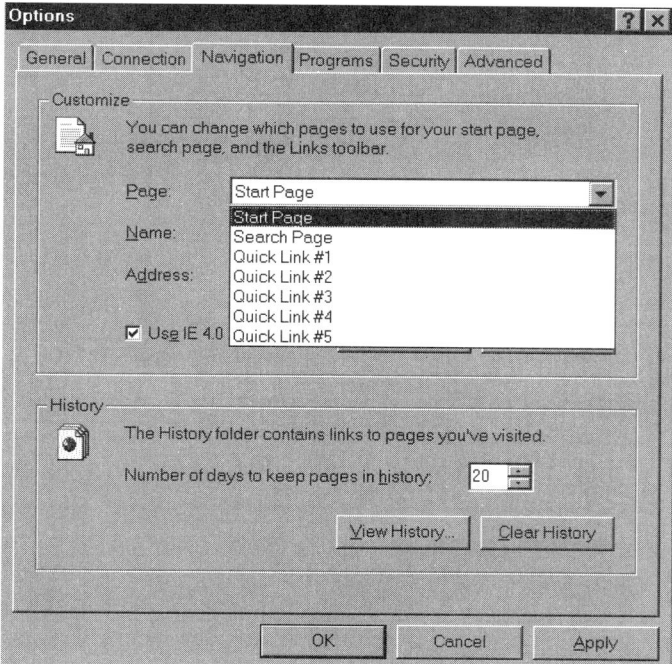

Figure 6.13 The Navigation tab of the Browser Options dialog box.

To configure this part of the Browser:

1. Pull down the list in the Page: field.

2. Choose which page you want to configure.

3. Type a name for the site in the Name: field, or accept the Browser's default. You can't change the name of the Start Page and Search Page. You can change the names of the Quick Links.

4. Type the URL for the site in the Address: field.

NOTE You can also navigate to the site you want to use before displaying the Options dialog box, then simply click on the Use Current button to set the url in the Address: field. Click on the Use Default button to use Microsoft's settings for these Web pages.

5. Click **OK** to close this dialog box and make the changes effective.

You can also adjust how Explorer handles the temporary history files it stores as you browse the Web. Change the number of days Explorer stores history files by clicking on the up and down arrows, or by selecting the value already in the Number of Days field and typing a new value. For best performance, this number usually should be set to a few weeks, say 20 days. However, keeping history uses disk space.

If you click on the View History button, Explorer displays all the files it is keeping in the history cache (see Figure 6.14).

You can drag this dialog box to a different shape if you need to so you can see all the fields. You can sort the list according to any of the fields in the history file simply by clicking on the field name by which you want to sort. To sort by Last Updated, for example, click on the title of that column. To delete a single entry, right-click it and choose **delete** from the pop-up menu. Close the history display with the **File Close** command sequence or by clicking on the **close** icon at the upper right corner of the dialog box.

Remove all entries in the history file by clicking on the **Clear History** button on the Navigation tab of the Options dialog box.

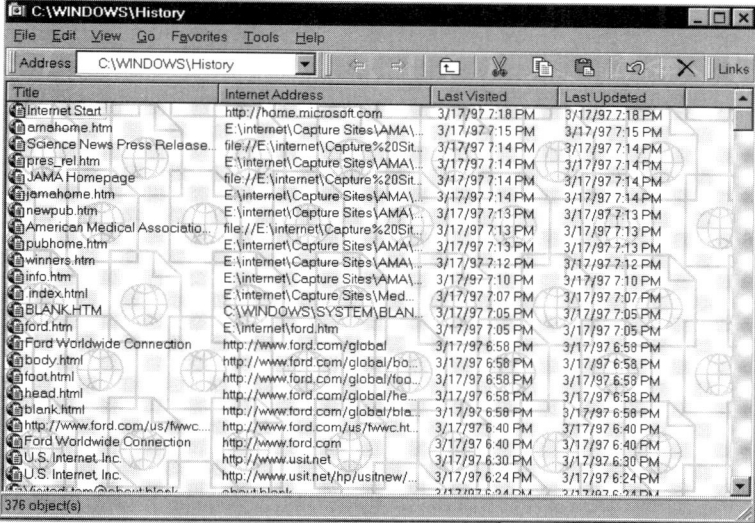

Figure 6.14 View History files dialog box.

The Programs Tab

The Programs tab (Figure 6.15) of this dialog box has three groups: Mail and news, Viewers, and Microsoft Wallet. This tab lets you set what programs Explorer will use to read and send mail, to access news groups, and to run programs or display files downloaded over the Internet. In addition, you can configure the operation of the Microsoft Wallet, a utility that helps you manage address lists and payments. A checkbox tells Explorer whether to check if it is the default browser when it loads.

By default, Explorer uses Outlook Express to manage your e-mail. This program installs as part of the Explorer package. If you are using Office 97—which includes the full Outlook application—or another e-mail package, you may want to specify something other than Outlook Express.

Explorer also uses Outlook Express for News, but you can change that if you wish.

However, you can't simply type in the name of a new mail or news program. Explorer will only present the names of applications you have previously installed and that it can find in your registry entries.

The File Types button in the Viewers group displays a File Types dialog box (Figure 6.16) that lets you associate file types with the applications required to display them. Windows is configured with a number of these files already, and for the most part these settings will be sufficient.

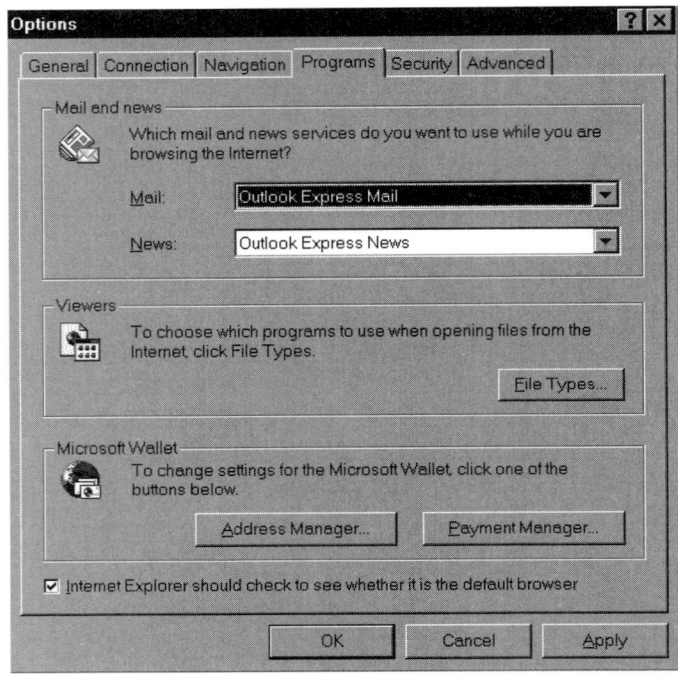

Figure 6.15 The Programs tab of the Browser Options dialog box.

Notice that as you click on a new file type, information about it is displayed at the bottom of the dialog box. You will see the file extension, content, and the program used to open and display it. You can add file types with the **New Type**... button, or remove a type with **Remove**. (Be sure to use Remove carefully. You might disable a desired functionality.)

You can get more information about a particular file type by selecting it in the Registered File Types: window and then clicking on Edit. You will see a dialog box similar to the one in Figure 6.17.

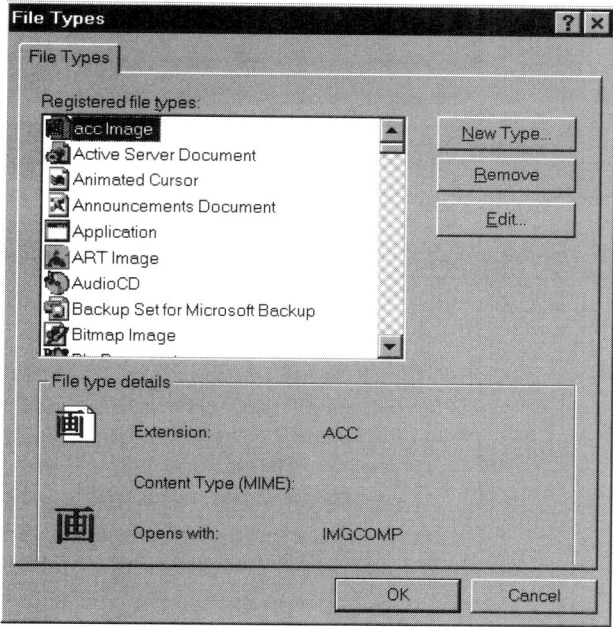

Figure 6.16 The File Types dialog box from the Programs tab of the Options dialog box.

Two options remain on this Programs tab, both part of the Microsoft Wallet utility. The Address Manager... button lets you view, edit and add to your personal address list. The Payment Manager... button helps you set up credit card accounts so you can use online shopping and pay automatically and safely.

ADDRESS MANAGER...

After you install Explorer 4.0, the Address Manager may be blank, or it may contain one name and address—yours. Remember that this is an intelligent product and it can pick up information from other locations in your system. You can view this (and other addresses, after you enter them) by clicking on the Address Manager... button on the Programs tab of the Options dialog (see Figure 6.18). Notice that this is a separate facility from the Windows Address Manager, also part of Explorer 4.0. This Wallet-based Address Manager is designed to hold address information for the people and companies with whom you do electronic business.

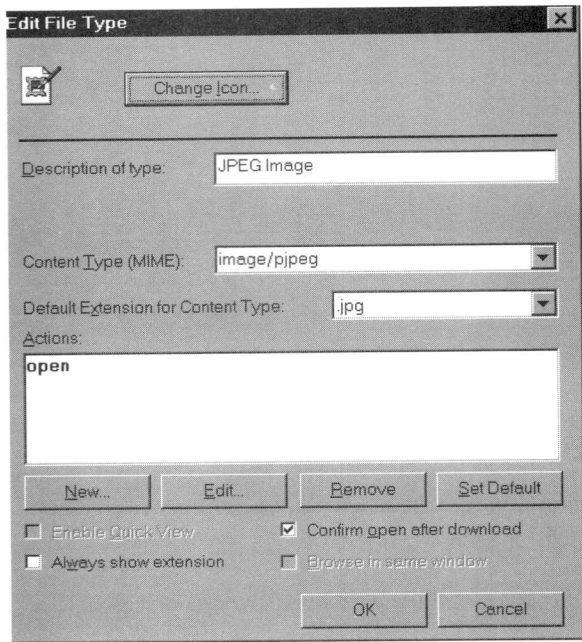

Figure 6.17 The Edit File Types dialog box.

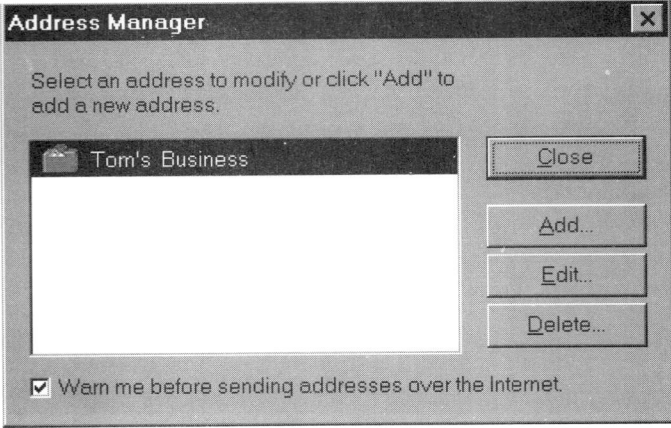

Figure 6.18 The Address Manager dialog box.

You can double-click on your address entry to review details or to edit the entry. Create a new entry by clicking on Add... to produce the display shown in Figure 6.19.

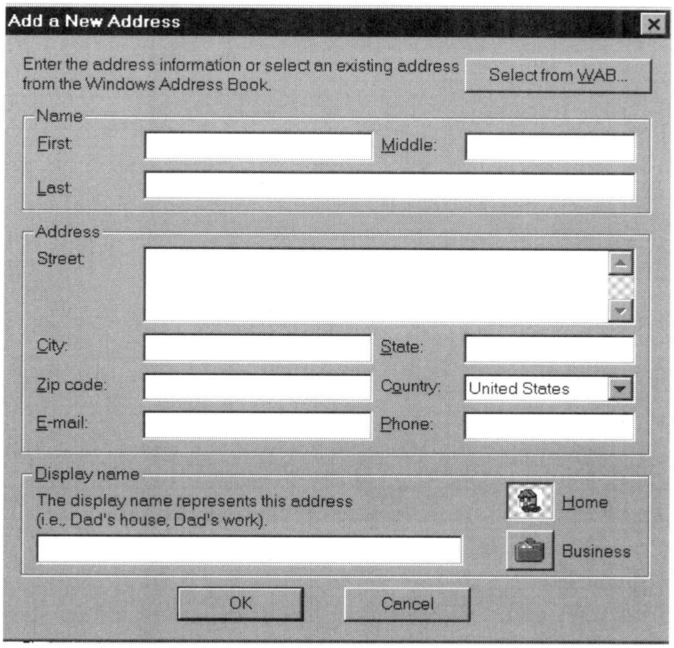

Figure 6.19 Add a New Address dialog box.

Type information into the fields of this address database, or click on **Select from WAB...** to display addresses in your Windows Address Manager. Choose a name from this list and it will be copied into the Wallet Address Manager.

Notice particularly the Display field at the bottom left corner of the Add a New Address dialog box. Put anything you want in this field to make the address easy to find. You can use a company name, a personal ID code, and so on. Also, click on the **Home** or **Business** button to indicate what kind of address the new entry is. Once you enter an address with one of these selections, you can't change its type. You can add a new entry for another location, if you wish.

Click on **OK** to close the Edit or New dialog boxes, as appropriate, then click **Close** to close the Address Manager dialog box.

PAYMENT MANAGER...

To enable and use the Payment Manager, do the following:

1. Click on the **Payment Manager...** button and click **Add** on the Payment Manager dialog box to produce the display shown in Figure 6.20.

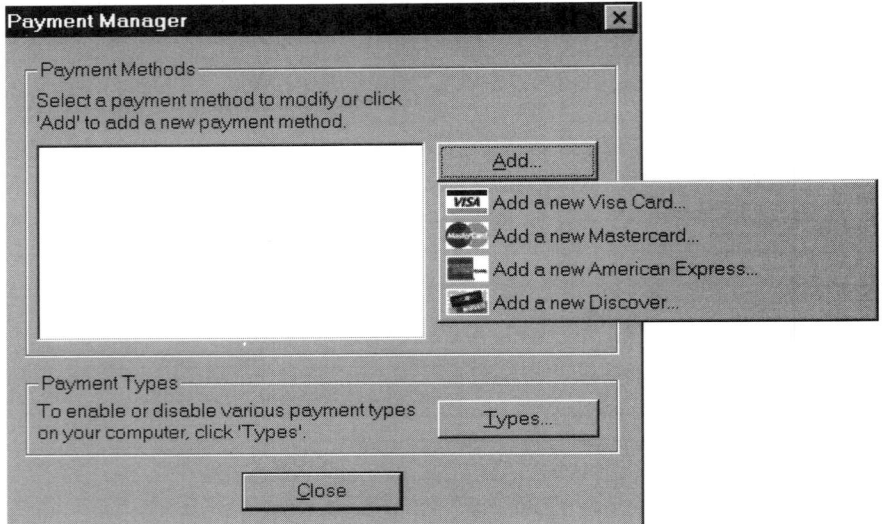

Figure 6.20 The Initial Payment Manager dialog box.

2. Choose a credit card from the list to add a payment type. You will see a Microsoft Wallet license agreement when you add your first credit card. Take special note of sections 7, 8, and 9, which explain Microsoft's liability in the event someone would obtain your Credit Card number from this software.

3. Click on **I Agree** to present the Add a New Credit Card screen shown in Figure 6.21. This dialog box summarizes the steps required to add a new credit card.

4. Click **Next** to continue the Wizard. You will see the screen in Figure 6.22.

5. Fill out the information for the credit card you are adding and click on **Next** to move to the following Wizard screen, shown in Figure 6.23.

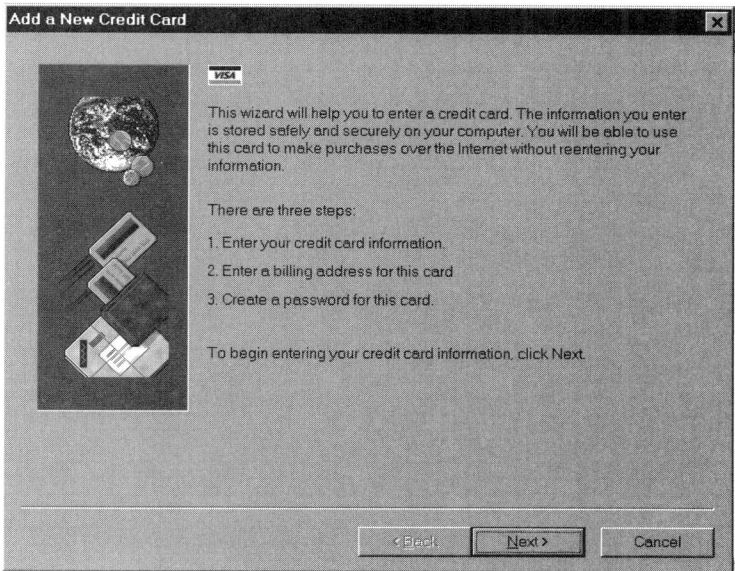

Figure 6.21 The Add a New Credit Card opening Wizard screen.

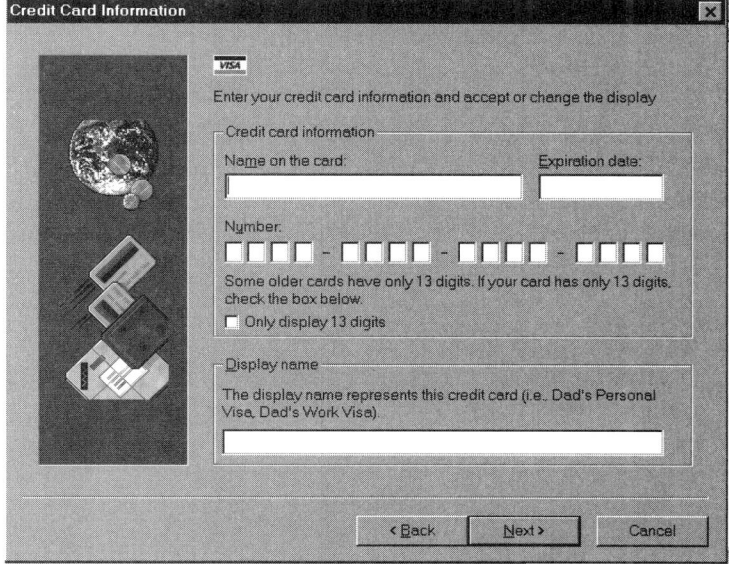

Figure 6.22 The Credit Card Information dialog box.

N O T E The Wizard will check the number you enter for accuracy. It can't know whether you enter precisely your correct number, but it does know whether the number you entered is reasonable for the type of credit card you are adding.

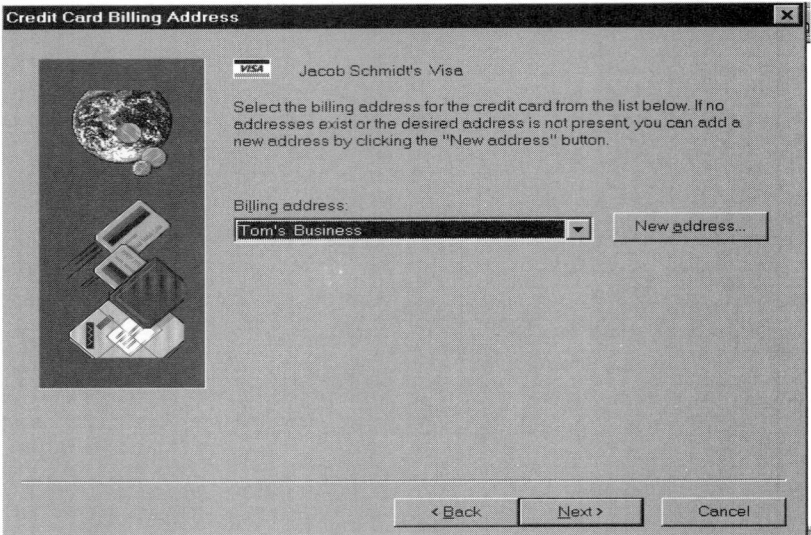

Figure 6.23 The Credit Card Billing Address dialog box.

6. Pull down a list of available addresses from the Address Manager. This is the mailing address that will be associated with this credit card. If the address you want to use isn't in the Address Manager, click the **New address**... button.

7. Click **Next** to display the Credit Card Password dialog box shown in Figure 6.24.

8. Enter the password you want to use for this credit card. You must enter the password twice, the second time as confirmation. You won't see the actual password as you enter it. Rather, the Wizard echoes asterisks instead of the actual characters you type. Be sure to remember the password; you will need it to use the credit card and to change or remove the credit card information.

9. Click on **Finish** to end the Wizard. The Payment Manager dialog box will be displayed with the new credit card information entered.

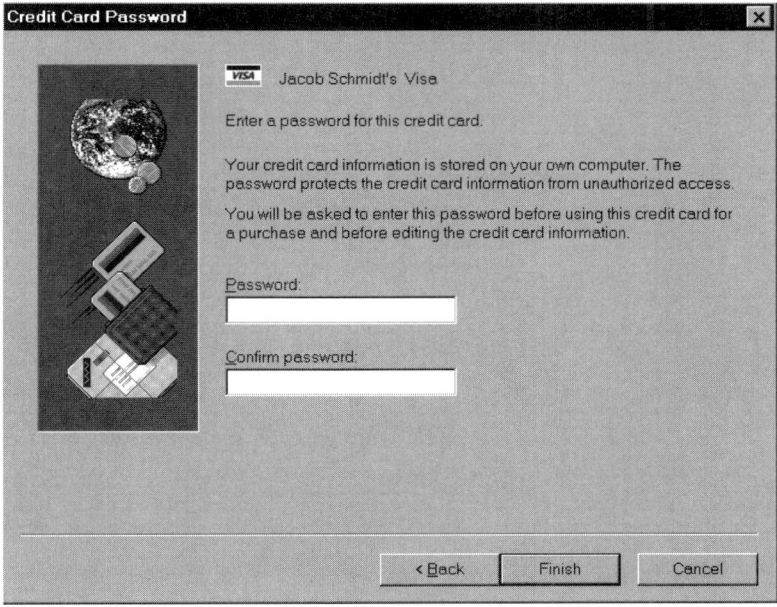

Figure 6.24 The Credit Card Password dialog box.

Now you can configure payments by clicking on the **Types...** button (see Figure 6.20) to produce the display shown in Figure 6.25.

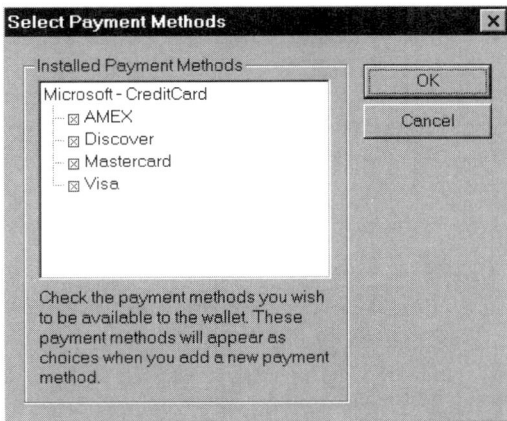

Figure 6.25 The Select Payment Methods dialog box

All available credit card types are selected by default. If you will be using only one or two cards, uncheck the cards you don't want to use for online purchases. The card types selected in this display will be offered as choices when you make a purchase. Reducing the number of choices here will streamline the purchase process. Also, you can edit information about an individual card by selecting the entry and then clicking on the **Edit** button.

Security

The Security tab of the browser Options dialog box has three groups: Content Advisor, Certificates, and Active Content. The default settings enabled when Explorer 4.0 is installed let you use the software quite effectively. However, you can make configuration changes to any of these areas if you wish.

CONTENT ADVISOR

There is a lot of concern, especially among parents and teachers, about some of the content available on the Internet. For some users, it may be desirable to limit access to some Internet locations. The Content Advisor can help you do this.

To use the Content Advisor, click on the **Enable Ratings...** button on the security Tab of the Browser options dialog box to present the Create Supervisor Password dialog box shown in Figure 6.26.

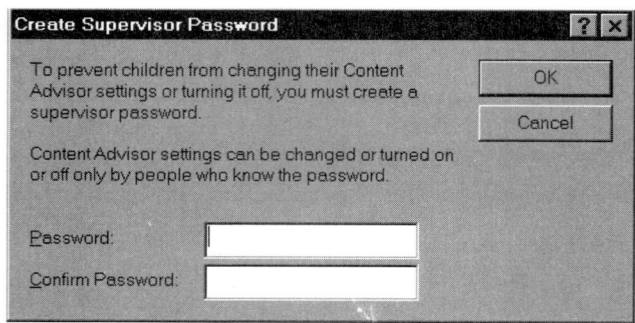

Figure 6.26 The Create Supervisor Password dialog box.

Type the password you want to use to control access to the Content Advisor and to restricted sites. Confirm the password by entering it again and click on **OK** to set the password and close the Password dialog box. The Content Advisor dialog box shown in Figure 6.27 will be presented.

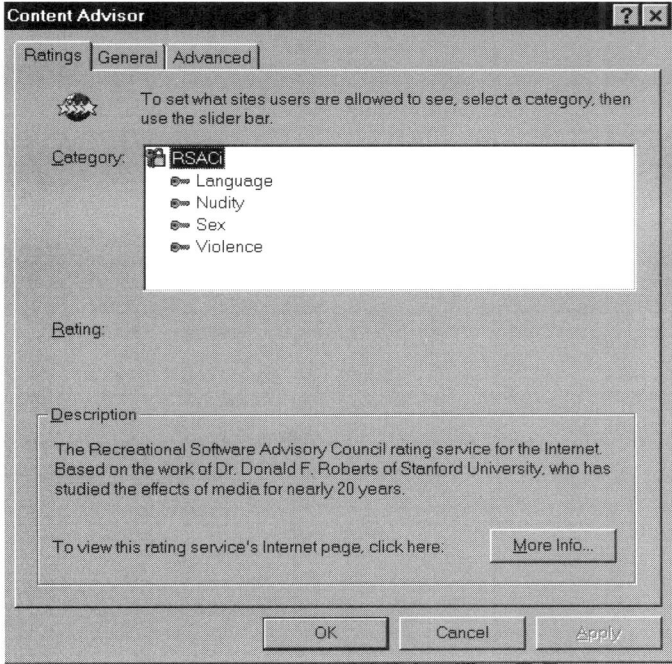

Figure 6.27 The Content Advisor dialog box.

This is a tabbed display with three tabs: Ratings, General, and Advanced.

Ratings

The Ratings tab is at the top of the display and the ratings of the Recreational Software Advisory Council (RSAC) are selected.

Choose one of the categories on this display, then use the slider in the middle of the dialog box (which appears after you make a choice) to set the acceptable level for that category. You are, in effect, setting a filter or a "not to exceed" level. If you choose Language, for example, the slider lets you choose a range of acceptable language from Level 0 (inoffensive slang) to level 4 (explicit or crude language). If you set the language level to 0, then this browser can only be used to access level 0 sites unless the user enters the administrator password you created earlier.

General

The General tab lets you change two settings (see Figure 6.28).

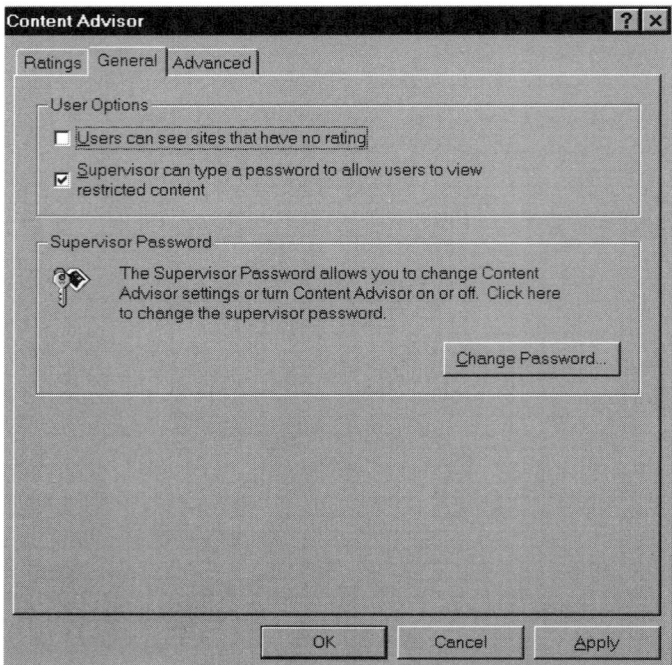

Figure 6.28 The General tab of the Content Advisor dialog box.

At the top of this dialog box are two buttons. One allows access to sites that have no rating—opening access to millions of unknown sites. When the second button is checked, sites without ratings can only be visited with the supervisor password.

At the bottom of this tab you can click on Change Password to change the supervisor password.

Advanced

The Advanced tab lets you add other ratings bureaus to the list of criteria Explorer can use, and you can specify an online source for ratings, a more secure setting but one that will slow down Web access. You can conduct a Web search for ratings to learn more about these bureaus.

N O T E

Be warned that the protective options here are not watertight. In some cases it will be possible to get to questionable content even though correct rating and screening setting were chosen. Human supervision may still be desired in many situations.

CERTIFICATES

The Certificates group of the Security tab lets you view available certificates used for authentication of companies and Internet sites. Click on **Personal**, **Companies**, and **Sites** to view available certificates. This feature is a relatively new concept that helps ensure safe and secure Web navigation. Certificates are electronic files stored on your computer and on the server computers at Internet sites. When you conduct certain actions, such as downloading a file or purchasing a product, your computer exchanges certificates with the host, validating your identity and the identify of the remote entity with which you are communicating or conducting business.

You can get more information on online certificates at the following Web sites: http:www.Microsoft.com/Workshop/prog/security/authcode/Codesign.htm, http://paradigm.webvision.com/developers/casetop.html/MoZmSq, http://www.thawte.com/certs/.

ACTIVE CONTENT

The Active Content section of the security tab of the options dialog box lets you specify what types of software a user of this Browser can download from remote Internet sites. All four types are selected by default. To disable one or more types, click on any entries to remove the check marks.

Although the default settings may be satisfactory for most users, for best security you should disable all four choices in this section. ActiveX and Java provide additional functionality, but they also can provide access to your local computer under some conditions.

The Safety Level button lets you choose High, Medium, or no security.

The Advanced Tab

The Advanced tab of the Options dialog box has two groups (see Figure 6.29).

The View Files... button in the Temporary Internet files group lets you view the Web sites stored in the cache area of your hard drive. Use the Settings button to tell Explorer how often to update the stored files. For best results, you should consider using the Every visit to page selection, and you should make your disk cache fairly large.

At the middle of this dialog box, the Advanced window lets you toggle on or off certain operational features of Explorer, including smooth scrolling, type of security used, how the printer functions, and so on. Click once to change the state of any entry; click again to return the setting to its previous state.

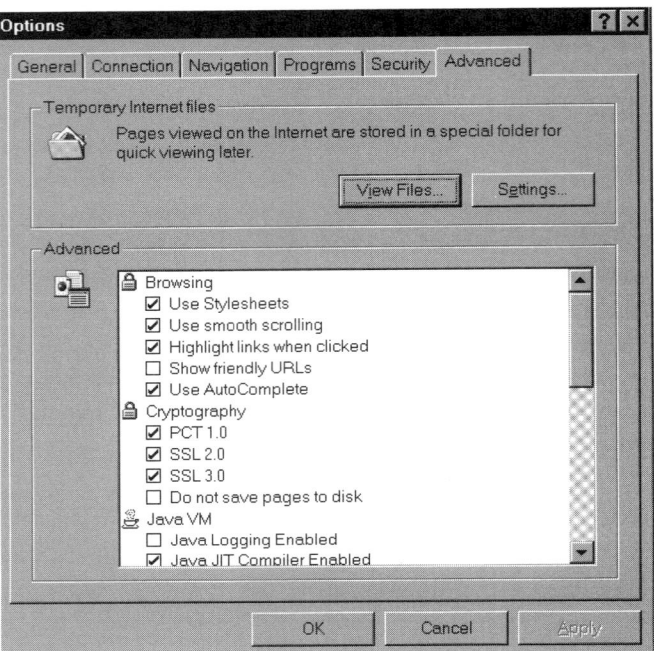

Figure 6.29 The Advanced tab of Browser Options dialog box.

Modifying the Task Bar

The Windows task bar is a convenient tool that normally rests at the bottom of your desktop. It contains icons of any running programs and also includes the *tray*, a section of the task bar that holds icons for utilities such as the scheduler, sound volume control, and so on.

Now, you can add Explorer 4.0 features to the task bar and control some desktop display features as well. Try this: Right-click the task bar to pop up the menu shown in Figure 6.30. Don't right-click an icon of a running program; choose a clear area of the task bar.

This pop-up menu is similar to what you are used to seeing in Windows, except that some of the terms on the rest of the menu are changed. Instead of saying simply "Cascade" as in original Windows, the modified menu under Explorer 4.0 now says "Cascade Windows." The "Tile Horizontally" and "Tile Vertically" menu entries now say "Tile Windows Horizontally" and "Tile Windows Vertically." Someone in Microsoft wisely reasoned that clearer information on menus makes for easier operation.

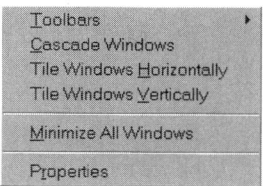

Figure 6.30 The Pop-up task bar menu.

Notice, too, the new menu item, Toolbars, at the top of this pop-up list. Point to **Toolbars** to produce the additional menu shown in Figure 6.31.

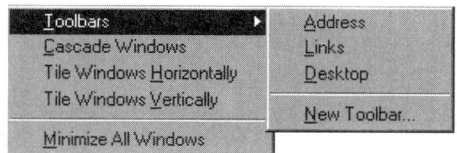

Figure 6.31 The Toolbars Pop-up on the task bar.

This menu gives you four choices: Address, Links, Desktop, and New Toolbar...

The Address and Links choices come directly from the Browser toolbar. Choose **Address** to drop the Address tool right onto the Task bar. Now you can use the pull-down list to show Web and local sites you have visited and jump right to them. Of course, you can type an address directly into the Address field to go to a new address. If you type a Web address, the Browser is launched and the specified Web address is displayed. If you enter a local drive path, the Windows Explorer (really a modified version of the Internet Browser, remember) is launched with the specified folder displayed. If you include a file name in your local or local area network path on the address bar then Explorer launches the application associated with the specified file and loads it for you.

You can also move this address bar around your desktop, turning it into a vertical bar or a rectangle anywhere on your desktop. Simply grab the **Address** bar and drag it where you want it on the desktop. For example, you could drag it to the top of your screen so it is always at the top of your desktop display.

The same is true of the Links bar. Turn it on, then move it wherever you want it on the desktop. To provide access to the shortcuts and other objects you have placed on the desktop, turn on the **Desktop** bar from this pop-up menu. This can be a useful way to customize your desktop display and provide access to local and remote facilities when you have turned off the desktop shortcut icons.

In addition to these standard toolbars, you can now create custom toolbars, similar to the way you can create custom toolbars for the Microsoft Office suite shortcut bar. Suppose you want to show the contents of your **My Computer** icon on the Desktop, for example. Here's how:

1. Right-click the task bar to display the pop-up Task Bar menu.
2. Point to **Toolbars** and choose **New Toolbar…** from the Toolbars menu. You will see a file navigation dialog box like the one in Figure 6.32.

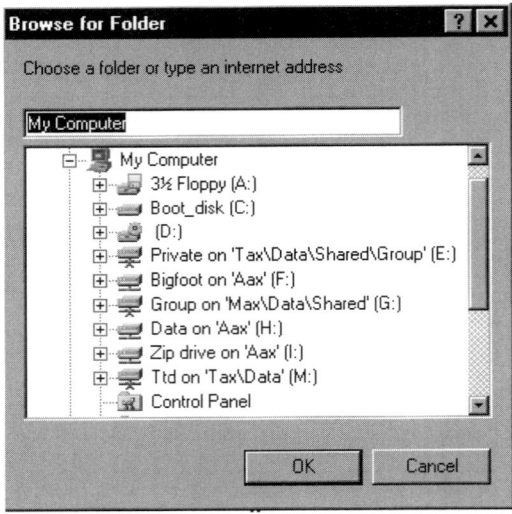

Figure 6.32 New Toolbar Browse for Folder dialog box.

3. Click on **My Computer** (or another folder if you want to display its contents on the Task Bar).
4. Click on **OK** to create the new toolbar.

Depending on how you had the task bar configured before you added the toolbar, you may now see only the new toolbar at the bottom of your screen. You can grab the top border of the task bar and drag it up, making it wider, so you can see the original task bar and the new toolbar at the same time. Of course, you can also drag the new toolbar away from where it is docked at the bottom of your screen and onto the desktop. This will produce a rectangular toolbar display that you can drag anywhere on the desktop. Figure 6.33 shows a My Computer toolbar as it appears on the Desktop.

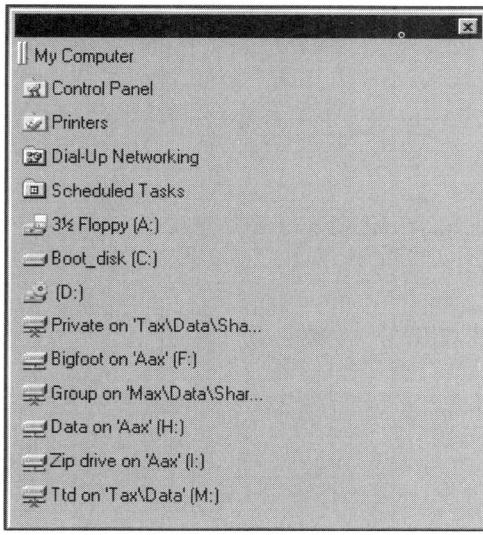

Figure 6.33 My Computer toolbar on the Desktop.

After you drag a toolbar away from its docking location, you can grab a border and drag the toolbar into nearly any shape you want. You can also dock the new toolbar at the side or the top of your desktop display, creating a Task-Bar-like toolbar in this new location. However, a toolbar such as My Computer contains a relatively large number of choices. With a toolbar like this one docked, you may not be able to see all of the choices because the toolbar consists of an icon and text. You can right-click the toolbar and turn off Show Text to produce an icon-only toolbar like the one shown in Figure 6.34.

Figure 6.34 An icon-only toolbar.

The location of the toolbar title and icons change as you move the toolbar around the desktop. Figure 6.34 shows the toolbar docked at the top of the Desktop. This produces an "always on top" display so you can access the toolbar no matter what other application is running. If you'd rather not see the toolbar until you need it, right-click the new toolbar to display a pop-up menu and toggle on **AutoHide**. Now, unless you move your mouse pointer over the location of the toolbar, you won't see it. When you move the mouse over the toolbar, it pops into view so you can select an icon from it. Choose **Large** from this pop-up menu to display much larger icons on this toolbar. When you are running in high-resolution displays, say, 800 x 600 and greater, the large icons help you locate the application you want to use from the toolbar.

Once you have created a new toolbar such as this, it acts like the task bar in that you can add other toolbars to it, or display the Address or Links bar. This kind of toolbar control let you create a highly customized desktop display.

To remove any of your new toolbar displays, right-click the bar and choose **close** from the pop-up menu, or drag the toolbar onto the desktop and click the **x** close icon at the upper-right corner of the display. Remember, you have to click on the bar and not on one of the icons on the bar. If the bar you want to close or move is too full to find a blank spot, locate the double vertical bar at the left of the bar. You can right-click here to display the menu, or grab the bar here to move the whole thing to a new location.

In addition to showing folder contents in a toolbar, there is more you can do. As with all other things on the desktop, the toolbar is an object and can contain most other objects. You can, for example, use FrontPad to make an HTML document, complete with backgrounds, links, and all other sorts of references. By following the procedure above, but typing the URL of the HTML document, you will get a toolbar that contains this HTML document. The document can be on your local computer, a server on the network, or even a server somewhere on the Internet. This is a feature that will enable many network administrators to easily modify the toolbars they present to their users, and that will enable such Web services as a toolbar that has a daily listing of the hottest new software, which you can then download with the click of your mouse, or a toolbar that lists your favorite Web pages. The possibilities are almost unlimited; nearly anything you can do in HTML can be incorporated in a toolbar.

EXPLORING LOCAL AND NETWORK DRIVES

If you have experimented with the configuration changes suggested earlier in this chapter you have some experience with many features of Windows

Explorer, the modified version of Internet Explorer 4.0 that lets you view and access local and networked drives. Although the Internet components of Explorer 4.0 are highly integrated into the Windows desktop, the Windows Explorer display is different from the Internet Explorer display. You can access components of each from the other, but the basic, default operation is different when you are exploring Windows and when you are exploring the Internet.

To use Explorer 4.0 to browse your local or network hard drives and other facilities:

1. Display the task bar if it is not already visible.
2. Click on **Start** and point to **Programs**.
3. Choose **Windows Explorer** from the programs list to present the display shown in Figure 6.35.

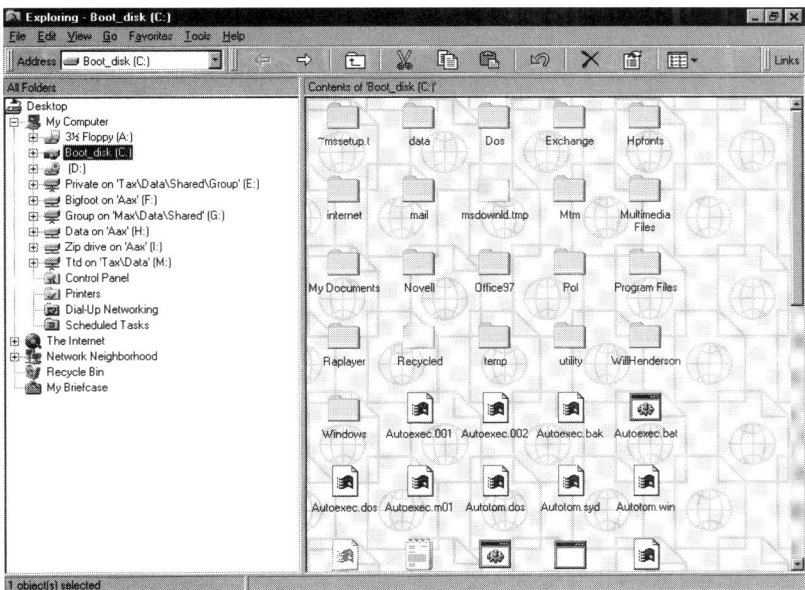

Figure 6.35 The Windows Explorer screen with large icons.

This display is a split screen, as in the original Windows Explorer, but there are some operational differences. The left part of the display shows folders and the right part of the display shows files within the folders plus subfolders within the main folder. This, too, is like the original.

The folder display on the left uses the conventional double-click method for opening any of the folders on the screen, while the right side of the display uses the Hyperlink convention where the mouse pointer changes to a pointing finger when you hover over an object. Once the pointer changes to a hand, you can single-click to select the object.

The toolbar has navigation arrows, like the Browser, to let you move back and forward in the directory structure of your computer or network. After you have navigated down a directory tree by clicking on successive folder names, you can step back up the tree with the back arrow on the toolbar. Similarly, return to lower directory levels with the forward arrow.

As with the original Windows Explorer, when you single-click a folder on the left side of the display, a list of folders and files appears on the right but the folder itself doesn't open on the left. Double-click a folder in the All Folders window to show subfolders on the left of the screen. You can also single-click the plus or minus sign beside a folder icon on the left side of the display to expand the list to include subfolders. When you do this, the file display on the right side of the screen doesn't change.

You can modify how the folders and files appear on the right side of Windows Explorer by pulling down the list of choices from the View icon (it looks like a two-column list display) on the main Windows Explorer toolbar. If you are pointing to a conventional folder on a local or networked drive, the choices available on this menu are the same as with the original Windows Explorer: Large Icons, Small Icons, List, Details. In most installations the Large Icons choice is the default and produces a display like the one in Figure 6.35. If you choose Small icons, the display shrinks as the size of the icons is reduced. The List choice provides a simple text table that shows the names of files and folders on the right side of the Windows Explorer display and the Details choice gives you additional information, such as the type of file, the date it was created, and the size in bytes.

If you point to the Favorites folder (**C:\Windows\Favorites**, unless you have changed the location), a new choice is added—Thumbnails. This provides a preview display for each file or document displayed on the right side of the Windows Explorer screen. If a site in your favorites list is not in your disk cache, Explorer will have to log onto the Internet to produce a Thumbnail display, so it could take a while to fill out the full Favorites list.

When thumbnail images are displayed, the Windows Explorer screen looks like the one in Figure 6.36.

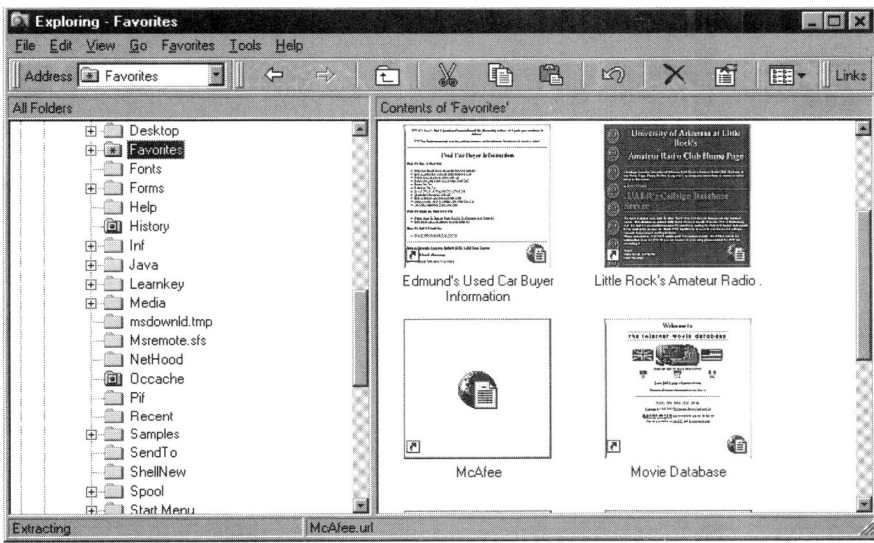

Figure 6.36 Windows Explorer with thumbnails enabled.

You can right-click a thumbnail view to present a menu that lets you select **Watch This Site**, and **Create Thumbnail** (see Figure 6.37). Choose **Create Thumbnail** if you want to update the current Thumbnail or create a thumbnail where none exists. The Watch This Site option is turned on by default and tells Explorer to periodically check the site for changes. Toggle this option off by clicking this menu selection.

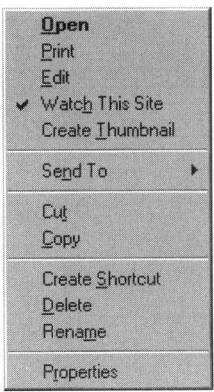

Figure 6.37 The Thumbnail pop-up menu.

This menu is another example of how Internet-aware Explorer 4.0 is. If you right-click another file in the Windows Explorer display you will see a similar menu, but it won't include the Watch This Site or Create Thumbnail selections. You can get more details about any file by choosing **Properties** from this menu to see a display similar to the one in Figure 6.38.

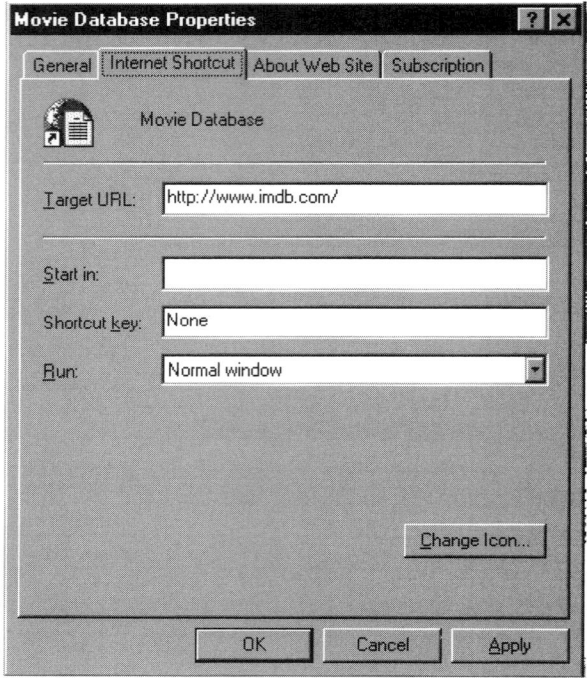

Figure 6.38 A File Properties display from Windows Explorer.

Again, the Properties display for an Internet site is different from the Properties display of a conventional file or document. Each Properties display provides the kind of information you are likely to need for a particular file type. Most objects, such as pictures, that you find on a Web site have their own properties box. You can get to this box in the same way: Hover the mouse over the Object, then right-click.

There may be another choice on the Views menu, depending on the type of folder that is selected in the All Folders window of the Windows Explorer. If you are pointing to the root directory of a local drive, you may see a Web view choice on this menu. Click on **Web** to produce in the Contents window a folder list that looks like a Web page.

Let's take another look at the Address bar at the top of the Windows Explorer display (Figure 6.35). You will see this Address bar on all implementations of Explorer 4.0, including the Browser, My Computer, and Windows Explorer. This bar lets you jump directly to a local or remote site by simply typing in the appropriate path. To display a specific directory (folder) that you can access from your computer, just type the drive letter and path into the Address bar.

For example, to display the contents of the networked E: drive, type **e:** and press **Enter**. To display a Web location, type the URL (universal resource locator) into the Address bar of Windows Explorer.

N O T E   You can display the contents of a shared computer on the network, even if you haven't mapped a drive on your local machine. Simply type the name of the remote host preceded by a double-backslash. For example, to view the shared resources on a computer named AAX on your Windows network, type **\\AAX** in the Address Bar. The information in the All folders window won't change, but you will see a list of shared resources on the specified computer in the Contents Window (see Figure 6.39).

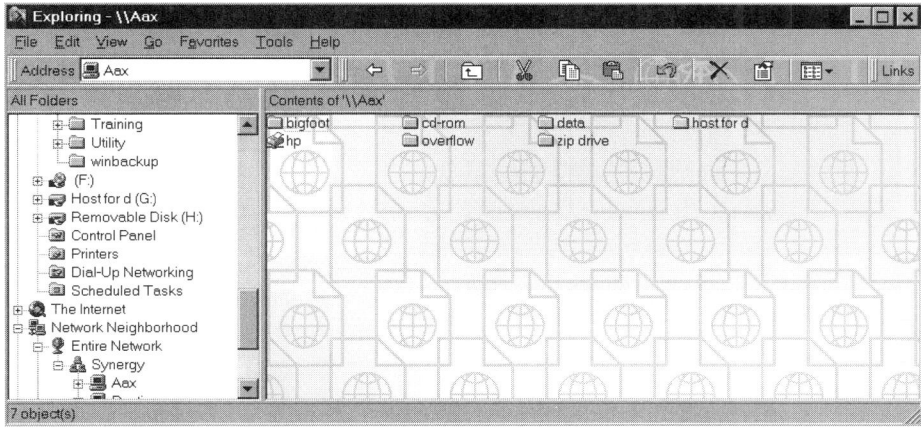

Figure 6.39 A Contents Window with Networked computer shared resources.

This feature is particularly useful when your computer is part of a relatively large network and you want to view available resources before mapping a drive to something specific. If you click on an icon that represents a remote disk drive, printer, or other resource, Explorer will open the display to show the contents. Of course, you must have at least Read rights to the remote host and any objects you open to be able to see anything there. If you do not have Read rights, or are not logged on to the network domain or network server, you will see a dialog box asking for your username and password.

EXPLORING THE WORLD WIDE WEB

In a way, it is redundant to talk about browsing the Web separately from browsing local and local area network resources. As I have said, the Windows Explorer and the Internet Explorer are really two different views of the same utility, Explorer 4.0. However there are some differences in the screens you see in each of these program implementations and things work a little differently.

To start exploring the Web the Explorer 4.0's browser, click on the Explorer 4.0 icon on the task bar.

N O T E I found with initial experiments with creating and moving toolbars that I accidentally lost the Explorer icon that was installed on the Task Bar when Explorer was installed. If this happens to you, restore the icon by creating a new toolbar that contains only **iexplorer.exe** (see description above). Right-click on the new toolbar and toggle off **Show Text**. Finally, grab the new toolbar and drag it wherever you want it to appear on the task bar and size it so it doesn't interfere with the rest of the icons on the task bar.

When the Explorer Browser launches, you will see the start or home page you have specified. If you haven't changed the defaults, you'll see the page at **home.microsoft.com**. This is a good starting point for your Web navigation unless you have an account through an ISP that has a good navigational page, or if you just have a favorite page anywhere on the net that you want to use.

Remember: You can change the default start page from the Navigation tab of the Options dialog box that you access from the View menu. This default start page doesn't have to be a Web location either. You could create your own HTML document that contains hyperlinks to favorite Web sites, local or network directories, and so on. You could use this custom page as a convenient starting point for the Browser or even as the permanent desktop interface you use with your computer.

N O T E

You could use Windows Explorer to customize the Favorites folder and create an HTML document. If you keep your Favorites list updated—including local programs and files you use frequently—this automatically generated page can serve as a useful desktop user interface and navigation tool.

Remember Explorer's ability to work offline. Once you have subscribed to one or more Web sites, you can use **File Work Offline** to force Explorer to assume that the sites you specify are stored on your local drive. Use **Favorites Subscribe** to view subscriptions and choose a site you want to display in Explorer. This ability reduces your online time and, in fact, lets you use information from favorite Web pages even if you don't have access to an Internet connection.

For more information on using specific features of the Explorer Browser, refer to the menu reference, in Chapter 11. In the next chapter, I'll discuss the operation of Outlook Express for e-mail and news.

CHAPTER SEVEN

Using Outlook Express

Outlook Express is another example of a Microsoft software marketing philosophy giving users a choice between an in-depth, full-featured product and a smaller, less capable version that maintains the user interface and many—but not all—of the features of the larger product. A popular example is Microsoft Works, a combination package that provides word processing, spreadsheet, and database services. The files created by Works can be read by members of the Microsoft Office software suite, Word, and Excel. Microsoft Works is marketed aggressively through computer manufacturers and is frequently included as part of the free software installed on new computers.

Outlook Express is another example of this two-stage software design. By providing users of Explorer 4.0 with the basic features of Outlook, Microsoft has introduced the integrated, groupware concept to millions of at-home and business users. The upgrade to the more capable Outlook—either as a stand-alone purchase or as part of the Microsoft Office suite—is virtually assured when users who like the Outlook concept and already are familiar with its operation need more functionality.

OUTLOOK EXPRESS COMPONENTS

Outlook Express is basically three online utilities combined. It is an electronic mail manager, a USENET News reader, and an address manager. This is a logical combination of features. Electronic mail is, with the World Wide Web, one of the most used features of the Internet. More Internet users claim electronic mail as the single most important aspect of their online life than any other application. And, like electronic mail, News—discussion groups, really—is a store-and-forward application, a messaging utility where users write messages and send them to a central host where they are stored for other people to read. And, if you are using electronic mail heavily, it makes sense that you need to track the e-mail addresses, names, and other information about the people with whom you are in contact.

Outlook Express handles all three of these tasks rather well, as you will learn in this chapter. I'll also show you how to move up to the full Outlook program if you wish, as well as how to use the name and address files you have created in Outlook with the Express version.

USING OUTLOOK EXPRESS ELECTRONIC MAIL

Slowly at first, then extremely fast over the past two years, electronic mail has changed the way we communicate. E-mail has eased accessibility of employees to management, it has opened new lines of communication between business and client and among businesses. Electronic messaging also is bringing far-flung families closer together. For some reason, people who rarely, if ever, took time to write a letter or even a thank-you note, now write weekly or even daily messages. E-mail is convenient because it transcends time and space. You don't have to play telephone tag or worry that people in a different time zone may be busy or unavailable.

However, it took friendly user interfaces, automatic mail checking, the ability to send nontext data easily, and a global network (the Internet) to make this fascinating and useful facility really take hold. Outlook Express is one product that fits these criteria, and in addition provides interesting integration with the Internet, news, and other online facilities.

E-mail Components

The basic e-mail handling component of programs like Outlook Express are frequently called *clients*. A software client provides user-side services such as accepting input from the keyboard, displaying data on the screen, and so on. Client software can't work alone; it requires the support of *host* or *server* software to do what it does. An e-mail server sits on a network and accepts incoming mail addressed to clients using that server. In the case of Internet mail, the server usually resides at your service provider and manages mail for the provider's customers. Larger ISPs (Internet Service Providers) may have two or more mail servers, allocating one server or set of servers for managing incoming mail (POP3 or IMAP) and another server or servers to manage outgoing mail (SMTP—Simple Mail Transfer Protocol).

I'll leave the components and operation of server-side software to the network gurus. As for Outlook Express facilities, you will find these basic components:

- E-mail Reader, a text screen that lets you view your incoming mail.
- E-mail Editor, a text editor that lets you write and edit your outgoing mail.
- Graphics and software viewers and filters, utility software that lets you load and view nontext files attached to your incoming mail. In most cases, this utility involves simply knowing what application to launch to allow you to view an attached file.

Configuring Outlook Express E-mail

When you installed Explorer 4.0 you were probably asked for information about your POP3 and SMPT mail hosts. To check or change this area of e-mail configuration:

1. Use **Tools Accounts…** to display a list of available accounts in the Internet Accounts dialog box.
2. Select the account you want to view or change and click on **Properties** to present the Internet Mail Account Properties dialog box, shown in Figure 7.1.

This tabbed dialog box gives you lots of opportunity for fine-tuning and changing your Outlook Express configuration. There are four tabs on this dialog box: General, Servers, Connection, and Advanced.

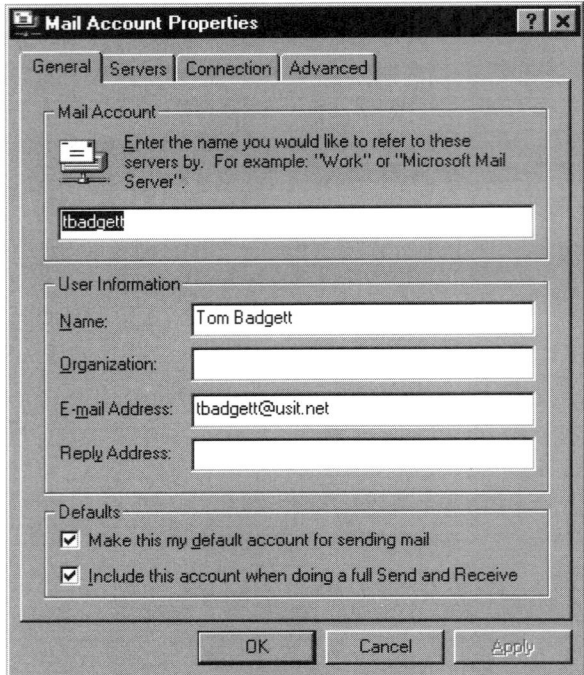

Figure 7.1 An Internet Mail Account Properties dialog box.

The General Tab

The General tab is presented first, by default, and is used to track the name for this account, your name (or the so-called public name you want to use for this account), your organization name, if any, and a different reply address, if you wish. At the bottom of this tab are toggles that control how Outlook Express uses this account as it handles mail.

The first field on this tab, the Mail Account Name, is simply used to identify this account. If you have multiple mail accounts, you might want to use the name of the provider of mail services. I have used the name of my e-mail account to identify this account.

If you want to identify the company or organization with which you are affiliated, enter the name in the Organization field of this dialog box, otherwise leave it blank.

Your e-mail address consists of your mail account user name, an "at" sign (@), and the domain name of your mail server. Enter your full e-mail address here, the address other people would use to send you electronic mail.

Normally, you receive mail to the same account you use to send it. However, if you want recipients of your mail to respond to a different e-mail address, type that address in the Reply Address field of this dialog box.

Click on **OK** to close the dialog box, or select another tab to make additional changes in your e-mail configuration.

The Servers Tab

The Servers tab of this dialog box (see Figure 7.2) lets you set the send and receive mail servers.

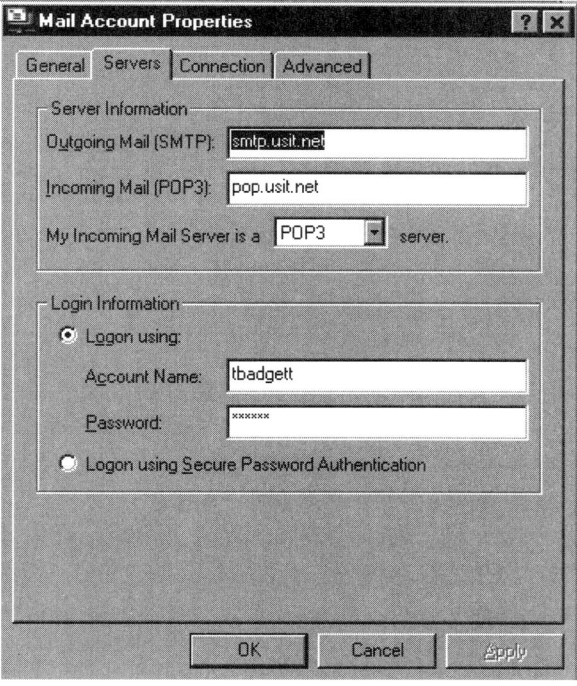

Figure 7.2 The Servers tab of Mail Account Properties dialog box.

This tab contains two groups, Server Information and Login Information. The Server Information group contains the server identifiers for sending and receiving mail and for specifying the type of mail host you are using. Enter the SMPT host name in the outgoing mail field. Then, if you are using a POP3 host, you will type the identifier for the POP3 server in the incoming mail field and use POP3 as the mail type in the Incoming Mail Server type field. If yours is an IMAP incoming server, select IMAP in the server type field and type the IMAP server identifier in the incoming mail field of this group. You will get the names of these servers, as well as the type of the mail server (IMAP or POP) from your service provider or network administrator. If you have the option to use either IMAP or POP, you will want to use IMAP, since it performs much better than POP does.

In the second group, choose the login method (check with your network administrator or ISP for this information). If you log into your mail account with a user name and password, type this information in the appropriate fields of this group.

Click on **OK** to close this dialog box and set the changes, or choose another tab if you want to make further adjustments to the e-mail configuration.

The Connection Tab

The Connection tab (Figure 7.3) lets you specify how you connect to your e-mail server and whether to connect only to download mail, or to stay connected after the mail transfer.

If you are using a LAN connection, including some ISDN links, click on the first choice in the Connection group of this tab. To connect manually, choose the second item; to use a modem, click the third choice. Additionally, you need to specify which dial-up networking profile to use to make the connection with a modem. You can pull down a list of available dial-up networking profiles, or add a new one if you wish.

Finally, click on **Disconnect when finished sending and receiving** if you want Outlook Express to dial up only to transfer mail and then disconnect the link. This is a good choice when you want automatic e-mail retrieval so you can read and create mail offline.

Click on **OK** to close this dialog box or choose another tab to make further changes.

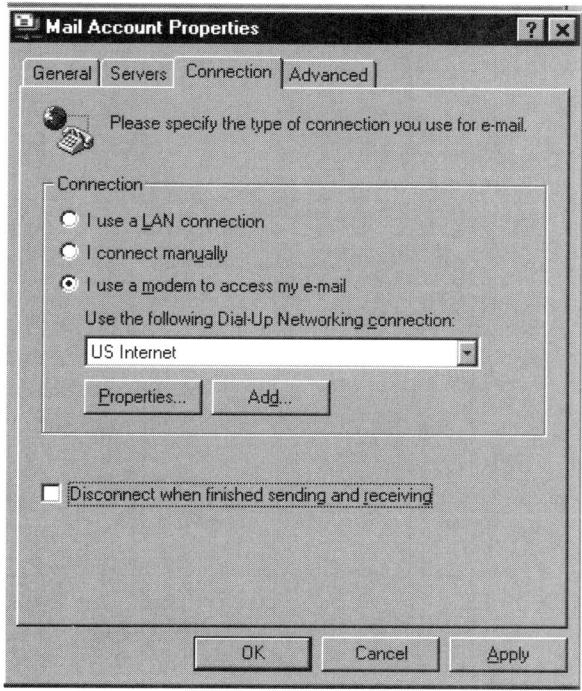

Figure 7.3 The Connection tab of Mail Account Properties dialog box.

The Advanced Tab

The Advanced tab of this dialog box (see Figure 7.4) has four groups: Server Port Numbers, Server Timeouts, Delivery, and Sending.

Advanced settings are just what the name implies, intended for users who know enough to change these defaults or who, because of special server circumstances, must change them. During installation the incoming and outgoing port numbers are set for you and, under most conditions, these settings should work fine. If you need to change the port data, simply select the field you want to change and type in a new number. You can also use the Port Numbers group settings to specify secure connections for your incoming or outgoing mail. Again, your MIS or networking administrator or someone from your ISP will tell you if such changes are necessary.

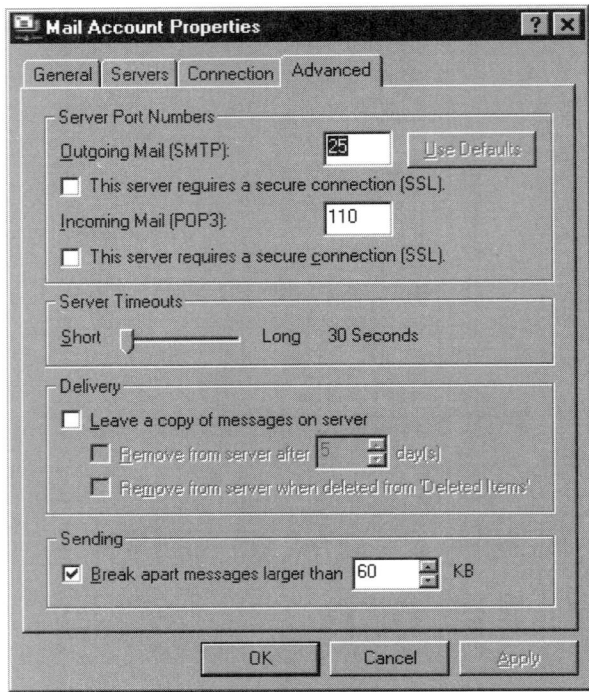

Figure 7.4 The Advanced tab of Mail Account Properties dialog box.

You probably want to leave Server Timeouts on the short side, but if you have problems with connection timeouts and everything else is correct, then a longer timeout setting may solve your connection or disconnect problems. Connections to service providers with heavily used mail servers can sometimes be problematic; increasing these timeouts can often solve the problem.

Under Delivery you can choose whether to leave a copy of your mail on the host. Normally, when you are using a desktop e-mail client such as this, you want the mail message to be downloaded to your computer, then deleted from the host. However, if you access your mail from more than one computer—one at home and one at work, for example, or from a desktop and also from a laptop machine—then you will want to leave a copy of your mail messages on the host. This way, you can download them to read on one computer, but they remain available for later download to another machine if you wish. Just remember that if you receive a lot of e-mail, the amount of storage you are using on the host machine can grow quite large. Depending on the hosting arrangement you have within your department or with your ISP, you may be asked to periodically remove old messages, or you may be charged for the additional storage space. In fact, with some server arrangements, your mail may even be terminated if you use more than a specified amount of e-mail storage space. Also be aware that mailboxes that are tens of megabytes in size often have problems and timeouts. These problems go away when you delete excessive mail to reduce the size of your stored mail file.

Finally, you may break up very long messages into shorter segments. Normally, you don't want to do this because it can make retrieving them on the other side somewhat difficult. However, if you are communicating with a server that has length limits for messages, you may have to change this default setting to send only small messages. Many users of Bulletin Board Systems cannot handle very large messages and require this setting.

Click on **OK** to close this dialog box and select another tab to make additional changes.

Mail Options

There's another series of e-mail settings you might want to change as well. Click on **Tools** on the main outlook Express menu bar and choose **mail options** to display the dialog box shown in Figure 7.5.

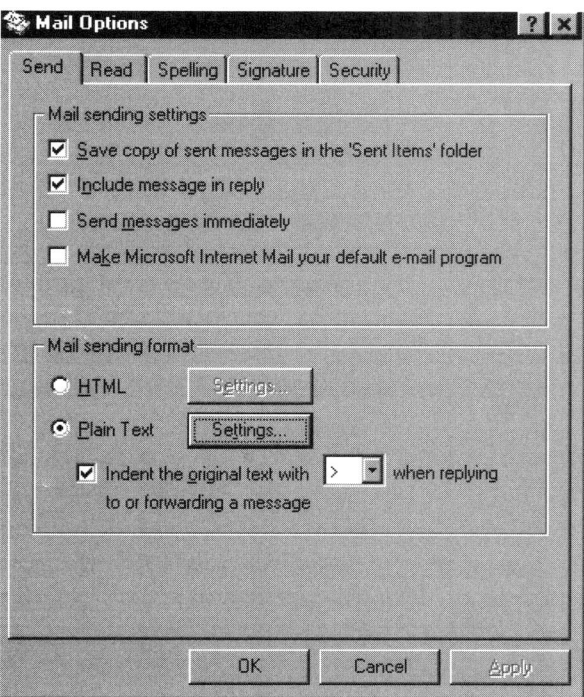

Figure 7.5 The Send tab of Tools Mail Options dialog box.

This dialog box shows five tabs: Send, Read, Spelling, Signature, and Security. The Send tab is on top. The settings in this dialog box help you control how e-mail messages are handled as you use Outlook Express.

The Send Tab

This tab has two groups, Mail sending settings and Mail sending format. By default, the first two sending settings are selected, and the last two are not. With the default settings, you will automatically save a copy of any sent messages in the Sent Items folder and include the original message when you reply to e-mail. You will also send new messages, including those you generate in reply to an original message, to a queue for transmission to the mail host the next time you log on to check mail. If you check Send messages immediately, Outlook Express will attempt to send new messages immediately instead of sending them to the queue. If you have a network or ISDN connection, then Send Immediately is a good choice. If you are using a dial-up modem connection, on the other hand, it is probably better to wait to send new mail when next you "send and receive" mail after you log on. This is fine if your computer automatically checks mail every so often—a setting discussed later. Otherwise, you need to manually "send and receive mail" for your messages to go out. Finally, if you check the Make Microsoft Internet Mail as your default e-mail program, then the mail program internal to the Explorer Browser will be used to send e-mail from the Internet.

The second group in this tab lets you specify whether to send messages in plain text or HTML format. Your choice here depends on who normally are your e-mail recipients. The HTML format can produce e-mail with eye appeal, but it requires some users to load a browser to display it, which could produce e-mail access delays for recipients of your messages. Some programs such as Outlook Express and Netscape Communicator can view these HTML encoded messages. Most, however, cannot. In general, it is better to use Plain Text until the HTML encoded Mail format becomes more widely supported. No matter which tab you select, you will be able to read HTML encoded messages with Outlook Express if they are sent to you.

The Read Tab

The Read tab (Figure 7.6) controls several interesting operations, including whether Outlook Express plays a sound when you get new mail, and whether to check for mail automatically. All of the selections on this tab are toggles, so you turn them off and on by clicking once to change state.

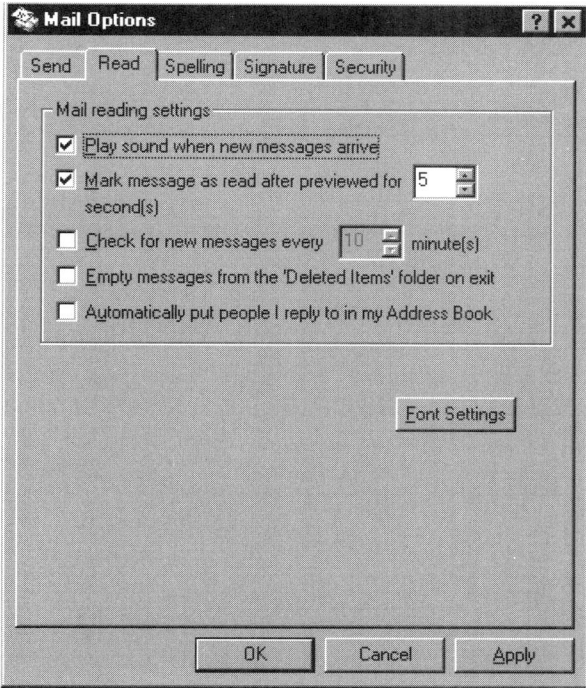

Figure 7.6 The Read tab of Mail Options dialog box.

Be aware that if you use a dial-up connection, your computer will dial in every time you have to check mail. If you select the "Check for new messages every X minutes" and then set X for a low number, you will find your computer dialing your service provider frequently. For users who do not have a dedicated phone line for the modem, or who pay for service based on the amount of time they use their network connection, this may get quite expensive. Checking mail also takes processor time, meaning that your computer will slow down a little as mail is being checked in the background. If you decide to check your mail every X minutes, 10 to 30 minutes is an acceptable interval for most people.

Whenever you delete a message from one of your mail folders, Outlook Express does not really destroy the message. Instead, it is moved to another folder that you will see in your folder list as Deleted Items. If you read and delete a lot of mail, this folder will get quite large, using a lot of disk space and somewhat slowing down Outlook Express. If you do not want to empty this folder on a regular basis, checking the "Empty messages from the Deleted Item Folder on Exit" may be a good idea.

The last tab can be useful to build up your address book, but be aware that if you are active on a mailing list with many subscribers, you may end up with an unmanageable collection of addresses!

Clicking the **Font** button will bring up a dialog box that lets you select the font that Outlook Express will use to display your incoming mail.

The Spelling Tab

Not too long ago the concept of spell-checking electronic mail was pretty unusual. Today, most desktop e-mail clients include the ability to check for correct spelling. A good thing too, since one major downside of e-mail is the lack of proofing and spelling that is considered required and commonplace in printed communications.

Use the Spelling tab of this dialog box (Figure 7.7) to control some of the spell-checking options in Outlook Express.

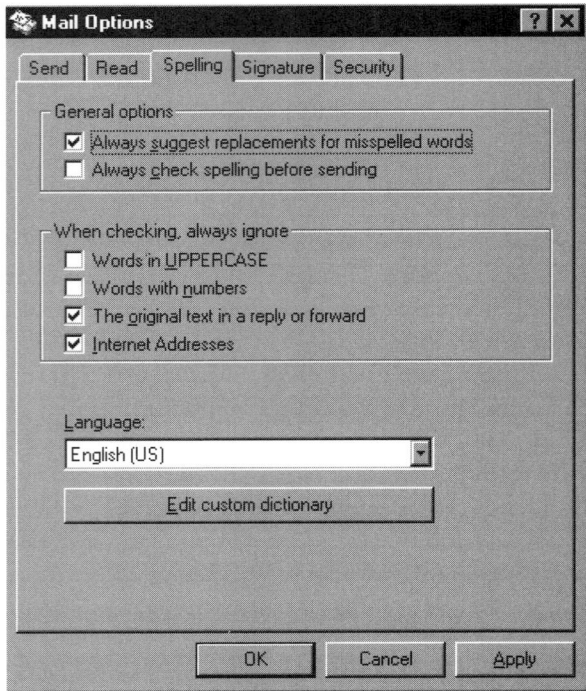

Figure 7.7 The Spelling tab of Mail Options dialog box.

The top group on this tab, General options, lets you tell Outlook Express whether to check spelling automatically and, when it does, whether to suggest a correct spelling. Unless you choose Always check spelling before sending, you'll have to spell check your messages on your own.

You can ease the spell-check process by telling Outlook Express what word types to ignore. If you frequently use abbreviations or material in upper case, you'll probably want to ignore anything in upper case during a spell check. You may similarly want to ignore words with numbers and, almost certainly, you want to ignore original material in received messages and in Internet addresses.

The Signature Tab

An e-mail Signature lets you automatically attach your company name and snail-mail address, your telephone or fax phone numbers, or any other tag line to all of your e-mail messages. To create or edit your signature, click on the **Signature** tab of this dialog box (Figure 7.8).

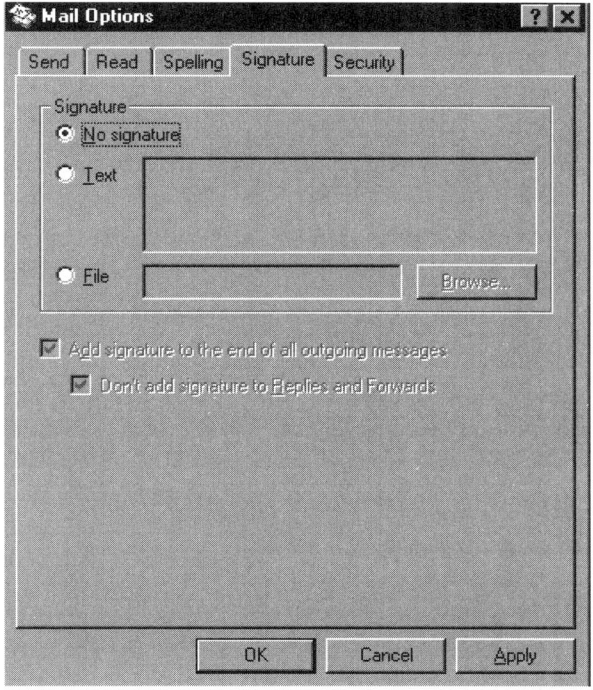

Figure 7.8 The Signature tab of Mail Options dialog box.

The default setting on this tab is No signature. You can click on **Text**, then type the content you want for your signature in the window to the right of this choice. Or, choose **File** and give Outlook Express the path to the file you want to use. You can include virtually anything you want in an e-mail signature, but use caution. It is easy to forget that an automatic message accompanies everything you send via e-mail. If you make it long, or too cute, people receiving your messages on a regular basis can tire of it surprisingly quickly. Also, it is simply considered bad manners to send complex or overly commercial signatures with your e-mail. It is OK to promote your business or services, but don't go on and on. And, unless your signature is simply an address and phone number, remember to change it regularly. Otherwise the impact you desire will be lessened. If you are using a signature, you have the additional options of automatic signatures at the end of all outgoing messages and also of suppressing your signature on replies and forwarded messages.

The Security Tab

The Security tab is a simple but powerful one. It contains only toggles for adding a digital signature to outgoing messages and for encrypting the contents and attachments for all outgoing messages. If you turn on either of these options, click on the **Advanced** button so you can specify what certificate to use and what encryption algorithm to use. There are no defaults for these choices. You will have to secure or install these elements to use with Outlook Express. To use these options, you will need to obtain a Certificate, a piece of code that identifies the message as coming from you. This can be important if you want to absolutely assure a recipient that it really was you who sent the message they are receiving. The details of using certificates are beyond the scope of this chapter., but you can find more information about the use of certificates, as well as obtain your own certificate from several places on the Internet. A good Web site to start looking would be VeriSign at http://www.verisign.com/. Among other things, you can obtain a personal certificate here. In addition, the whole certificate concept is so important, I have included a more detailed description of certificates and how to use them in Outlook Express in Appendix A. Study this information if you want to know more about how this rising online facility works.

Creating New E-mail Messages

Once you have all of these configuration issues behind you, you are ready to actually start using Outlook Express. Luckily, using this product is a lot simpler than configuring it. When you are ready to send an e-mail message to someone else, here's how:

Click on **Compose** and choose **New Message**. The New Message dialog box shown in Figure 7.9 is displayed.

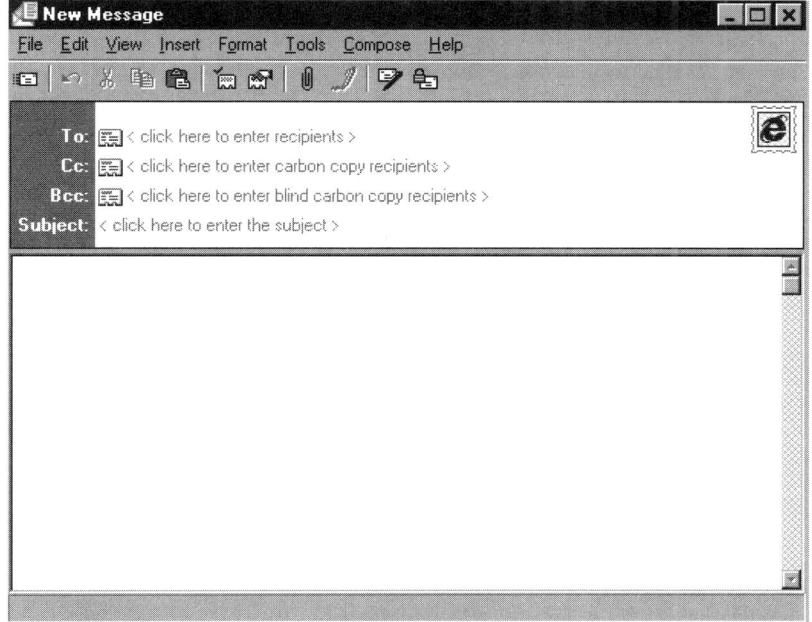

Figure 7.9 New Message dialog box.

There are two parts to this dialog box: the message header and the message body. The header includes the address of the recipient or recipients and a subject. The message body contains the actual message you are transmitting.

If you have chosen to use HTML as your Mail Sending Format, you will see a formatting toolbar at the top of the message text section.

Hover the mouse pointer over objects on the New Message screen to view a pop-up identifier or instructions for these objects.

N O T E

To enter a To: address, simply click in the **To:** field and type the address. A local e-mail address may simply be a person or computer name; an Internet address consists of a user name, an "at" sign (@), and a server name or domain name. Separate multiple To: addresses with a semicolon or by pressing the **Enter** or **Return** key after each address. Include addressees you want to receive a carbon copy of this message on the Cc: line, and type addresses for blind carbon copy recipients (people who will receive the message but whose addresses don't appear to other recipients) on the Bcc: line.

You can also use the Address Book (Contacts Manager) to enter the addresses automatically. Click on the card icon in the front of any of the address lines to launch the Address Book and choose an existing address. I'll show you more about using the Address Book later in this chapter.

Try to put descriptive wording in your Subject line. As you will see later, the sender name and Subject line are the first two things you see when you look at your mailbox. A descriptive subject will be appreciated by people who get a lot of e-mail.

When you are ready to enter the text of the message, click in the message area (or press the **Tab** key until the insertion point moves into the message body area), and start typing your message text. You can include existing files—including graphics files or documents from other applications—with any e-mail message as well as plain text. To include a file, click on **Insert** on the main Outlook Express menu and choose **File Attachment...** to display the dialog box shown in Figure 7.10.

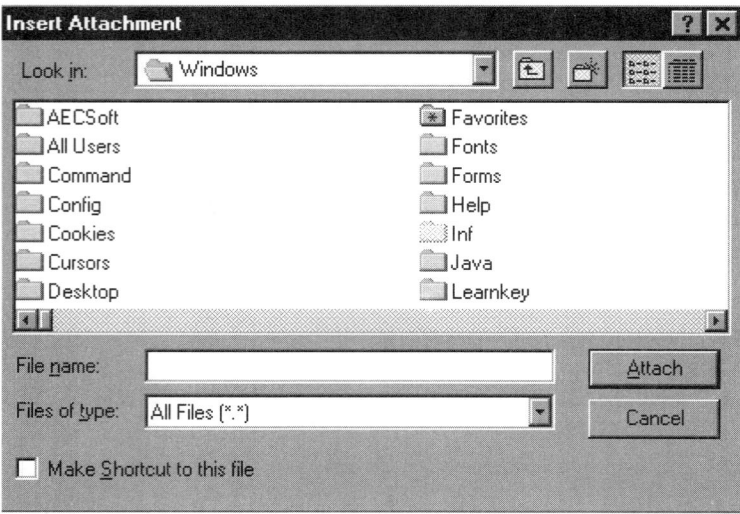

Figure 7.10 Insert Attachment dialog box.

In addition to external graphics, word processor, spreadsheet, and other application files, you can insert text files as part of your e-mail as well. Click on **Insert** and choose **Text from File**.... You will see the same file manager screen shown in Figure 7.10.

In either case, navigate to the file you want to attach and double-click it or select it and click on **Open**. Outlook Express inserts an icon that represents the file into the message body area of the New Message screen if you have chosen a non-text file. If you are inserting a text file, you will see the text inserted into the body of your new message.

You can also insert Hyperlinks as part of an e-mail message. Suppose you want to tell someone they simply must view the Web site at www.lookatthis.com. You can simply type the address in text and when you press the space bar after completing the address, Outlook Express will insert it as a Hyperlink so that the recipient can jump directly to it—in most cases, by simply clicking on the link. If the recipient's e-mail program does not recognize Hyperlinks, they simply copy and paste it into the Address: line of their browser. Additionally, you can insert a Hyperlink anchored to a piece of text. Here's how:

1. Select the text you want to use as a Hyperlink. You can use the Web address, or any other text.

2. Click **Insert** and choose **Link** to display the dialog box. If you are using HTML as your Send format, you can also click on the Link button in the toolbar.

3. Pull down the list of available links to produce the display shown in Figure 7.11.

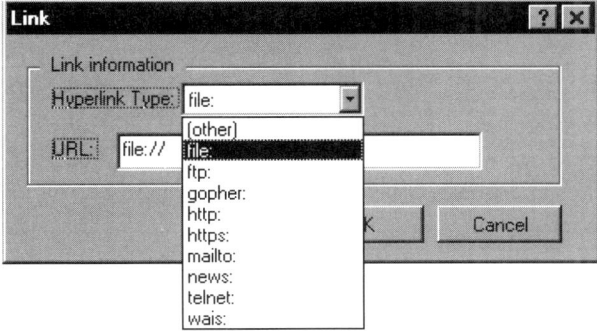

Figure 7.11 Insert Link dialog box.

4. Choose the type of link you want to insert. For example, for a Web link, choose **http**.

5. Type the path, URL, or other address information for the link in the URL: field of this dialog box.

6. Click **OK** to complete the link. The selected text is underlined and changes color to reflect its link status.

WARNING

The Insert Links function doesn't work with early beta releases of Explorer.

I showed you earlier how to set the default format for your messages, text, or HTML. You can also specify an HTML format for just the current message before you send it. To send the current message as an HTML document, click on **Format** and choose **HTML Format**. When the recipient gets the message, it will either appear as a Web document (if the recipient's e-mail client can read it), or it will be sent as an attachment that can be read with a Web browser.

You can also insert pictures (or other graphics), and other types of links in your e-mail message before sending it. The advantage of using HTML as your message format is that you have more control over how the message appears. You can use different styles and sizes of text, bulleted lists, and any other formatting that HTML allows. As mentioned earlier, the chief drawback of using HTML is that many e-mail readers do not yet support it. For this reason, do not use the HTML format unless you are *sure* your recipient will be able to read it.

Sending and Receiving E-mail

When you have finished composing a new message, click on the **Send** button on the message toolbar or use File Send Message (**Alt+S**) to send the message. Unless you have chosen Send Immediately (see configuration instructions earlier in this chapter), you will see a message reminding you that the message will go into a queue to be sent the next time you check your mail. You can click on a toggle button on this dialog box to disable future messages if you want. However, don't forget to choose Send and Receive mail sometime soon, or you will think you have sent e-mail when you haven't.

When you choose **Send and Receive** from the main toolbar or use Tools Send and Retrieve (**Ctrl+M**) from the main menu, Outlook Express establishes a connection to the Internet, logs into the SMTP server first to deliver any mail waiting in your local queue, then logs into the POP3 or IMAP server to retrieve any mail waiting on the host for you.

If you have any new mail you will hear a beep (if you have enabled sound notification on new mail), and the new messages will appear in your inbox. In addition, a little e-mail symbol will appear next to the Clock in the status toolbar.

Reading E-mail

When you receive new mail, Outlook Express displays the From: and Subject: lines from the message header, plus the date and time the message was sent (see Figure 7.12). Notice that if you are viewing the Outlook Express screen in less than full screen size, you may not be able to see the Received date and time. Click on the maximize button or use the horizontal scroll bars at the bottom of the Inbox summary area to view the Received information. You can change the size of the headings, making the columns wider or smaller to suit your needs. The messages can be sorted by date, subject, or Sender. You choose the sort method simply by clicking on the column heading. A little arrow will appear next to the heading you have selected. Clicking again will change the direction of the arrow, representing the choice of ascending or descending sort. Ascending sort by date is the method most often used in normal operation. If you are looking for a message from a certain person, sorting by sender can be a handy tool, since it brings all messages from one sender to one spot.

At the bottom of the Inbox display is a message window that shows all or a part of the selected message in the Inbox. How much of the selected message you will be able to read depends on the length of the message and the size of the window you are using for Outlook Express. The message displayed in Figure 7.12 is the automatic message that is installed with Outlook Express. It actually comes off your installation files and not over the Internet. This sample file shows you how e-mail appears in the Inbox and, when you open it, how message headers look.

You can read any message in the Inbox by selecting it with a single click and then scrolling through the text in the bottom window of the Outlook Express display. Or, double-click on the message you want to read to open it in a message display window like the one in Figure 7.13.

Once you are in the full message window, you have a number of action options, including:

Delete the message. Click on the **X** on the toolbar or use **File Delete**, or press **Ctrl+D**.

Save the message to a file: Use **File Save As...** and provide a path and file name.

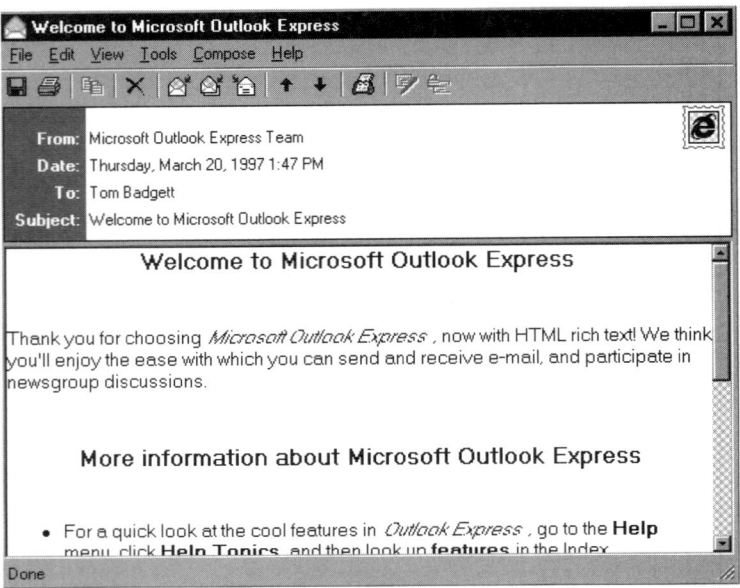

Figure 7.13 The Message display window.

Print the message. Click on the **Print** icon on the toolbar or use **File Print...**, or press **Ctrl+P**.

Reply to the Author. Click on the **Reply to Author** icon on the toolbar or use **Compose Reply to Author** (**Ctrl+R**) on the Menu Bar. You can reply to a message without opening it in the full message window. Simply select the message and click on the **Reply to Author** icon on the main Outlook Express toolbar.

Reply to All. Click on the **Reply to All** icon on the toolbar or use **Compose Reply to All** (**Ctrl+Shift+R**). This will send a message to everyone on the recipient list in the message header.

Forward. Click on the **Forward** icon on the toolbar or use **Compose Forward** (**Ctrl+F**) on the menu bar. This lets you send this message to someone not on the recipient list in the message header.

Display the next message. Click on the **down arrow** on the toolbar or use **View Next** to choose which message to view, or press **Ctrl+>**.

Display the previous message. Click on the **up arrow** on the toolbar or use **View Next** to choose which message to view, or press **Ctrl+<**.

When you respond to a displayed message by replying to the author, all recipients, or forwarding the message to someone else, Outlook Express opens a message editing window with the original address and text in it. You can then add any addresses, if you wish, and then type the text of your reply of introduction to the forwarded message.

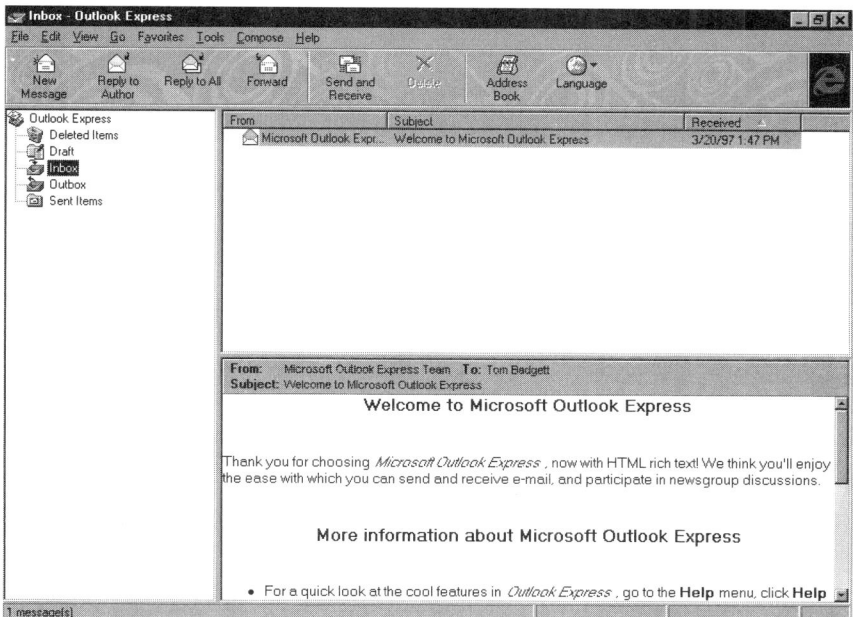

Figure 7.12 Inbox: Outlook Express folder display.

By current convention the new part of the message goes at the top of the page and the original text goes at the bottom. Several years ago, the opposite was true and you mostly saw the original message at the top of the page followed by any new text added along the way. Today, you may see it either way.

In addition, although Outlook Express copies the entire contents of the original message to your reply or forward, unless the message is really short, you don't want to include the full text. Use standard editing keys (backspace, delete) to remove all but the very necessary parts of the original message when you are sending a reply. Of course, if you are forwarding a message, you'll want to include the entire message.

As when you are sending an original message, when you are ready to send the reply or forwarded message, click on **Send** and the message editor will close. Outlook Express has sent the message to the queue where it waits until you check for new mail again, at which time the message will be sent to the host.

NOTE Remember that the Inbox Assistant (on the Tools menu) can help you orga-nize e-mail by sending incoming messages to specific folders according to contents, author, or recipient. I showed you how to do this in Chapter 5.

As you collection of e-mail grows, you may have a need to locate a message you know is in there somewhere but that you can't find. In this case use the **Edit Find** sequence from the main Outlook Express menu to display the Find dialog box shown in Figure 7.14.

Type the text you're looking for, send any search perimeters, such as Match case, and click on **Find Next** to start the search. When the text you specified is found, Outlook Express highlights it and waits for you to close the search win-dow, look for the next occurrence of the text, or start a new search.

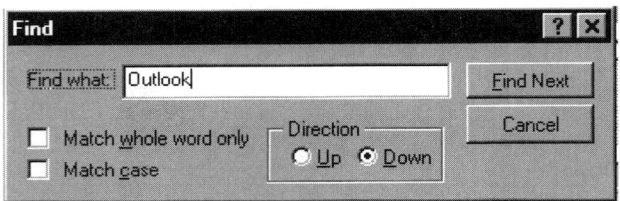

Figure 7.14 The Outlook Express Find dialog box.

Notice also the list of folders at the left of the Outlook Express display (If you don't see a list of folders, use **View Folder List** to turn it on). You can choose which group of messages to display by clicking on the appropriate folder list. You can move information among the folders by opening one folder, then drag-ging a message to a folder in the left side of the display. Copy a message into another folder by holding down the **Shift** key as you drag.

NOTE Use the Draft folder to store messages you have started but not finished and mailed. Use **File Save As...** from inside the message edit screen to save a message-in-progress to the Draft folder.

To create new folders to store messages about different topics, do the following:

1. Use the **File New Folder...** command sequence. You will see the dia-log box shown in Figure 7.15.

2. Choose the existing folder you want to use as the parent for the new folder.

3. Type the name for the new folder in the Folder Name field of this dialog box.

4. Click on **OK** to close the dialog box and create the new folder.

If you have created a new folder beneath an existing folder, you won't see the new one until you open the parent folder by clicking on the plus sign (+) next to it.

Remember, too, that Outlook Express stores any new messages you create in the Outbox prior to sending them to the host. If you change your mind about sending a message, or you want to add something to a message you already have sent to the Outbox, just open the Outbox and choose the message you want to delete or edit. Obviously, you do not have this option if you use Immediate send. Once a message is sent to the mail host it is removed from the outbox and a copy is placed in the sent mail folder.

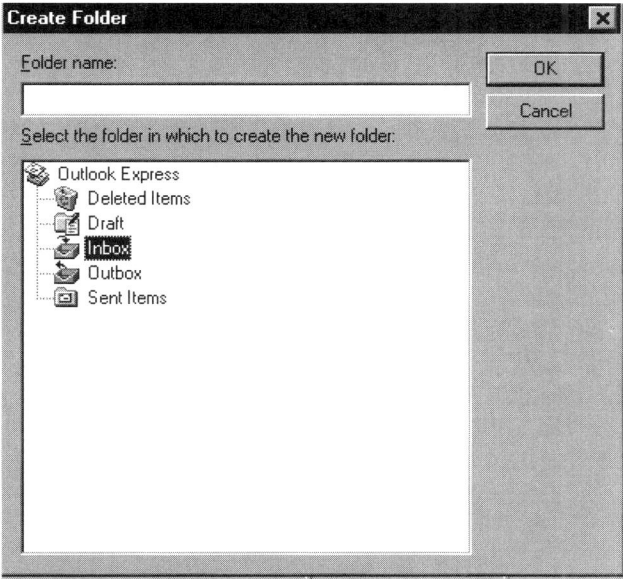

Figure 7.15 Create Folder dialog box.

Keep in mind that if you click on the Outlook Express folder, you will see a graphical display in the right side of the Outlook Express screen that shows all of the components of this package.

USING OUTLOOK EXPRESS NEWS CLIENT

USENET News is a little like e-mail, except that messages are sent to a group instead of to individuals and the messages remain on a host where multiple readers can review them. These messages are grouped by subject. Internet users use News to research a business or personal topic, to share information with other users, and to have fun.

News Client Components

Reading and posting News is similar to sending and receiving electronic mail. The editor and reader screens will be quite familiar if you have spent any time with e-mail in Outlook Express. The main components of Outlook Express News are:

- News reader, a news organizer and text reader that lets you view USENET news topics and documents.
- News Message Editor, a text editor that lets you post messages to groups or send e-mail to individual users.
- Folder List, individual folders to hold the topics and messages for individual news groups.

Configuring Outlook Express News

There is a configuration screen similar to the e-mail configuration screen that lets you set some New operational features. Use Tools News Options to display the dialog box shown in Figure 7.16.

You can see the similarity between this dialog box and the one used to configure e-mail. Some of the terms have changed slightly, but the functionality is virtually the same. You can select specific tabs and make changes as required. Once you get some experience reading News, these options will become self-explanatory.

Using the Outlook Express News Reader

To read news, click on **Outlook Express** in the folder list and choose **Read News** to launch the configuration Wizard. Details of this process are in Chapter 5.

After you complete the Wizard, you should see a blank News window and a Newsgroup icon on the toolbar. Click on the **Newsgroup** icon to produce the dialog box shown in Figure 7.17.

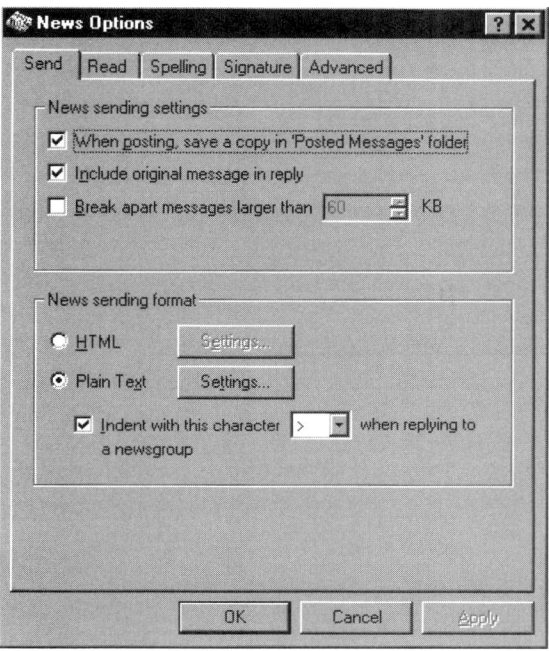

Figure 7.16 The News Options dialog box.

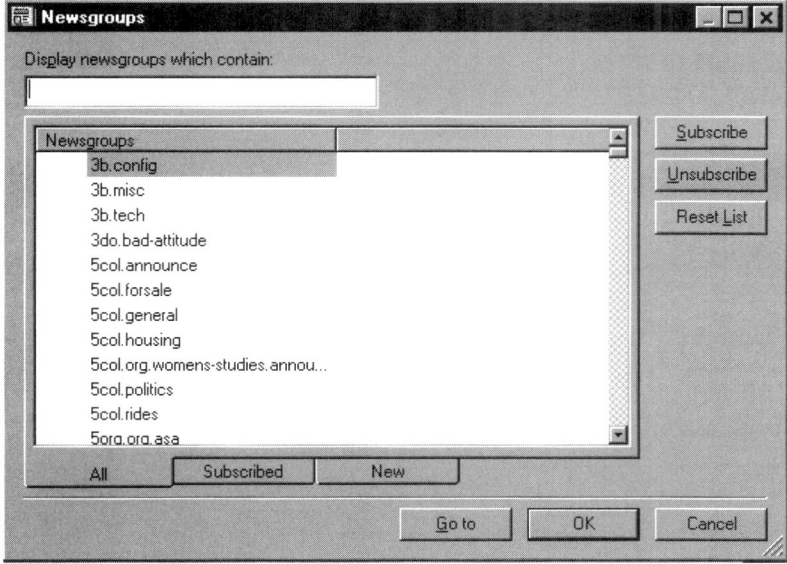

Figure 7.17 The Opening the Newsgroups dialog box.

The first time you access the News reader, Outlook Express will log onto your specified News host and download newsgroup names. This may take several minutes, depending on the speed of your link and the number of newsgroups maintained on your News host. There are more than 35,000 USENET News groups as this book is written, with more coming online all the time.

The Newsgroups list is in alphabetical order. You can scroll down the list and press Enter to open one you want to read. You can also find groups that contain specified text in the title by typing the word or words you want to find in the Display newsgroups which contain: field that appear at the top of this dialog box.

Select a newsgroup and click on **Subscribe** to add the selected group to your subscribe list. Once you have built a subscribe list, you can tell Outlook Express to show you only subscribed groups by clicking on the Subscribed tab at the bottom of the Newsgroups display. You can also double-click group names to toggle the Subscribed flag on or off.

Traditionally, News groups are named with certain codes to help you understand at least the general type of information they contain. A group whose name begins with *edu*, for example, is generally educational information, while a group whose name begins with *comp* is computer-related. Groups that contain *sci.* in the name are scientific topics, while *alt.*, originally intended to group together those that didn't fit the relatively small list of topics, now defines newsgroups that discuss anything you can imagine. There are even *alt.sci*, *alt.edu*, and so on, indicating alternate versions of traditional topics.

In general, the titles are quite descriptive, so in conducting your search, type the topic you hope to find and chances are it will be there. If you don't see a group with the topic you entered, try changing the name by shortening it or by adding a period between components.

To read the contents of a group, select a group in the Subscribed list or All list, and press **Enter** or click on **Go to**.... You will see a display similar to the one in Figure 7.18.

When you subscribe to one or more newsgroups, Outlook Express goes to the host and downloads the header information for them. Then if you select a message to read, the full text is download as you ask for it.

Just as with your e-mail, you can view News messages in the window below the message list, or double-click a message title to open a larger window for that message. From the full message window or the main Outlook Express display you can post a reply to the group or send private e-mail to the author by clicking on the appropriate icon on the toolbar or using the Compose menu. Choose **Reply to Group**, **Reply to Author**, or **Forward** to respond to a specific message.

Outlook Express also keeps all messages you have sent in the Sent Items folder. Should an addressee say they didn't receive a message, open the Sent Items folder and send it again.

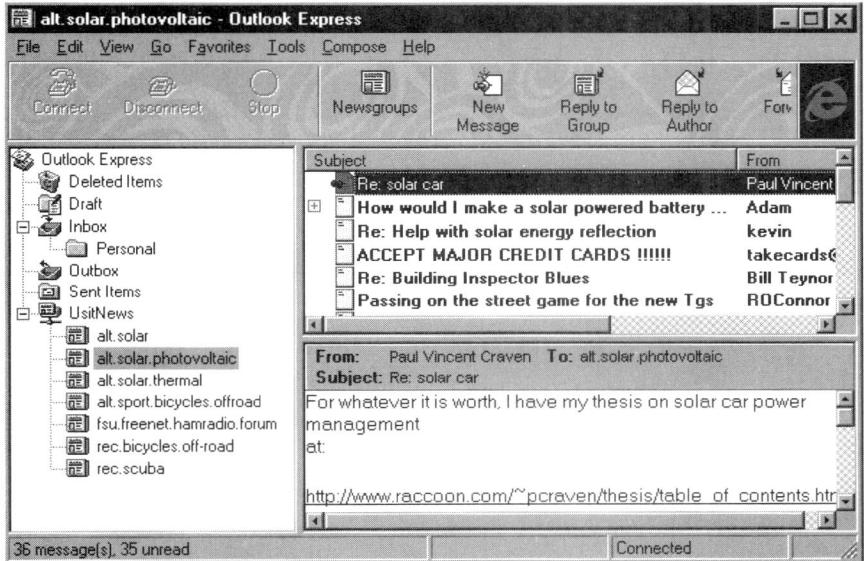

Figure 7.18 Newsgroups folder and header display.

And, like e-mail, any responses you make to news groups or individual authors are placed in your outbox queue until you check mail. Then all of your outgoing messages are uploaded to the server, unless you have Immediate Send already set, in which case the messages are uploaded as they are finished.

To remove a group from your folder list, display Newsgroups and **Unscribe** to the group you want to remove.

USING OUTLOOK EXPRESS CONTACTS MANAGER

The Outlook Express Contacts Manager or Address Book can be a very useful addition to your online toolbox. Although you can access the Address Book components from the Start menu as a standalone application, it is also readily available from inside Outlook Express e-mail. You can use this facility to track individual e-mail addresses, but it also stores full names, business and home addresses, telephone numbers, and more.

Address Book Components

The basic components of the Contacts Manager are:

- Address Book, a database of names, addresses, telephone numbers, and e-mail addresses that you can access through Outlook Express.

- Database Editor, a user interface that lets you add or edit names and associated information to the list.

- E-mail Manager, a dialog box that lets you choose e-mail addresses from the database for inclusion in new e-mail messages or forwarded messages. You can also create groups of e-mail addresses so that you can specify a single group-member address on an e-mail message but have that message sent to all members of the group.

Configuring Address Book

For the most part, the Address Book is configured for you when you install Explorer 4.0. There are, however, some display options you can set to change the way the utility works. For example, to change how information appears in the Address Book, click on **View** and choose a display configuration: **Details**, **Small Icons**, **Large Icons**, or **List**. From this View menu, you can also specify how the information will be sorted.

Using Address Book

You can open the Address Book display in a number of ways:

- When creating a new e-mail message, click on the address card beside any of the address lines in the message header.

- Use **Tools Address Book** from the main Outlook Express menu.

- Click on **Start** on your desktop, point to **Programs**, and choose **Windows Address Book**.

You'll see different screens depending on how you launch the Address Book. For example, if you choose Address Book from the Tools menu, you will see a display similar to the one in Figure 7.19.

This shows a display with Large Icons. Your display may look different if you have a different type of display selected. Double-click on one of the entries to display the tabbed dialog box shown in Figure 7.20. Notice that the Address Book stores detailed information about each person in the database.

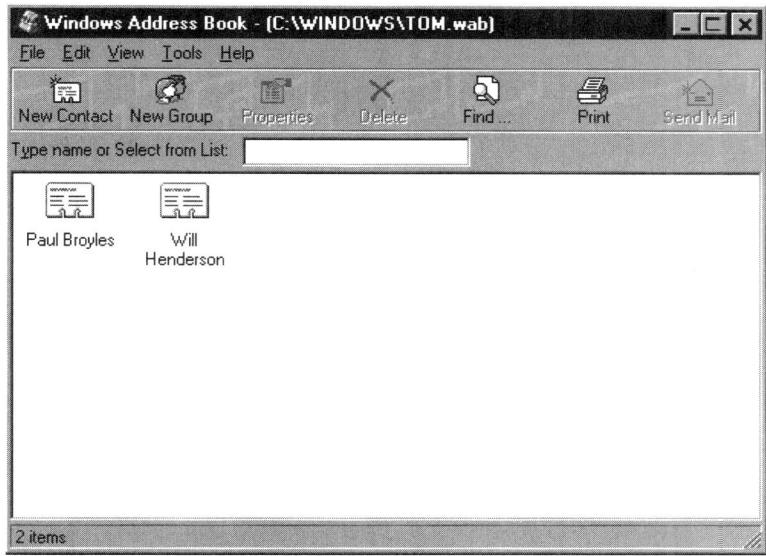

Figure 7.19 Tools Address Book dialog box.

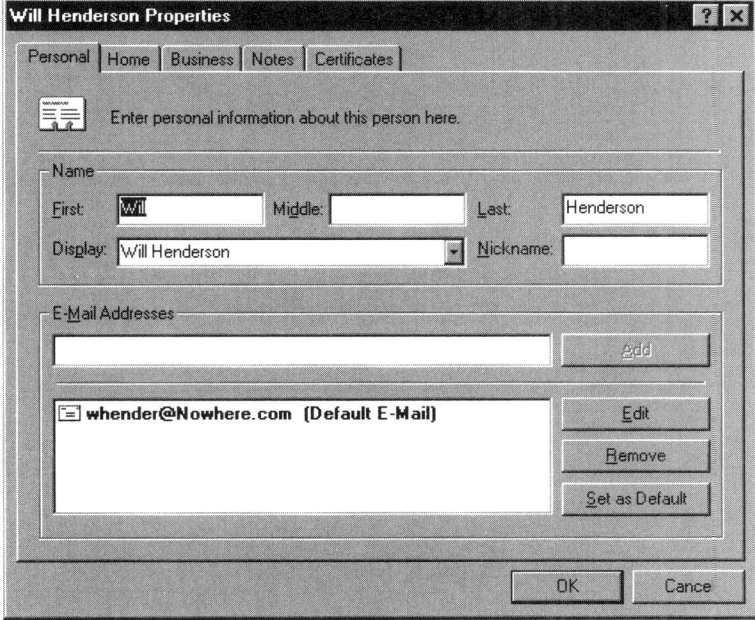

Figure 7.20 A Tabbed Address Book database record.

Click on each tab to display more information about this entry. You can add new information or edit the data already there. For example, you can store multiple e-mail addresses for each person. On the Personal tab of this dialog box enter an e-mail address in the E-mail Addresses field and click **Add**. The new address will be moved into the window at the bottom of the dialog box. Click the **Set as Default** button to mark one of the addresses as the one to use automatically.

The Home tab lets you enter this person's home address and personal Web page (see Figure 7.21).

The Business tab of this dialog box contains similar information, but with fields more oriented to business-related information. You can enter as much or as little of the total amount of information possible. A name and e-mail address are enough to make this facility useful to you in using e-mail. However, if you want to track sales contacts, family members or other Address information, you can fill out complete address and telephone information. If you plan to use many of the groupware features of the full version of Outlook later, it would be a good idea to complete as much of this information as you can.

The Notes tab is a simple text editor that lets you type information about each person in the Address Book database. You might enter a Notes line or lines each time you talk to this person on the phone or receive an e-mail message, for example.

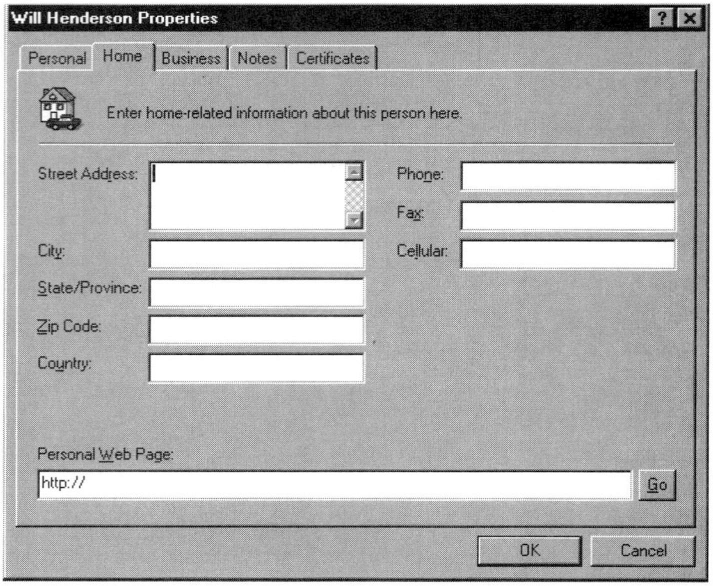

Figure 7.21 The Home tab of the Address Book dialog box.

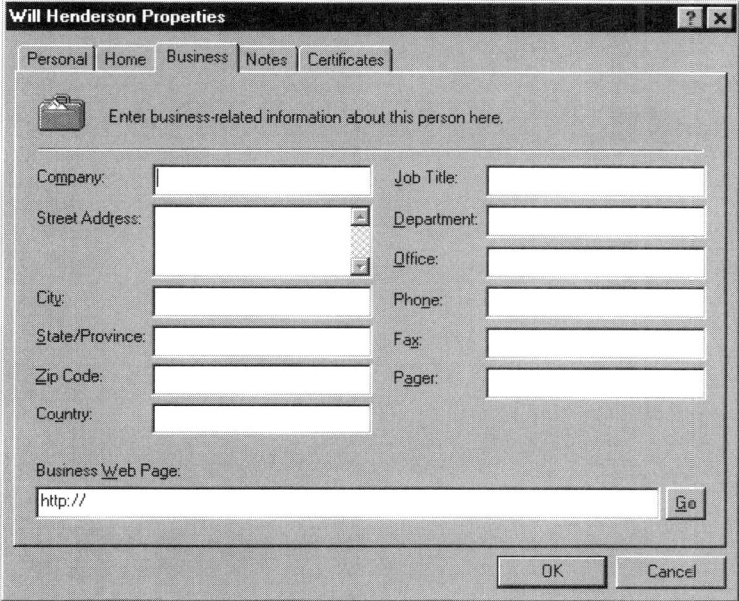

Figure 7.22 The Business tab of the Address Book dialog box.

Finally, the Certificates tab lets you store and track personal certificate information about each person in your database. Certificates can be used to verify that electronic messages that appear to be from a certain contact did indeed originate there. A good starting point to learn more about the use of certificates can be found on the World Wide Web at http://www.verisign.com/.

When you click on **OK** from the Address dialog box, the new or edited information is saved to disk and you are returned to the main Address Book dialog box.

If you access the Address Book from inside the e-mail or New editor, you will see a different screen, the one in Figure 7.23.

The left side of this dialog box lists the names in your Address Book database. On the right are windows for e-mail recipients in the To:, Cc:, and Bcc: fields of an e-mail address header. Click on a name in the left side of the screen and click on To:, cc:, or BCC, depending on the e-mail header section in which you want to insert the name. The chosen name will be copied into the e-mail address area on the right.

If you select a name in the left side of this dialog box and then click on Properties, you will be able to edit information in this person's record. (Properties is the same tabbed dialog box you saw in Figure 7.20.)

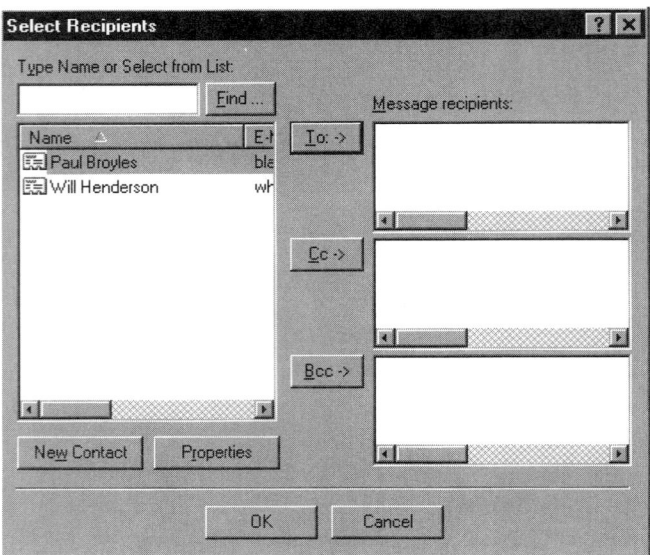

Figure 7.23 An E-mail Address Manager dialog box.

You can also add a new address from this dialog box by clicking on Add. You will see a blank database record where you can add the information.

To create a new address group, display the main Address Book dialog box (Figure 7.19), and click on the **New Group** icon on the toolbar. You will see the display in Figure 7.24.

Type a name for this group in the Group Name: field of this dialog box. You might use Accounting as a name, for example, or Engineering, or Family. Then click on the **Select Members** button to display the records in your Address Book. Choose the records you want to include in the group. Click **OK** to close the New Group dialog box and return to the main Address Book display. Now the name of the group appears in the Address list along with individual entries. You can use this group name as if it were a single address, sending e-mail to everyone on the list.

Importing and Exporting Data

If you are using another address manager program or you want to upgrade to the full-featured Outlook program, you can import address records from another program, or export them from Outlook Express to use in another application.

The import/export converter supports several file formats, including vCard, your Windows card file manager program. To import a file, click on **Tools** and choose **Import**. A menu pops up for you to choose Address Book or vCard. If you choose vCard a file manager screen is displayed so you can navigate to the file you want to import.

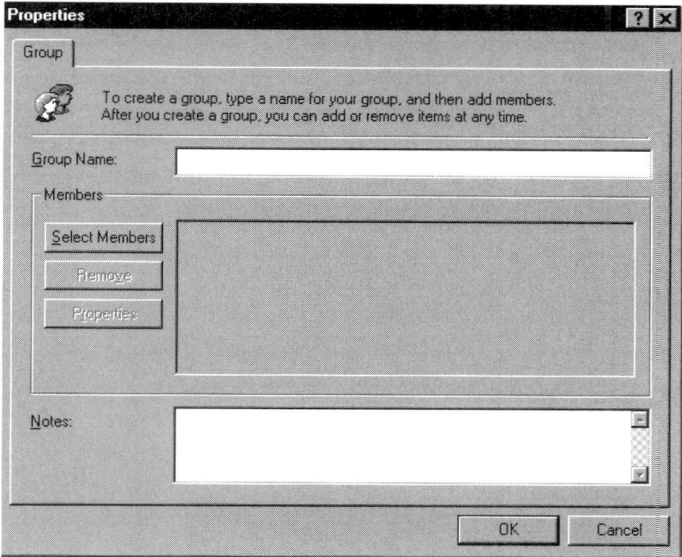

Figure 7.24 The New Group dialog box from Address Book.

If you choose Address Book, you will see the file type selection dialog box shown in Figure 7.25.

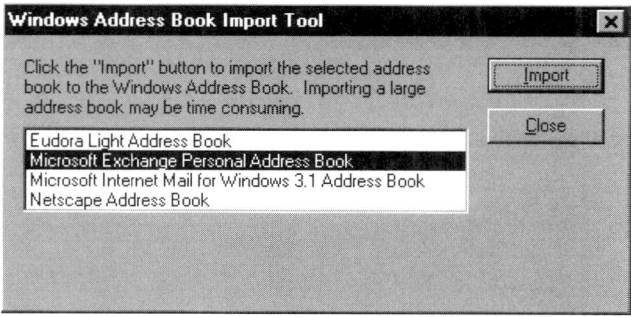

Figure 7.25 An Address Book Import dialog box.

This facility lets you import address information from Eudora Lite, Microsoft Internet Mail, Microsoft Exchange, or Netscape Addresses. Choose the Address

Book type you want to import and you will see a second dialog box that asks for additional information. This second dialog box varies with the type of Address Book you are importing.

Because the Windows 95 registry tracks the location of these resources, so you should be able to just sit back and watch the Wizard work.

Exporting data from inside the Address Book database is the reverse of the import process. Choose **Export** from the Tools menu and select the type of address information you want to export. If you choose Address Book you will be given two choices, Microsoft Exchange and a delimited text file.

If you want to send Address Book data to Excel, Access, or another data management application, the text format is a good one. If you choose a text file, an Export Wizard is launched and you can answer questions and follow the steps to create the file.

The second Wizard screen lets you select the fields you want to export (See Figure 7.26 on the following page).

The information is exported to a comma-delimited file in the same order the field names appear in the list in Figure 7.26. You may need to copy down this order or print the screen to make it easier to import this information into another data management program.

There's more to this program, of course, but the rest of it should be fairly straightforward. The best teacher is do-it-yourself. Try using the program and learn your way around.

In Chapter 8, I'll show you more about the NetMeeting program.

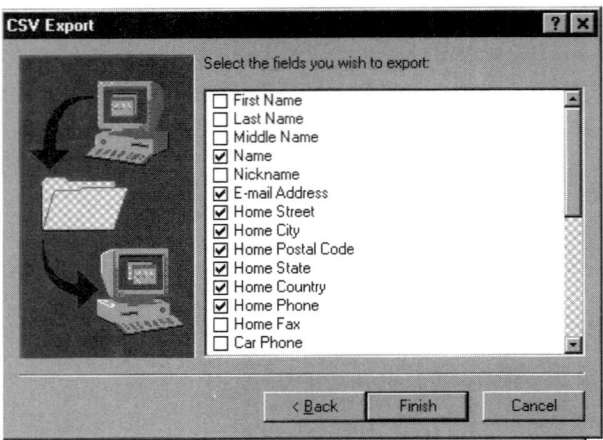

Figure 7.26 Address Book text file Export Wizard fields.

CHAPTER EIGHT

Using NetMeeting

NetMeeting is an interesting and versatile program that provides a variety of communications features. These features take advantage of Internet connectivity to demonstrate the potential of real-time, global multimedia communication. In addition, NetMeeting integrates well with the features and design of Explorer 4.0.

NetMeeting is not new with Explorer 4.0. It was released in an earlier version with Explorer 3. This updated version has additional features and makes better use of the Explorer design and integration.

NETMEETING COMPONENTS

NetMeeting is a multimedia communications tool that includes the following components:

- *Chat*—a conventional computer communications tool that lets you converse with the keyboard, using a split-screen display. The words you type appear in one part of the screen; the words typed by others appear in another part of the screen.

- *Whiteboard*—a graphics-based communications tool. The Whiteboard has the look and feel of the Windows Paint program, letting you draw pictures, use colors, and send text to communicate ideas. When you open a Whiteboard, other users on the call can also see it and any one of them can add or modify the sketches on the Whiteboard.

- *Audio Communication*—an audio communications tool that uses a microphone, speakers, and sound card to let you talk to other users. If your sound card can support it, you can conduct full duplex communications, like a telephone. Older sound cards are limited to one way at a time, more like push-to-talk radio communications.

- *Video Communication*—a video communications tool that uses a black and white or color camera to send images across the Internet. You can communicate one-to-one or with groups via a NetMeeting server.

- *Sharing Applications*—a data sharing tool that lets you launch an application while you are in a NetMeeting call. Other users on the connection can see the data in your application and can work with the data.

CONFIGURING NETMEETING

The basic NetMeeting configuration is done the first time you run the program (see the description of this configuration Wizard in Chapter 5). Beyond this initial configuration, however, there are settings you can change if you wish. Notice the tabbed dialog box, shown in Figure 8.1, which is displayed with the Tools Options... menu sequence.

This dialog box has six tabs: General, Protocols, Video, My Info, SpeedDials, and Directory. The settings on these tabs are, for the most part, straightforward. I will discuss the major points of each in the following sections.

The General Tab

The General tab has three groups: General, Network bandwidth, and File transfer. You set the Bandwidth section with the configuration Wizard when you first started NetMeeting, and the location of saved files (the last group, File transfer) was set for you automatically. You can change either of these simply by selecting the appropriate button or field and entering the new information.

The first group, General, was also configured automatically, but there may be a good reason to change some of these settings. The first toggle, the Show Microsoft NetMeeting icon on the task bar, creates an icon in the tray section of the task bar when NetMeeting is running. You can pop-up a toolbar that launches many NetMeeting functions from this tray icon.

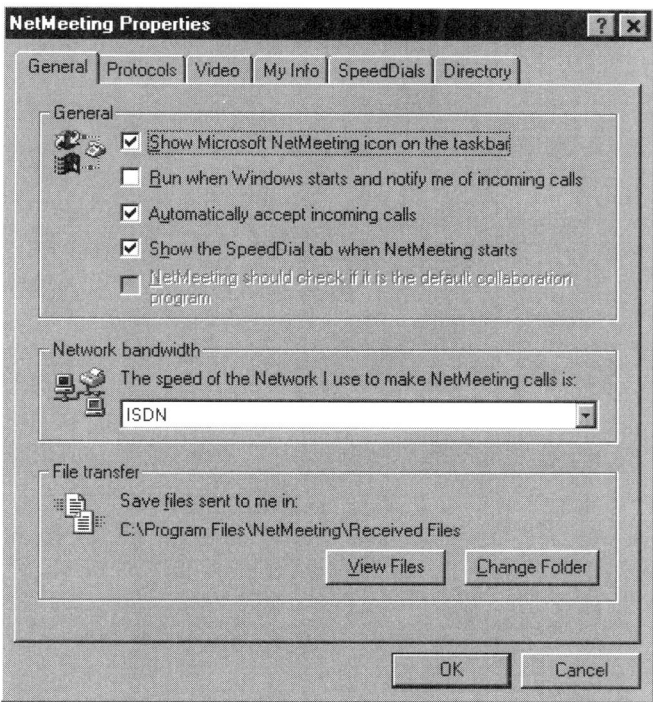

Figure 8.1 The NetMeeting properties (options) dialog box.

The second toggle, when active, automatically runs NetMeeting when you open Windows and sets the program to notify you of incoming calls. Unless you are using NetMeeting regularly, you probably should toggle this off. NetMeeting requires a fair amount of memory and other system resources, so unless you are actively using it, leave it off.

The third toggle tells NetMeeting whether to answer incoming call automatically. You probably do not want this feature enabled, especially if your system is equipped with audio and video facilities. If your camera is turned on and your computer automatically answers a call, whatever image is being captured by your camera at the time can be transmitted to the caller. I personally want to control whether a caller can access images or sound generated by my computer.

Select or de-select the last two toggles at your preference. By default, NetMeeting displays the SpeedDial tab of the main screen when the program starts. If you prefer to see the Directory tab instead, turn off this toggle. And, if you have more than one conference software package installed, you can tell NetMeeting to check whether it is the default conferencing software.

The Protocols Tab

The Protocols tab (Figure 8.2) lets you specify how you will connect to other computers to use NetMeeting features. At least one protocol should have been selected when you ran the configuration Wizard. However, if you wish you can turn on more than one protocol.

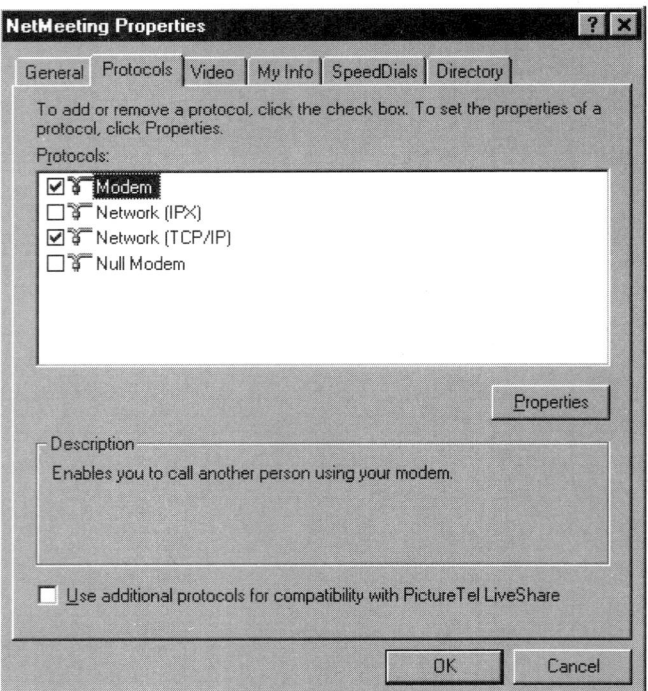

Figure 8.2 The Protocol tab of the Properties dialog box.

If you are using the Internet to connect with NetMeeting, choose **Network (TCP/IP)**. You can also connect directly to another computer with a modem. If this is how you want to use NetMeeting, choose this protocol as well.

The Video Tab

The Video tab of this dialog box (Figure 8.3) contains settings that control some of the operational features of your video hardware. There are four groups on this dialog box: Sending and receiving video, Send image size, Video quality, and Video camera properties.

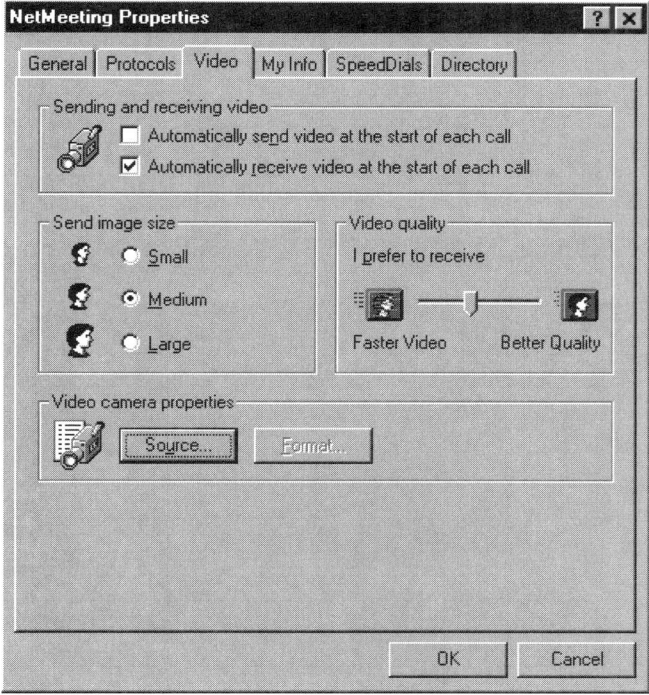

Figure 8.3 The Video tab of the Properties dialog box.

The sending and receiving default settings automatically receive video if it is available when a call starts, but it doesn't automatically send video.

You can speed up call connection times by disabling video sending or receiving. Then you can enable video sending and receiving after the call is established.

Similarly, the smaller image size gives you a faster connection, and you can choose whether to improve performance or quality in the video quality group. The Video camera properties button displays settings and information specific to your video hardware.

The My Info Tab

You filled out the My Info tab when you installed NetMeeting or when you ran it for the first time. (See chapter 5 for details.) It contains personal information, including your "public" or "display" name, your e-mail address, and so on.

The SpeedDials Tab

The SpeedDial feature is like a Favorites list for NetMeeting contacts. It stores the names and connection information for the people you contact with NetMeeting. Particularly if you use direct modem-to-modem contacts, storing the dial-up number in the SpeedDial area can make the call go faster.

The SpeedDial tab (Figure 8.4) lets you control whether NetMeeting automatically adds new contacts to the SpeedDial list, and how often to refresh the SpeedDial information.

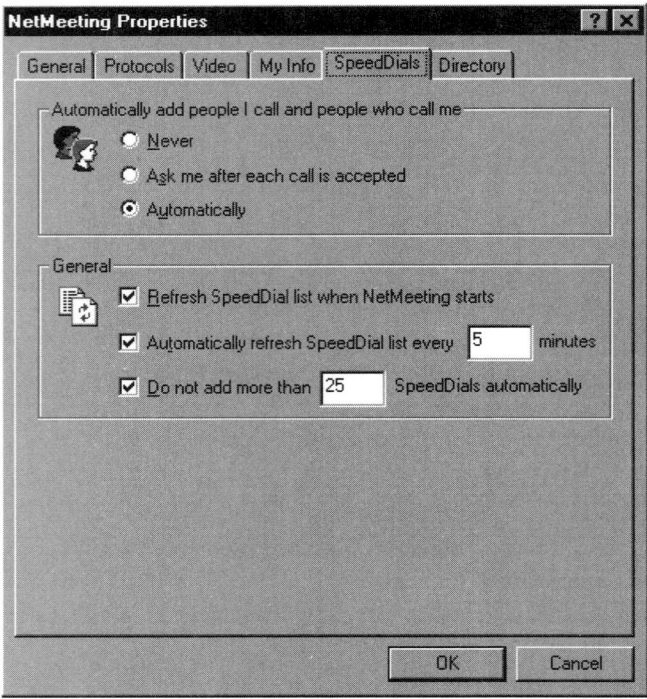

Figure 8.4 The SpeedDial tab of the Properties dialog box.

The Directory Tab

While you can use NetMeeting by connecting directly to another computer via a modem, or over a network, the larger application is through directory servers that let you pick someone to contact from a list. The Directory tab of the Properties dialog box (Figure 8.5) lets you choose which directory server will be the default connection when you launch NetMeeting.

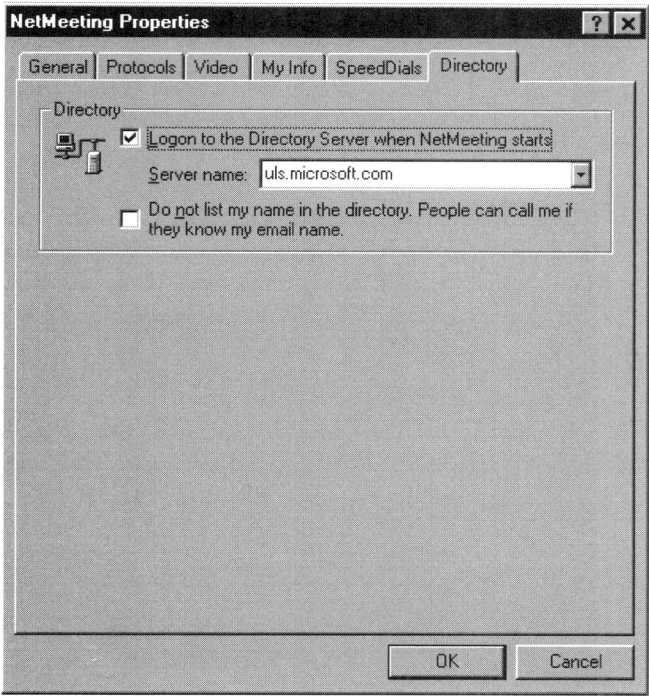

Figure 8.5 The Directory tab of the Properties dialog box.

You can also tell NetMeeting to repress display of your name in the online directory. Other users on the directory can still contact you if they know your address, but they can't browse the list and contact you randomly. Expect to see many corporations and network service providers starting to provide directory services for intra-company use in the future.

ESTABLISHING A CONNECTION

Getting connected with NetMeeting may require one or two steps, depending on the type of connection you want to make. Once you have established one or more SpeedDial entries, connecting may be as simple as choosing one from the list. This method works if you are using a direct modem connection to the remote party's computer, or if you are using a permanent Internet connection.

 **NOTE** By default NetMeeting creates up to 25 SpeedDial entries for you automatically each time you contact someone. You can create a SpeedDial entry of your own with the SpeedDial button on the toolbar (or by clicking on **SpeedDial** and choosing **Add SpeedDial** from the menu). You can also disable automatic SpeedDial creation by toggling off this option on the SpeedDials tab of the Properties dialog box.

If you don't have a SpeedDial entry for the person you want to contact, of if you want to browse an online directory to find someone, then the procedure is a little different. Suppose you simply want to connect to one of the available NetMeeting directory servers and see who is available. The general procedure is to establish a connection to the Internet or other network where the directory server resides, specify the directory server, and choose a name.

How you establish a connection to the network depends on what kind of network and the type of connection you use to log in. You should have already established your modem or network connection information as described earlier in this chapter.

If you are using the Internet to connect to one of the Microsoft NetMeeting directory servers, for example, do the following:

1. Establish an Internet connection. Use Dialup Networking if you connect to the Internet via a dialup connection. If you have a network connection, then this part of the process should be automatic for you.

2. Choose a directory server from the pull down list beneath the toolbar.

NetMeeting should attempt to log you in automatically. If not, use **Call Logon to <servername>** from the main NetMeeting menu to start the process. Within a few seconds you should begin to see a list of e-mail addresses and names of the people currently connected to the specified server.

NOTE

When you choose a directory server, you should see a list of participants within a few seconds. However, there may be hundreds or even thousands of people logged into the server you have chosen. It may actually take several minutes to complete the list. You can view the progress of the directory display by watching the progress report in the lower left corner of the NetMeeting display. Also, you shouldn't try to contact any of the people on this server until the status message in the lower right corner of the NetMeeting screen says "Logged into <servername>."

On the other hand, suppose you want to talk to a specific person using a modem connection. You either must make arrangements in advance to make the connection, or you must know that the recipient of your call keeps NetMeeting running all the time and will be available to take your call. When you are ready to contact a particular individual with a modem call, here is the process:

1. Click on **Call** on the main NetMeeting menu and choose **New Call** (or click on the **Call** icon on the toolbar) to display the dialog box shown in Figure 8.6.

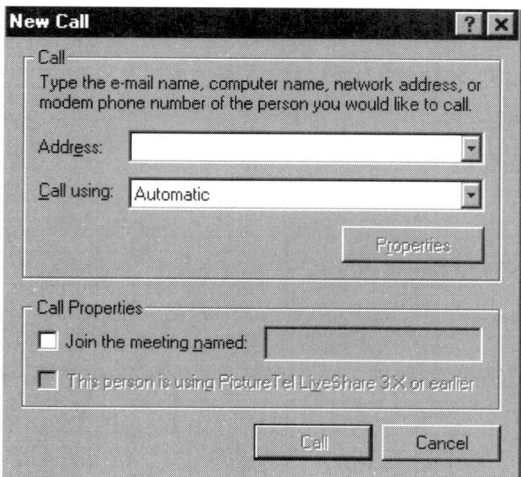

Figure 8.6 New Call dialog box.

2. Type the telephone number of the person you are calling in the Address: field of this dialog box. Pull down a list of call options in the

Call using: field and choose **Modem**. Remember, you must have already established the Modem protocol by previously using the Protocols tab of the Options dialog box available on the Tools menu.

If the number you are calling is for a machine hosting a meeting (see about opening a host session later in this chapter), then click on the **Join the meeting named**: button and type the name of the meeting you want to join.

N O T E

3. Click on the **Call** button at the bottom of this dialog box. After a few seconds the modem should go off hook and the number will be dialed. NetMeeting will establish a connection with the remote computer and you then should be able to communicate.

You will see the hourglass while the connection is being built. Assuming that the party you are calling does indeed answer and accept your call, you will see their name appear as one of the participants in the current conference, and the two video windows will appear. Because the bandwidth of modems is limited, it may take a while for video and audio to start streaming. You can launch NetMeeting and make a call in one operation by using the **Run** command on the Start menu and the **Address** toolbar or any Address window in Explorer by using a specific URL. Here's how:

1. Click the **Start** button, and then click **Run**.
2. Type: **callto:<servername>/<e-mail address>**

For example, if you are calling tbadgett@usit.net, who is logged onto uls.microsoft.com, type: **callto:uls.microsoft.com/tbadgett@usit.net**.

You must have established a network connection (to the Internet or local area network) that will allow you to log on to the specified server for this process to work.

N O T E

If the person you are calling is logged onto the same server as you are, you may need to use only their e-mail address. You can use this procedure whether or not NetMeeting is running. However, the process is faster if NetMeeting is already running in the background.

N O T E

Note that using a callto: URL may not start NetMeeting but some other tele-conferencing software if that software is installed as the default. You can change this with the Tools:Options Menu sequence, as described above. You can use the callto: syntax to help someone call you directly from your Web page or e-mail. Just add a link on the Web site or in the e-mail message. Here's how:

In the HTML for the Web page, use the syntax: **callto:<servername>/ <e-mail address>**.

For example, if I wanted to place a link on my Web page so that other people could call me using one of the Microsoft directory servers, I would insert text and tags similar to this:

Call me using Microsoft NetMeeting at <A HREF="callto:uls.microsoft.com/ tbadgett@usit.net">

uls.microsoft.com/tbadgett@usit.net</A>

ACCEPTING A CALL

NetMeeting answers incoming calls for you, whether you are logged into a directory server or receive calls via a direct TCP/IP or modem connection. However, you can control whether NetMeeting asks for confirmation before answering, and whether you automatically send video once the connection is made.

Set these features from the Options choice on the Tools menu. On the General tab of this dialog box (the Properties dialog box, which you display with the Tools:Options Menu sequence), turn on **Automatically accept incoming calls** if you want NetMeeting to answer all calls. Then on the Video tab, click on **Automatically send video at the start of each call** if you want to turn on your camera and send video to the calling party automatically.

If you have turned off the automatic accept feature, when you receive a call a window appears near the task bar. Click **Accept** in this window to answer the call and begin a conversation with the caller. To reject the incoming call, click **Ignore**.

You can also reject incoming calls in advance by turning on the **Do not disturb** toggle on the Call menu. If you turn on **Do Not Disturb**, you will see the warning message shown in Figure 8.7. If you turn on Do Not Disturb, callers will be told you are refusing calls.

Click **OK** to accept the **Do Not Disturb** setting. This is a toggle, so you can turn it off to accept calls by clicking on **Do Not Disturb** a second time. The check mark beside this menu entry should be removed when you want to accept calls.

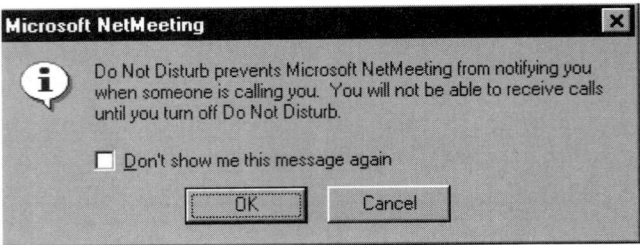

Figure 8.7 The Do Not Disturb warning dialog box.

USING NETMEETING COMPONENTS

Once you answer a call (or a remote party has answered your call) you are connected with the remote user or meeting and are ready to use the specific communications features of NetMeeting. If you're familiar with other Internet communications facilities, then these utilities will soon be second nature. "Learn by doing" is the best way to become familiar with all the ways to communicate with NetMeeting. I'll show you the basics in this section. Then you're on your own to become proficient in the ones you want to use. You should note that there is only a limited amount of bandwidth available among any machines on any network. *Bandwidth* is a measurement of how much information per second can be sent between machines. Every additional feature you enable will take up some of the available bandwidth and potentially slow down other aspects of your connection. Video and audio tend to use the most bandwidth of any single application, followed by application sharing, the Whiteboard, and Chat. Especially when using a modem or slow Internet link, you may consider turning off video when you are using a shared application to increase speed.

Chat

The Chat feature is the traditional way of communicating with other network users. Network operating systems, UNIX, and the Internet have supported split-screen, text-based conversations for a long time. To enable Chat, once you have connected with another user, use Tools Chat (**Ctrl+T**) to display the dialog box shown in Figure 8.8.

Information typed by people participating in the chat session is displayed in the top window of this dialog box. The name or online ID of the person who typed the message appears to the left of the message. Notice that this display includes your messages as well.

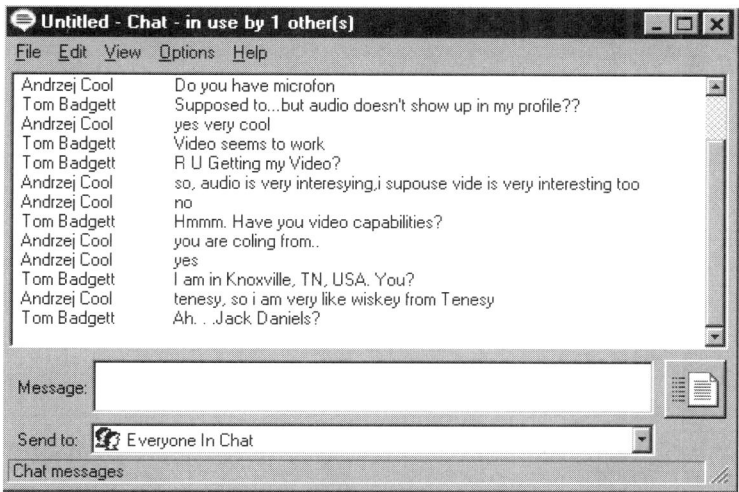

Figure 8.8 The NetMeeting Chat dialog box.

To send a message to the group, click in the lower window of this display and type what you want to say. The message isn't sent to the chat session until you press **Enter**, so you can edit mistakes or change the message before you actually send it.

You can also change the way this Chat window appears. Click on **Options** and choose **Chat Format…** from the Chat dialog box to display the configuration screen shown in Figure 8.9.

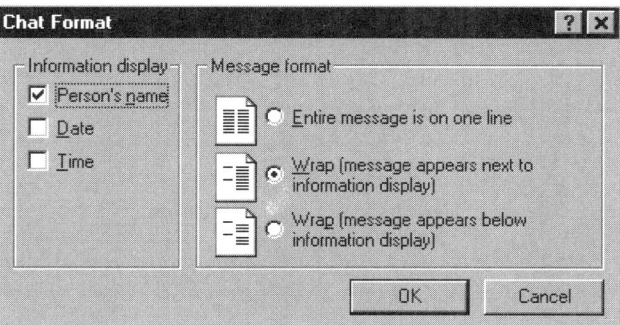

Figure 8.9 The Chat Format dialog box.

You can turn on date and time display for each message typed, and you can control how NetMeeting Chat handles message display. These changes take effect immediately after you close this Chat Format dialog box.

The Options menu also lets you control the font used for Chat displays, and you can save or print the contents of the Chat window if you want. If you are using the Chat connection for a business meeting, particularly, the save and print feature is a useful way to track what was discussed and to help you remember any action items for which you are responsible.

Use **File Exit** from the Chat dialog box to close the Chat session and return to the main NetMeeting window. You are still connected to the remote user at this point. To disconnect the call, click on the **HangUp** icon on the toolbar, or use **Call Hang up** from the main NetMeeting menu.

Notice that in the bottom section of the Chat window you can choose who will see your messages. In addition to sending messages to everyone in a meeting, it is possible to send messages to a specific user.

Whiteboard

The NetMeeting Whiteboard lets you share drawings, doodles, and other graphics objects with remote users. After you are connected with one or more people through NetMeeting, use Tools Whiteboard (**Ctrl+W**) to display the Whiteboard dialog box shown in Figure 8.10.

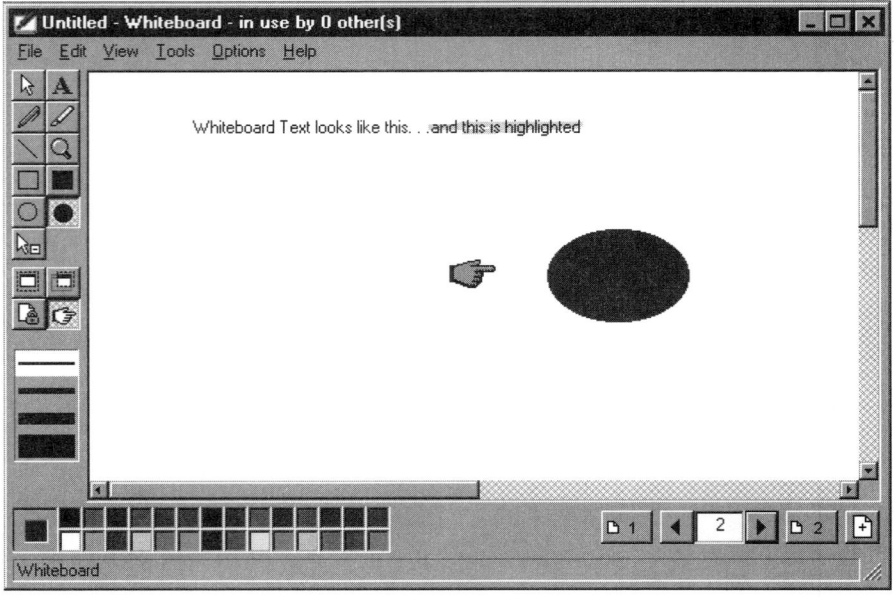

Figure 8.10 Whiteboard dialog box.

If you are familiar with the Windows Paint utility, then the Whiteboard will be easy to use. Most of the Paint tools are available, including the Text tool, filled objects, and the freehand drawing pen. You can also erase lines and objects with the eraser, and you can use the highlight tool to highlight text or objects to call the attention of remote users to them.

Click on the **Remote Pointer** tool to turn on the remote pointer (shown in the middle of Figure 8.10). This feature lets remote users point to objects on your screen and you point to objects on their screen.

You can have multiple Whiteboard pages open simultaneously. Step among open pages—or open a new page—with the right- and left-facing arrows in the lower right corner of the Whiteboard display. You can see from Figure 8.10 that screen 2 is being displayed in this sample. If you are using the remote pointer on a new screen, you'll first have to turn the pointer off by clicking again on the Report Pointer tool or by using the Tools Remote Pointer menu sequence. Then turn the pointer on again after selecting the new screen.

Two Interesting buttons on the Whiteboard toolbar let you insert an open window on your desktop, or insert a selected area of your desktop right on the Whiteboard. Suppose you want to show someone what the screen of a software application looks like, for example. Here's how:

1. Click on the Window tool. You will see a message that says the next window you click will be inserted onto the Whiteboard.

2. Click **OK** to close the message dialog box.

3. Click on the Window you want to insert onto the Whiteboard.

N O T E
If you are using the Whiteboard in full screen mode, click the **Restore** button to reduce the size before selecting the Windows tool. Also, make sure that the window you want to insert onto the Whiteboard is open.

Figure 8.11 shows a Whiteboard display with the PointCast software window inserted. When you insert a window in this way, the new window covers up whatever is already on the open screen of the Whiteboard. The original contents are still there, but you'll have to drag the inserted window to one side or use the **Edit Send to Back** menu sequence to see it.

Don't forget the Remote Pointer. You can move it around the inserted window to point up specific areas of the Whiteboard display. And, remember that you can use File Print or File Save As... to save versions of the Whiteboard display. Use File

Exit to close the Whiteboard utility and return to the main NetMeeting display. Note that when other participants in your meeting are controlling the pointer, their initials are tagged to the bottom of it, letting you know who is manipulating the Whiteboard. Especially in larger meetings, this is an important facility.

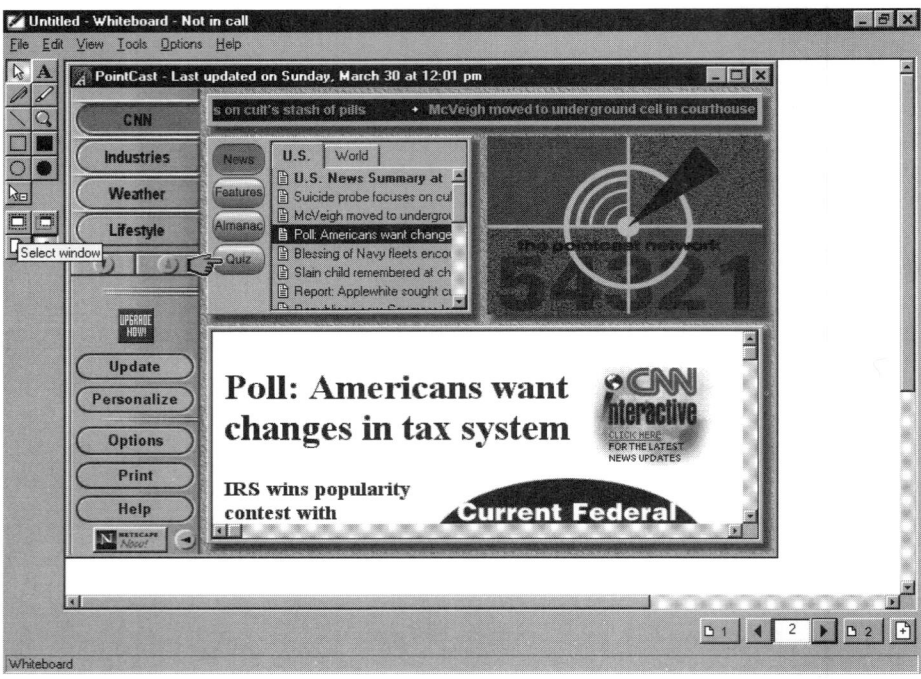

Figure 8.11 Whiteboard with PointCast Window inserted.

Audio

NetMeeting audio facilities are pretty much automatic. If your computer has a compatible sound card installed and you are connecting with a user who also has a version of NetMeeting that supports audio on a computer system properly equipped, you should be able to talk. You can tell who has audio support when you log onto a directory service by checking the icons displayed in the Directory window. A yellow speaker icon beside a user's name indicates they have audio support.

Many users also include information in their personal information profile saying whether they can or will use audio as part of a NetMeeting contact.

If you establish a connection with someone, but find you can't talk to each other, there are some things you can try:

- Use **Tools Audio Tuning Wizard...** to launch the audio tuning wizard. You should have used this program during installation to test your audio board and set its configuration. However, running this utility again will tell you whether your audio card is compatible with NetMeeting and how it is configured.

- Make sure the party on the other end of the link can support audio. If their configuration doesn't support audio, you can try to talk to them and it will appear that your audio system isn't working.

- NetMeeting audio only works with TCP/IP network connections. You can't use audio over a modem-to-modem connection. You can use a modem with audio, but you must be connected to the Internet or another TCP/IP network rather than directly to the modem of the remote user.

- If you are hosting a session (see the information on hosting a NetMeeting session, later in this chapter), you can't use audio.

- You can use audio only between two people. You can be in a meeting with more than one other person, but you can use audio features of NetMeeting with only one user at a time.

N O T E

Microsoft maintains an excellent troubleshooting Web site for NetMeeting. Online Wizards help you diagnose and correct a number of audio and other problems with NetMeeting. Point your Browser to **www.microsoft.com/support/tshooters.htm**. You can also try backing up one level to **www.microsoft.com/support** for a general support page that may be helpful with a range of Microsoft products, including NetMeeting.

In addition, your sound card may be able to support only half-duplex operation where only one party can talk at a time. This is like a two-way radio connection that uses push-to-talk. If yours is a full-duplex sound card, then the connection operates more like a telephone where both parties can talk at once.

You can control who on a meeting receives your audio. Display the Current Call window, then click on the audio icon next to the name of the person you want to disconnect from your audio stream and choose **Stop Sending Audio and Video.** You can switch audio sending to another user by clicking on the audio or video icon next to the name of the person you want to receive your audio in the Current Call window. Then click on **Send Audio and Video** to turn on audio and video communication to the specified user.

Video

If you have a video capture card and a camera, you can probably use live video in your NetMeeting conferences. By default, NetMeeting doesn't automatically send video when you connect to another user, but you can start sending video after the connection if you wish. After you establish a connection as described earlier, use the **Tools Video** menu sequence to display the pop-up menu shown in Figure 8.12.

Figure 8.12 Pop-up Tools Video menu.

A check mark beside any entry on this menu indicates that the feature is enabled. Notice in Figure 8.12 that all items are checked. You can also see the local and remote video windows on the screen. The Detach options open your video windows to the full size specified in the video configuration and move the windows out of the NetMeeting window. With the video windows detached and configured for Always on top, you can move the video anywhere on your desktop, even while you work on other applications.

If you have audio capability, for example, you can shrink NetMeeting, detach video, and work in your word processor or spreadsheet while you see and hear someone else on the remote link. If you don't have audio—or if the person on the other end of the link doesn't have audio—you can still share video images and communicate with the Chat window. You type what you want to say and read what the other person says while you view their transmitted image in the Receiving video window.

Of course. you are not limited to video images of yourself sitting in front of your computer. You can pick up your video camera and point it at anything you want to show the other person. If you have a color camera, the images at the remote site can be quite clear, even if you are transmitting at a slow frame rate. Normal full-motion video transmits at 30 frames per second, but your computer hardware and Internet link probably will limit video transmission to 15 frames per second or less. This produces a jerky motion, but lip sync can be surprisingly close and a fixed image, such as a book, comes through very well.

For this book, I have used the U.S. Robotics BigPicture video kit, which includes a small, high-quality color camera and its own video capture card for the PCI bus. I was able to produce very good quality video, in color, and transmit it all over the world. This particular camera—and many others you might use—has a good depth of field and even supports some macro capabilities so you can show genuinely close-up images such as your keyboard, a printed page, a photograph, and so on. I have used these video capabilities from the floor of a convention hall, for example, and was able to share images of the convention and of the people that visited my booth with other people at my home office.

Applications and File Sharing

After you have established a connection with a remote user, you can share an application that runs on your computer and you can send and receive files over the NetMeeting link. These features add another level of sharing that can be useful in a business environment where you want to discuss a spreadsheet or document and for personal use when you want to send the remote user a picture of yourself, a graphics image, a shareware program and so on.

To share an application after you have established a NetMeeting link:

1. Launch the application you want to share and open any documents you want to use with this application.
2. Click **Share** on the toolbar or use the **Tools Share Application** menu sequence to display a list of all open programs.
3. Click on the application you want to share from the pop-up list. You will see a message confirming that you want to allow others to view the selected application and telling you that they will not be able to make use your application unless you click Collaborate on the toolbar.
4. Click **OK** on the warning dialog box to begin application sharing.

The application and whatever file is loaded with it will appear on the remote computer within a few seconds. Now anything you do with the chosen application can be seen over the NetMeeting link. This one-way connection is good to show other users a particular file such as a word document, an excel spreadsheet, or a drawing. If you want to allow others to interact with your application, click on **Collaborate** on the toolbar or use the **Tools Start Collaborating** menu sequence. You will see the information dialog box shown in Figure 8.13.

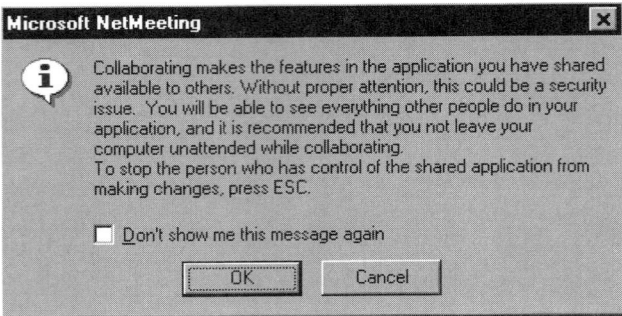

Figure 8.13 Start Collaborating information dialog box.

Once you turn on Collaboration, other people on the NetMeeting connection can interact with any shared application you have running on your computer. Interestingly, shared applications appear on the task bar of remote computers as if they were running locally. At the remote site, users will see a pop-up window instructing them to click the mouse button to take control. If you lose control of your screen, click the mouse button to regain control. This sort of collaboration takes some practice. Each user on the conference has to take a turn in controlling the shared program or programs. Otherwise, you will have chaos with no one in control.

Notice that once you have enabled collaboration, everybody's mouse movements are visible and no one can control the local desktop—including features of NetMeeting—until they click the mouse button to take control. However, no applications are shared with remote users until you specifically share them with the Share icon on the toolbar (or the Tools Share Application command).

One example of how to use application sharing follows. Suppose you have a document in Microsoft Word that you want to review and edit with a group. You launch Word and load the document you want to edit. Use **Tools Track Changes Highlight Changes**... from the Word menu to turn on tracking. Now when anyone makes a change to the document the changes are marked by a vertical line in the margin beside the paragraph that has been changed, and the new text appears in a different color from the main body of the document.

WARNING

You should be aware that all functions of the application you share are available to all users you share it with. Accidents do happen, and it is strongly suggested that you make copies of the documents you will be working with and put them in a safe place. You should also keep a close eye on what is happening, so that you may be able to take control before fatal mistakes are made. Once you share an application and turn on collaboration, other users have full control of the shared application.

You can also use this connection to transfer files to the remote user. To transfer files after you have established a connection with a remote user, do the following:

1. Click on **Tools** and point to **File Transfer** to pop up the Files menu.
2. Choose **Send Files** from this menu to display a file manager dialog box.
3. Navigate to the folder that contains the file you want to send.
4. Choose the file to send by double-clicking on it or by clicking on it once and then clicking on **Send**. NetMeeting transfers the file to the remote computer and stores it in the default file transfer folder. You will see a message indicating when the file was successfully sent to the remote user. This again uses part of the available bandwidth between your computer and the recipient. When you send large files, you may notice that other components of your meeting respond slower.

By default, NetMeeting stores the received file in the Received Files folder beneath the NetMeeting folder. You can view any received files by clicking on **Tools**, pointing to **File Transfer**, and selecting the **Open Received Files** folder.

OPENING A HOST SESSION

So far, I've talked about using NetMeeting to contact another specific user or to answer a call from someone browsing a directory server or who uses your modem number. You can also configure your computer as a host to coordinate several connections. This might be useful on your corporate LAN or intranet to collaborate on a document or to conduct a brief staff meeting when you don't want to get everybody together in a conference room.

To set up your computer as a host, do the following:

1. Launch NetMeeting.
2. Click on the **Host** icon on the toolbar or use **Call Host Conference** from the main menu. You will see the dialog box shown in Figure 8.14.

Figure 8.14 The Host Conference Information dialog box.

3.   Click on **OK** to close this dialog box and begin the hosting.

NetMeeting will bring the Current Call tab to the front of the display and show your local profile at the top. The system is waiting for others to call you. Generally, when you host a conference, you will notify potential participants via e-mail or a telephone call. Then when you are set up for the conference, the other users can call you and connect or disconnect as they need to. To facilitate easy access to the conference, you should turn on automatic call answering by displaying the **Options** dialog box on the Tools menu and checking the **auto answer** button on the **General** tab.

When you open a host session, users who call you will see a message saying that you are already in a call, even if no one else is connected to the system. They should answer **Yes** when they are asked if NetMeeting should try to join the conversation.

As the host of a conference you cannot use audio or video, but you can share applications and use Chat and the Whiteboard.

NOTE

NetMeeting isn't a product for everyone, but it can be quite useful for business applications, and for keeping in close contact with family and friends located in many different places. Not only do you save on long-distance telephone calls, you add the depth of video, drawing, and application sharing as well.

In Chapter 9, we'll look at Explorer's broadcast facility, NetShow.

CHAPTER NINE

Using NetShow

Microsoft NetShow is a multifaceted product that provides one more link in the networking of corporations and of providing desired information directly to consumers. NetShow can be considered a broadcast facility for delivering streaming audio, and/or illustrated audio, video, and other computer files over a LAN, intranet or the Internet. Microsoft is promoting this facility heavily on its corporate Web sites and is providing regular updates and online documentation. I will introduce NetShow in this chapter, but I'll leave you on your own to gather in-depth information about this series of products if you want it.

NETSHOW COMPONENTS

Although the full NetShow package includes many facilities, the program is basically two components: server software and client software. The server software includes several components to help you install and configure the server, for administering NetShow files and delivery channels, and for creating NetShow-compatible files for network delivery. Microsoft lists three types of utilities that I would consider server-side components:

> *NetShow Server*—This is a Windows NT software system that can send audio, video, and computer files over a network to single users who ask for them (unicast), or to multiple users simultaneously (multicast).

> *NetShow Administrator*—This is a set of utilities that manages NetShow channels, programs, and streams and that also configures and monitors NetShow Services.

NetShow Content and Conversion Tools—These utilities are used to convert live audio and video information to Active Stream Format (ASF) and an Active Stream Format editor that can be used to assemble, synchronize, and compress audio and video files into a single ASF file.

On the client side, there are programs for playing active stream media and for handling multicast file transfers. The full NetShow package includes four clients:

Nsplayer.exe—A standalone ASF file player that renders active stream media, including video, audio, images, URLs, and scripts

Nsplay.ocx—Renders active stream media, like **nsplayer.exe**, but the **.ocx** file is an ActiveX control that you can embed in other applications such as Internet Explorer or any Visual Basic, C++, or Office application that is ActiveX-enabled.

Nsrtpaud.ocx—ActiveX control that renders audio

Nlfile.ocx—ActiveX control that handles multicast file transfers

The version of NetShow that shipped with Explorer 4.0 as this book was written was 1.0 and included only the On-demand player, a Help file and some sample files. In fact, the On-Demand player file was renamed to **nsoplay.exe**, presumably to differentiate it from the client files that are delivered with the full NetShow package. And, during installation of the Explorer package, the installer creates a shortcut to the **nsoplay.exe** program named **On-Demand Player**. Yet before the public beta for Explorer 4.0 was shipped, Microsoft was promoting NetShow 2.0, which included server- and client-side software and considerably more documentation than was shipped with Explorer.

You can download the latest version of NetShow and read additional online documentation about the program. Here's how:

1. Launch the On-Demand Player: Click on **Start**, point to **Programs** and then **Microsoft NetShow**. Choose **On-Demand Player**.
2. Click on **Go** and choose **NetShow Software Updates**. The Explorer Browser will be launched and in a few seconds you will see a NetShow Web page within the Microsoft site.

CONFIGURING NETSHOW PLAYER

You can't use NetShow Player without a server somewhere. If you download the complete NetShow 2.0 package from Microsoft, you can set up your own corporate server, but the On-Demand Player application delivered with Explorer 4.0 lets you access any compatible NetShow server to which you have access rights.

There are a few settings you may want to change to control some of the operation features of the NetShow client player. Here's how:

1. Launch the On-Demand player (use the **Program** list on the **Start** menu).
2. Click on **View** and choose **Play Settings...** to display the dialog box shown in Figure 9.1.

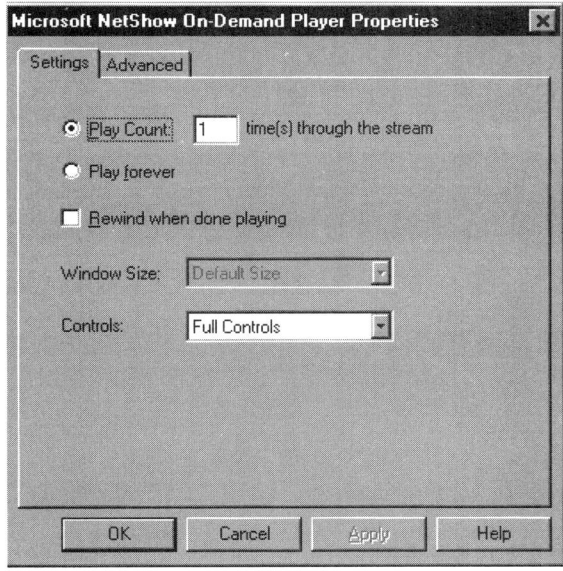

Figure 9.1 The NetShow On-Demand Player Properties dialog box.

This is a two-tab dialog box that lets you control settings for playing media streams.

The Settings tab includes five configuration settings that you can control:

Play Count—You can click on **Play Count**, then enter a number from one to 999,999,999 times.

Play Forever—You can click on **Play Forever** to turn on a loop display that keeps playing the current file until you stop it.

Rewind when done playing—This choice will leave the pointer at the end of the file, or at the beginning of the file, after the media stream is finished.

Window Size—Notice that this option is not available unless a file is loaded into the Player.

Controls—You can streamline the player display by turning off all controls, or you can choose simple controls, or turn on all controls. If you are playing a file "forever," then no controls are necessary in many cases. If you want full access to the Player's controls, then set Full Controls.

3. Click on the **Advanced** tab to display an additional three choices, shown in Figure 9.2.

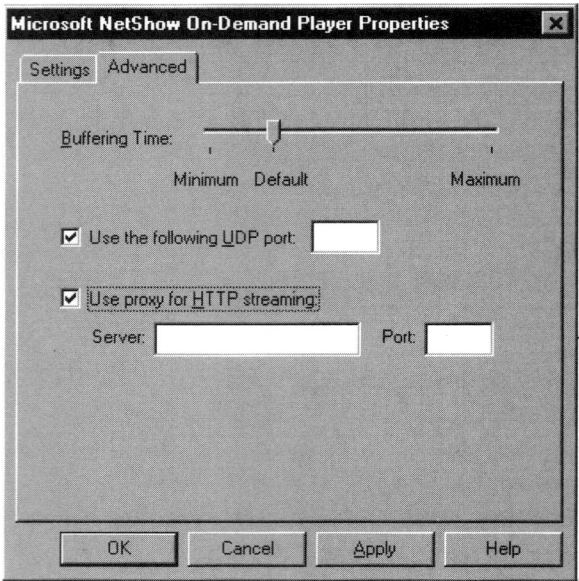

Figure 9.2 The Advanced On-Demand Player Properties dialog box.

You can probably leave these settings alone for most applications, but if you have a lot of RAM on your client machine, you may be able to improve play performance by increasing the local buffer size. Simply slide the marker from the default setting to the desired location. Try several settings, testing after each change to judge the effect. A larger buffer setting means it will take longer after you connect to a remote site to start seeing images and hearing audio, but, in my experience, a larger buffer often produces better quality images.

If your server uses other than the default UDP port, enter a value in the following UDP port field of this tab. And, if you access the NetShow server via proxy server, enter the information about your proxy server in the final area of this tab.

4. Click on **Apply** to change your settings without closing the Player Properties dialog box, or click on **OK** to make the change and close the dialog box.

There's another setting on the View menu you might want to change. Toggle on Always on Top so the NetShow Player stays visible on your desktop even if you run other applications.

USING NETSHOW COMPONENTS

Again, the NetShow package is more comprehensive than the player application delivered with Explorer 4.0. But the Explorer 4.0 player is a good way to get started with the NetShow environment. In fact, there are files on the Microsoft streaming server that can provide additional information about NetShow and, at the same time, show you how to use the Explorer intrinsic player:

1. Launch the NetShow On-Demand Player.
2. Click on **File** and choose **Open Location**….
3. Type the suggested location into the Open: field of this dialog box: **mms://msnetshow.microsoft.com/nsoteach.asf**. If you have access to the Internet, within a few seconds a streaming file that describes the ASF editor (part of the server software offerings) will start playing (see Figure 9.3).

You can use the controls to pause the playback and to jump forward and backward in the file.

N O T E

Click anywhere on the displayed image to pause the playback. Click again to resume playback.

The quality of the images you see and the sound you hear depend on several factors, including the speed of your network connection, the type of computer you are using, other applications that you are running, the speed of the server, server load, complexity of the file being played, and so on.

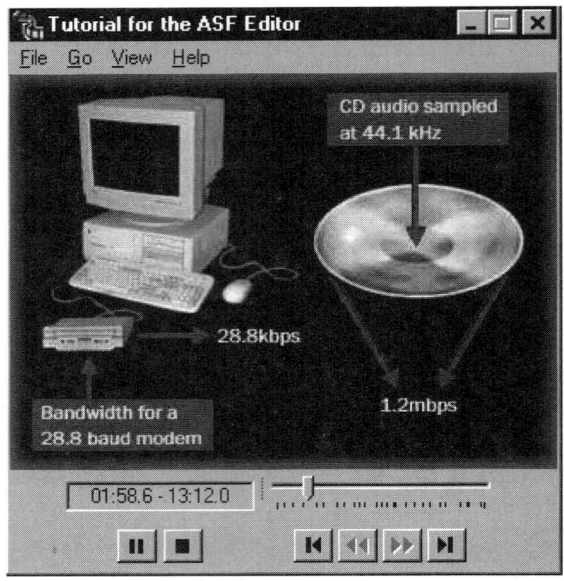

Figure 9.3 nsoteach.asf loaded in On-Demand Player tutorial.

I found that with a 128K ISDN link to the Microsoft server shown in Figure 9.3, the sound produced was reminiscent of listening to a short-wave broadcast with a fading signal and some interference. The frequency of the sound changed during the playback and at times the illustrations (slides) that accompanied the audio stream were incomplete. Splotchy holes sometimes appeared within the images. However, I could rewind the file and sometimes get a complete image. In addition, setting a larger buffer sometimes improved the image quality. Interestingly enough, the motion or animated parts of the file seemed consistently clearer than the still images that accompanied the audio stream.

You can learn more about a file you have loaded into the On-Demand Player with the **File Properties** command sequence, which displays the Properties dialog box shown in Figure 9.4.

You can click on the various tabs of this dialog box to view information about the file you are playing. Two tabs that may be of particular interest are the Statistics tab (Figure 9.5) and the Markers tab (Figure 9.6).

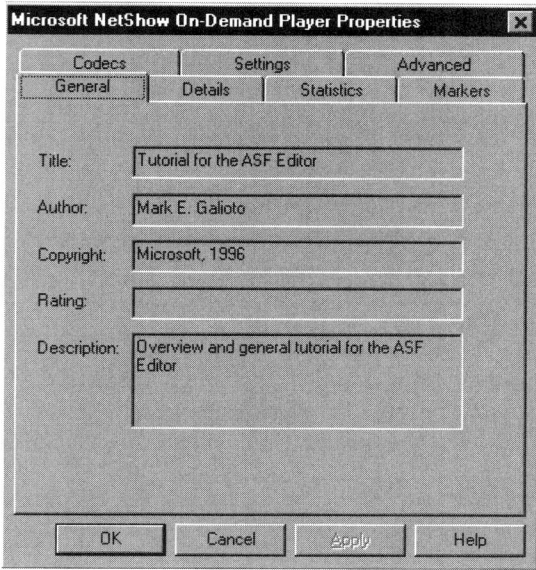

Figure 9.4 The Properties dialog box for the **nsoteach.asf** file in On-Demand Player.

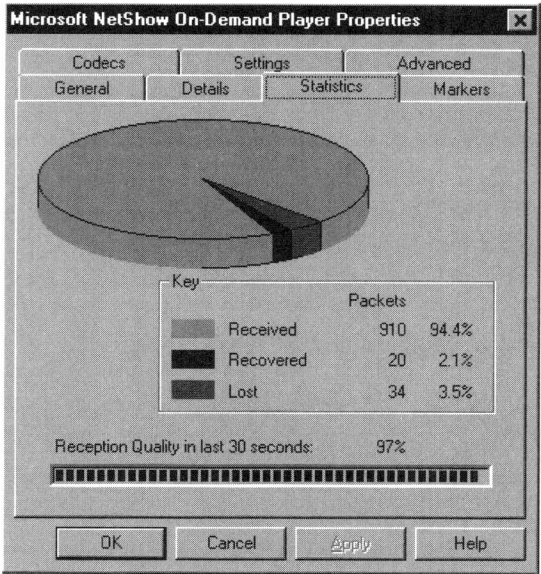

Figure 9.5 The Statistics tab from the Properties dialog box.

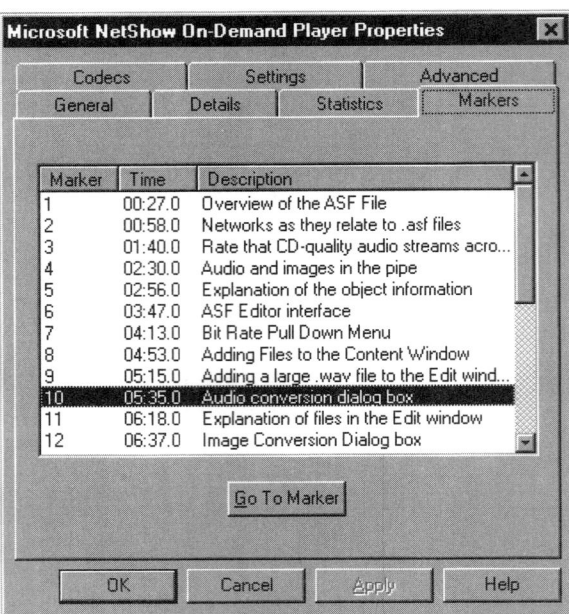

Figure 9.6 The Markers tab from the Properties dialog box.

The Statistics tab shows you how successful the download has been over the past 30 seconds. You can see from Figure 9.5 that a number of packets have been lost in this transmission, perhaps accounting for the choppy audio and incomplete pictures. In Figure 9.6 you can see all of the sections (markers) of the file. You can use this tab to jump to a specific section, if you wish, by simply clicking on the section you want to view to select it, then clicking on the **Go to Marker** button at the bottom of this tab.

Although NetShow files aren't currently widely available, look for an increase in the number of these files as the technology catches on. In general, you will probably access these files directly from a Web page by choosing from a list. As the file downloads, it can launch the NetShow player and start the display on your local desktop. Also expect to see more and more Web pages incorporate these files in ActiveX controls, resulting in audio and video streams being launched when you load a page and becoming yet another object in your browser.

In Chapter 10, I will introduce you to the FrontPad HTML editor and Web site design package, another of the exciting and interesting features of the Explorer 4.0 package.

CHAPTER TEN

Using FrontPad

The World Wide Web has enjoyed a quick rise to prominence. When developers first started adding a graphical interface to the Internet it was a novelty and was not widely used. The early Web offered only limited graphical capabilities, making it a challenge to produce a decent-looking Web site. Moreover, in the early days (a couple of years ago), programming a Web site for a graphical interface required a fairly deep understanding of computer programming techniques. Finally, the tools used for Web site development were text-based editors, not object-oriented graphical utilities.

The Web world is different today, very different, and FrontPad is one of the products making a difference. FrontPad—a more limited version of Microsoft's FrontPage Web development utility—helps make it possible for virtually anyone to develop at least a basic Web site. As you learn more, you can readily upgrade to the full FrontPage program.

FrontPad introduces you to the Microsoft Web development environment. Your only cost is the effort you expend in learning how to use it.

A Web site is no more than a series of specially marked-up text files, as mentioned in Chapter 2. The language used is Hyper Text Markup Language, or HTML. FrontPad is no more than a simple, graphically based HTML editor. In addition to making Web sites, it can be quite useful in making objects for your desktop.

FRONTPAD COMPONENTS

FrontPad is actually several products in one, including:

Web Document Viewer—You can load local files or remote files over the Internet and view them directly in FrontPad, with some limitations. For example, you can't see image files and other inserted objects from most online sites.

HTML Object Editor—You can use WYSIWYG (what you see is what you get) editing to create new Web pages or to edit existing Web pages.

HTML Source Viewer and Editor—As you become more familiar with HTML coding, you can use FrontPad to view, create, and edit directly in HTML source code. While the graphics editor in FrontPad lets you do most anything you are likely to need to create a Web site, working directly in HTML code can offer greater flexibility if you understand how to use this programming language.

Included with the editor/viewer utilities within FrontPad are facilities to insert and edit objects, create HyperLinks, and edit or insert text. Once you create or change an HTML document, you can also use the Web Publishing wizard to have FTP (file transfer protocol) upload the document to your Web server. For more advanced users, other methods are available as well.

CONFIGURING FRONTPAD

FrontPad is a comprehensive product that comes pretty much preconfigured. You make custom changes to the current Web document, but there is very little in the way of general configuration settings to contend with.

You can specify a default font set and set default proportional and non-proportional fonts by clicking on **Tools** and choosing **Font Options...** to display the dialog box shown in 10.1.

For the most part you will use the default settings for US/Western European fonts. If you are creating pages in multiple languages, or if you want to change the default settings for proportional and fixed-width fonts, you can pull down lists on this dialog box to choose the fonts you want to use.

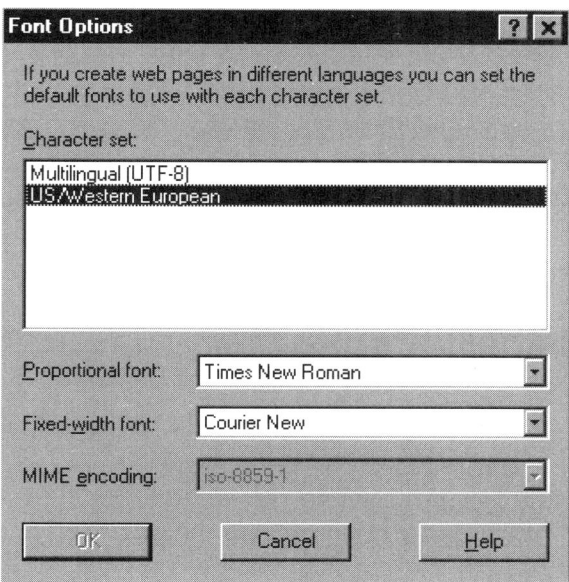

Figure 10.1 Tools Font options dialog box.

You can control the choice of objects displayed as part of your FrontPad editing screen. Pull down the View menu and notice the list of objects with checkmarks beside them. By default, FrontPad shows you three toolbars—standard, format, and status—plus format marks. If you normally use menus instead of tools, you can turn off the toolbar display and give yourself a little more room on the editing screen. Similarly, remove the status bar if you find you aren't using its information. You can always toggle these objects back on if you want them.

Finally, if you have multiple documents open, use the Windows menu to arrange them in cascade or tile format so you can view portions of all of the windows simultaneously and choose the document you want to edit or browse.

USING FRONTPAD COMPONENTS

Probably the quickest way to discover the features of FrontPad is to load an existing Web page off your local computer or from the Internet, then select different views, edit some of the content, add objects, save the file, and then load it into the Explorer Browser. You may have a page of your own that you'd like to use. If not, you can use a page from the Microsoft Web site. Here's how:

■ Launch FrontPad. Click on **Start** on the task bar, point to **Programs**, then to **Accessories**, and choose **FrontPad** from the pop-up list of available programs. You will see the opening screen shown in Figure 10.2.

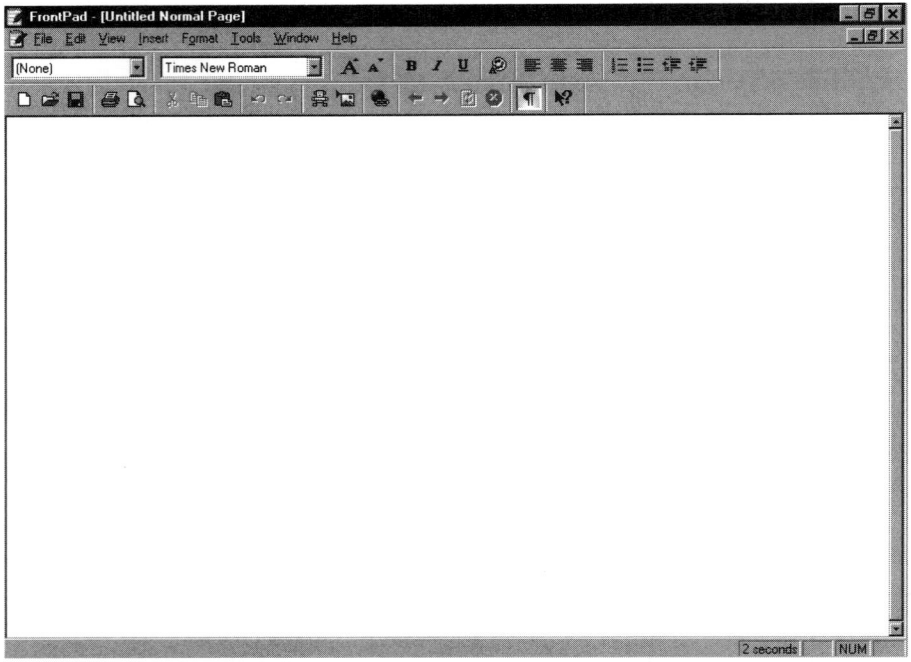

Figure 10.2 The FrontPad opening main screen.

■ Use **File Open…** (**Ctrl+O**) to display the Open File dialog box.

■ Click on **From Location** to produce the display shown in Figure 10.3.

■ Type **www.microsoft.com** (or another Internet URL address) in the From Location: field of this dialog box, and click on **OK**. FrontPad will launch your Internet access facility (the precise process depends on the type of Internet connection you use), locate the specified site, and display the opening page at this site (see Figure 10.4).

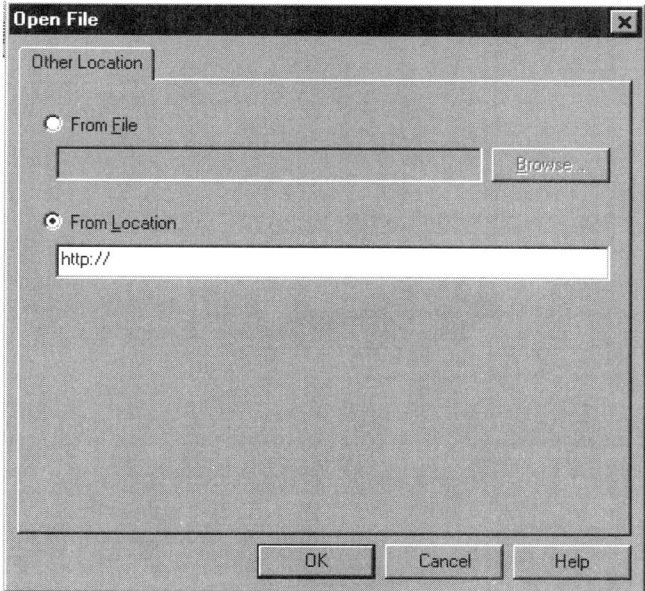

Figure 10.3 The Open File From Location dialog box.

N O T E

With the Microsoft and other sites, you may see a warning that you have received a "Cookie" and asking if you want to accept it. You won't see this message if you have turned off Cookie notification in Explorer. A Cookie is simply a way for your computer and the Web site hosting computer to identify you. It is stored on your computer, and the Web Server will look for it the next time you connect. If it does not find it, it will issue you a new Cookie. Accept or reject this Cookie as you wish, but be aware that rejecting a Cookie will probably result in not getting all objects from the server.

You can see from Figure 10.4 that FrontPad doesn't necessarily load all the objects that are part of the chosen Web page. Figure 10.5 shows the same www.microsoft.comsite as viewed from within Explorer Browser.

What's missing in Figure 10.4 is the full WYSIWYG display, primarily. In Figure 10.5 you can see the split screen, the left side of which holds links to other parts of the site. On the right side of the screen is the contents of the current page.

All the features of the original Microsoft page are there, but FrontPad doesn't display the page properly. Let's experiment with this page you have loaded into FrontPad. First, save a copy of the page to your local hard drive. Here's how:

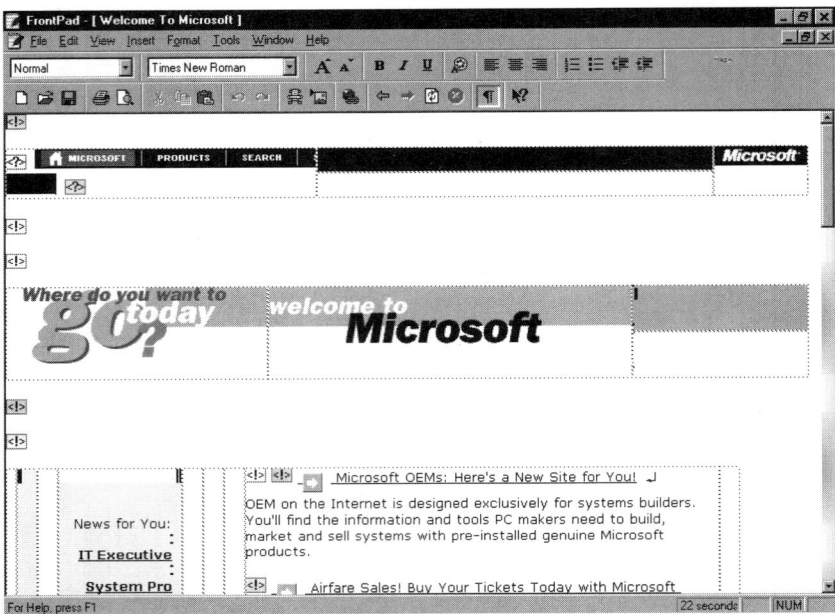

Figure 10.4 The opening file at www.microsoft.com.

Click on **File** on the main FrontPad menu and choose **Save As…** to display the Save As dialog box shown in Figure 10.6.

FrontPad automatically assigns a title for the page and inserts the source path to the page as the save location.

You can't save a Web page on the Microsoft server. You can try, but the remote computer would never let you in. You can, however, save the Microsoft page to your local hard drive. To do this, click on the **As File…** button to produce the display shown in Figure 10.7.

Because this is a typical Windows file manager dialog box, you can navigate to the directory where you want to save the current document, give it a name if you want to use something other than the original name, and click on **Save**.

Next, you will be asked for confirmation on graphics image file names and a path for saving them. Normally, you will want to save the associated graphics images in the same folder as the file itself.

You should note that sometimes FrontPad will not be able to open the page as Explorer would. The results you get with this technique may vary. Also, FrontPad slightly modifies the HTML code when you use the Save As command, so some unexpected things may happen.

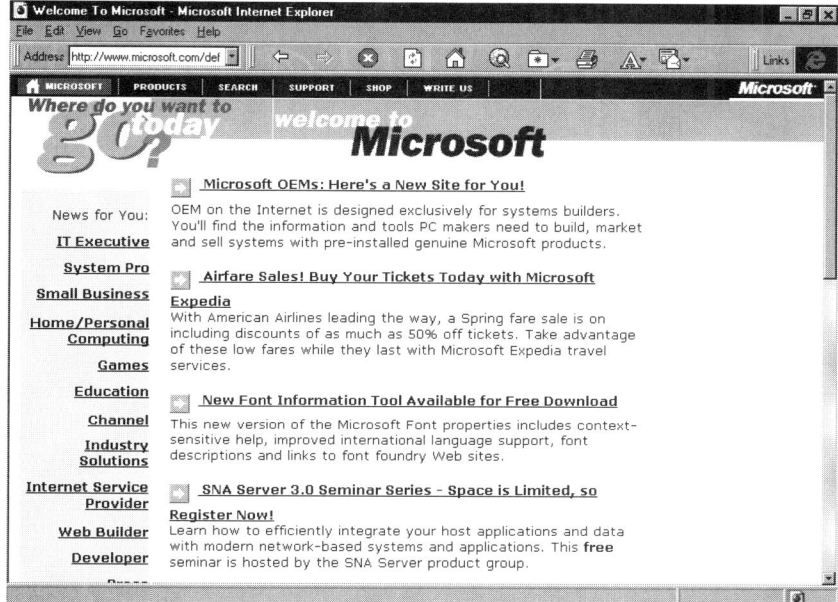

Figure 10.5 www.microsoft.com in Explorer Browser.

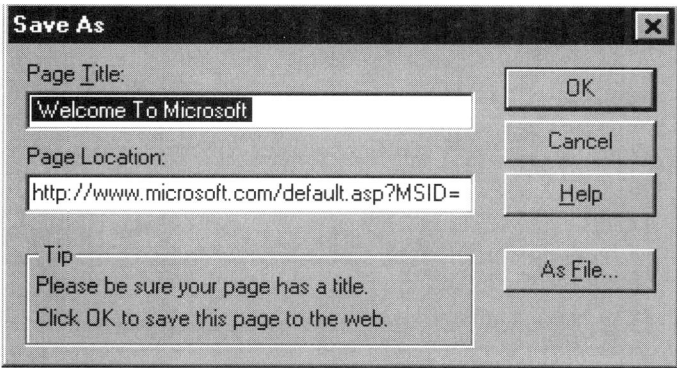

Figure 10.6 The FrontPad Save As dialog box.

Once you have saved the page to your local hard drive, you can test the file by opening it in the Explorer Browser. Also, you now have on your hard drive an HTML document with some associated images that you can use with FrontPad to learn your away around the program.

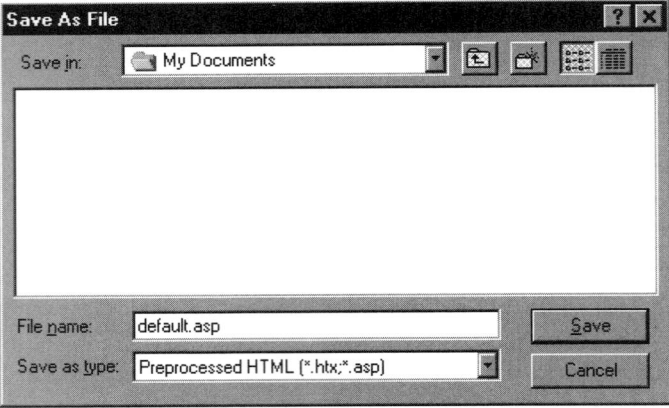

Figure 10.7 The Save As File… dialog box.

For example, check out the Properties dialog box for the current file by choosing **Page Properties** from the FrontPad File menu. If you have loaded the Microsoft page I described, you will see the dialog box shown in Figure 10.8.

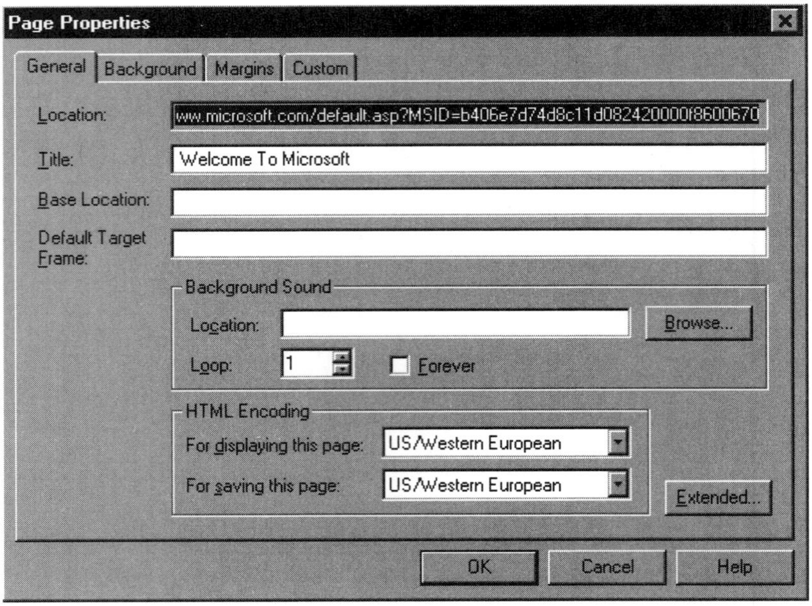

Figure 10.8 The Page Properties dialog box.

This is a tabbed dialog box that includes tabs for General, Background, Margins, and Custom settings. Click on each tab to view the contents or make changes.

The General Tab

As you can see from Figure 10.8, the General tab shows you the Location and Title of the page currently loaded in FrontPad. You can't change the location; that's a fixed property that changes only if you change pages or save this page somewhere else. However, you can change the title, if you want.

In addition, the General tab lets you specify a Base Location and a Default Target Frame. The base location is something that you leave blank in most cases. It is used to complete "Partial URL's." The Default Target Frame indicates in what frame this page should be loaded if no specific frame is specified. A frame can be a new Window, or a specific part of a Window on a Web site. Both of these are advanced properties beyond the scope of this book.

The Background Sound group lets you specify a file name, including path (a local file) or location (an Internet file) to play as background sound for this page. Try this one out. It is really simple to specify a .WAV file, for example, as the background sound for a page. Then when you open the page in Explorer Browser the specified file will play. This can provide an interesting greeting to the new site visitor. You can specify whether the file plays once, many times, or keeps playing as long as the user is viewing the page.

The HTML Encoding group lets you set the default fonts for display and saving, and if you click on Extended you will see a dialog box that lets you add attribute/value pairs to the currently-selected tag. These values will show up as arguments in the <BODY> tag, offering you the possibility of using options that FrontPad does not know about. For example, you could include the option-value pair BGPROPERTIES-fixed, which does the same as checking the Watermark button under the Background Tab. In general, you should avoid using this option.

The Background Tab

The Background tab shows you the current background colors—or the background image, if any—and lets you change them if you wish. If you have loaded the Microsoft page, the Background tab looks like the one in Figure 10.9.

The background for the current page is white and the other page objects are in shades of black and gray. Given the appearance of this page in FrontPad or the Explorer Browser, the selection makes sense, doesn't it? You can change any of this information on the Background tab. Think of these tabs as styles in Word or another word processor. Any change you make to attributes here are global, appearing throughout the current page.

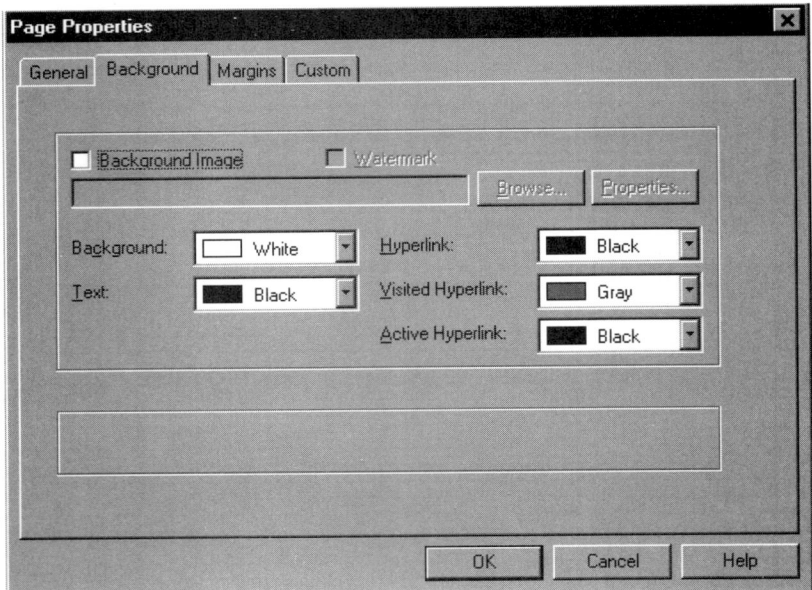

Figure 10.9 The Background tab from the Page Properties dialog box.

For example, try changing the HyperLinks from Black to **Red** and notice the change to the page appearance. (You have to click on **OK** to close the Page Properties dialog box and make the changes effective.)

You can add an image as a background—though that will make this particular page a little busy. Try it. Click on the **Background Image** button to toggle it on, then enter a file name and path to a graphics image for the background. This will change drastically the appearance of the current page in FrontPad. You can also click **Browse** to display a browse dialog box where you can specify a file on a local or network drive, or choose a location on the Internet to supply the image. A ClipArt tab on this dialog box lets you choose from available clip art images for the background.

If you choose Watermark from the Background tab, then you can insert an image, but it is displayed in a light shade instead of at full brilliance. Also, the image will not scroll with the page when viewed in Internet Explorer, it will remain stationary on the background.

The Margins Tab

You have two choices on this tab: top margin and left margin. You can use the pull-down list associated with each of these fields to set the margins, or you can simply click in the field you want to change and enter a new value. The default value for each of these is zero, which means that there will be no top or left-side offset. If you set a top or left-side margin, the current page will be displayed, offset by the number of pixels you specify. This is a useful tab if you are concerned with exact spacing: Different browsers on different computers have different standard margins. It is a good idea to explicitly define the margins you want.

The Custom Tab

The Custom tab contains two groups: System Variables and User Variables (see Figure 10.10).

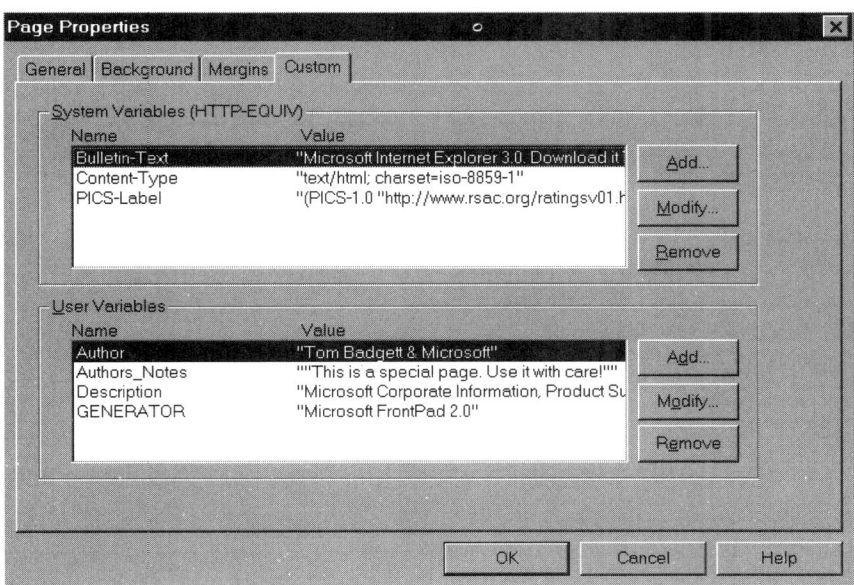

Figure 10.10 The Custom tab from the Page Properties dialog box.

These variables are inserted in the header area of the current page. Variables are used to reduce errors in displaying repetitive data and to make it easier to make global changes within an HTML document. Notice the entries on the Custom tab, then close this dialog box and use **View HTML** to display the source code for the current page. You'll see this variable information near the top of the page in HTML code.

There are many more objects you can add to an existing Web page and you can use FrontPad features to edit existing material. For example, you can use the Insert menu to add images, lines, and symbols. You can insert a Web View object, such as a folder from your local or networked disk. You can use the Insert menu to insert a video sequence into your page, add background sound (in addition to using the Page Properties dialog box), show a marquee display, or use a WebBot programming sequence.

I'll step through a couple of those Insert choices. Then you can practice on your own with other options.

Suppose you want to insert a video sequence into a page you are developing or editing. Here is the process:

1. Click on the page where you want the video sequence to appear.
2. Click **Insert** and choose **Video** to display a file manager dialog box.
3. Navigate to the folder where the video file is stored and select it by double-clicking on the file name. You can also choose a location for the file instead of a folder on your local hard drive or network. FrontPad inserts a small icon to hold the specified video file, but you won't see any images or title on this image.
4. To view information about the inserted video clip, double-click on the icon to present the Image Properties dialog box shown in Figure 10.11.

You can use this dialog box to fine-tune the operation of the video clip. Set the number of times it plays when selected, for example, or when the file plays. You can accept the default and have the video clip play when the file is opened, or you can play the file when the mouse pointer is hovered over the image.

WARNING

This function was buggy in the earliest release of FrontPad for Explorer. When you insert a video image and save the file to disk and try to open it in the Explorer browser, FrontPad may be opened with the page in it instead of the page being displayed in the browser.

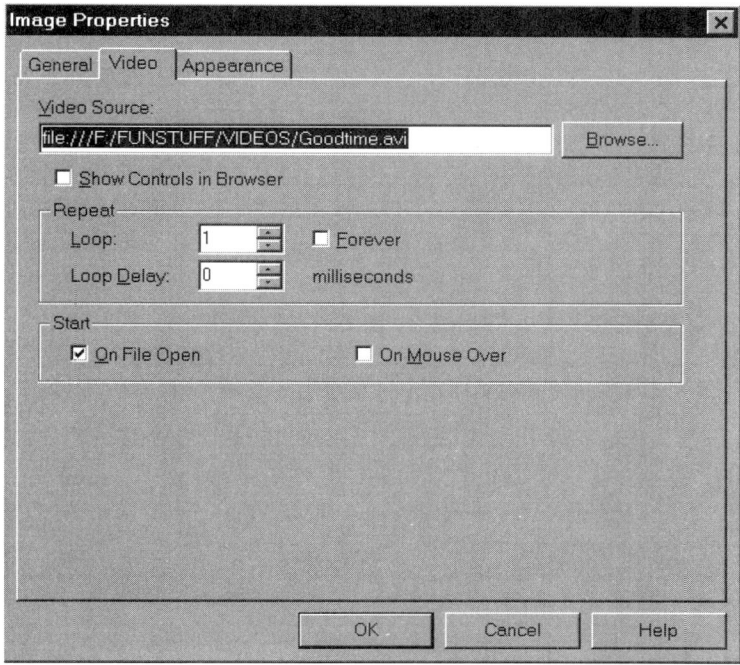

Figure 10.11 The Video tab from the Image Properties dialog box.

WebBot components are preprogrammed applets that you can insert on a Web page to conduct common tasks, such as search a page for information. Try inserting a WebBot:

1. Position the insertion point where you want the program component to reside.

2. Click on **Insert** and choose **WebBot Component** to display the dialog box shown in Figure 10.12.

3. Click on **Search** and then on **OK** to display the WebBot Search Component Properties dialog box, shown in Figure 10.13.

4. Make any changes you want to the Search Component, then click on **OK** to insert the WebBot into your page (see Figure 10.14).

You can insert a marquee display in the same way. A marquee is animated text that scrolls across the screen in an attention-getting display that can prompt the user to do something, or simply provide additional information about the topic covered on the page.

Use the **Insert Marquee** menu sequence from the main FrontPad menu to display the Marquee Properties dialog box shown in Figure 10.15.

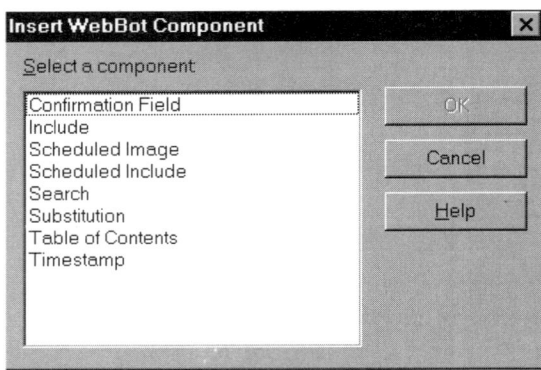

Figure 10.12 The WebBot Component list dialog box.

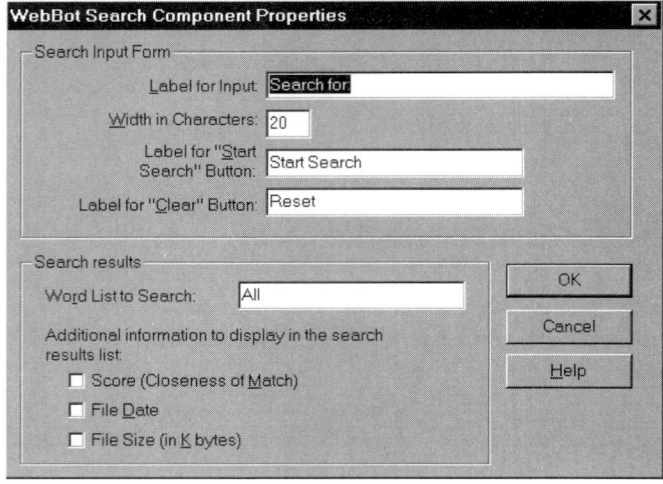

Figure 10.13 The WebBot Search Component Properties dialog box.

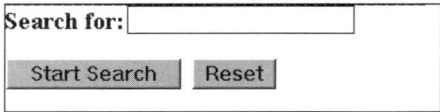

Figure 10.14 The WebBot Search Component display.

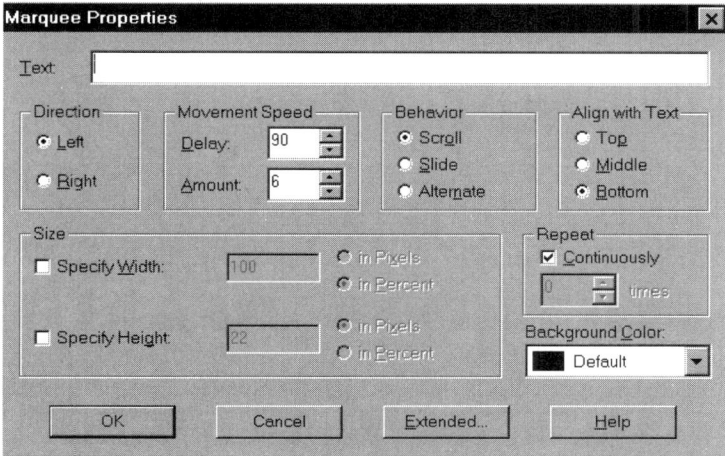

Figure 10.15 The Marquee Properties dialog box.

Type the text you want to display in the marquee in the **Text**: field of this dialog box, make any adjustments to the properties, and click on **OK** to insert the new marquee into your Web page. You can change the text and other properties of this marquee any time by double-clicking the marquee object in FrontPad. The Properties dialog box will be displayed.

These examples show how object-oriented FrontPad is and how easy it is to add relatively sophisticated objects to your Web page design. Don't forget that FrontPad includes templates and other tools to help you develop a page from scratch. To start building a page of your own, use **File New** to display the New page dialog box shown in Figure 10.16.

Choose the type of site you want to develop and click on **OK**. If you choose a template, FrontPad loads the template so you can make changes. If you choose a Wizard, you will be prompted through the basic page-creation process. If you choose the Personal Web Page Wizard, for example, you will see the opening Wizard screen shown in Figure 10.17.

Add or remove components for your personal home page and click **Next** to continue the Wizard. Fill out each of the Wizard screens with the data you want to include in your site and click **Next** to move on to the next screen.

The final screen in this Wizard tells you to click **Finish** to complete the process. When you do, the basic home page with hyperlinks to other pages will be displayed. Use **File Save As...** to store the page before you do any editing on the design.

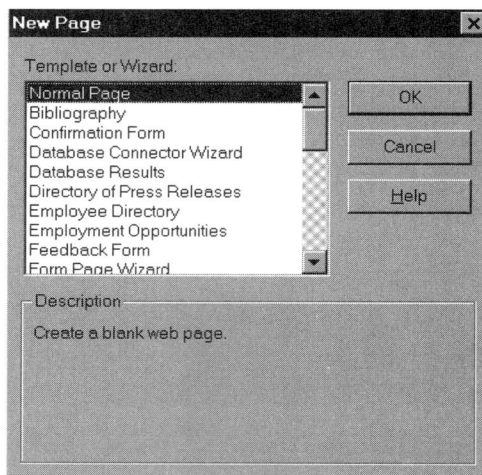

Figure 10.16 The New Page dialog box.

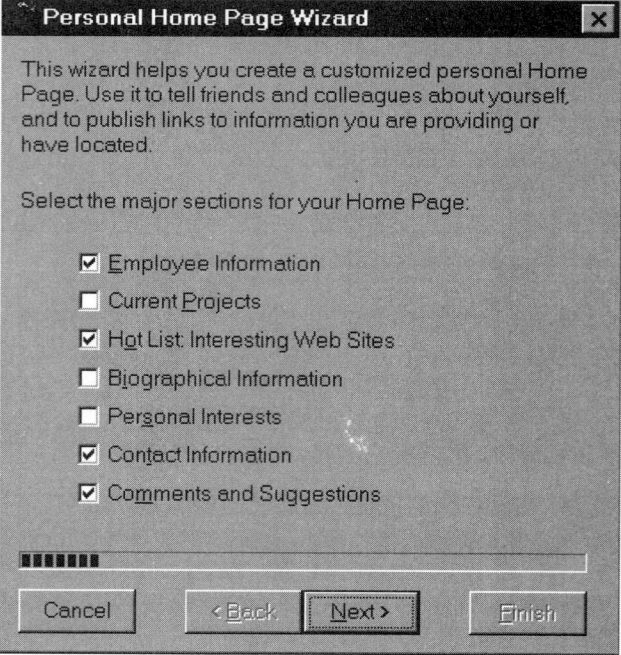

Figure 10.17 The Opening screen, Personal Web Home Page Wizard.

Using templates and Wizards, you can develop a professional-looking Web site for yourself, your business, or your organization. Combine the basic design with one or more of the WebBot components, and you will have an impressive and functional Web site.

One more thing. Pull down the Tools menu for a look at another set of tools and utilities you can use during page development and to help make your page interesting and professional. There's a spell checker, a To Do list, an image editor, and more. Enjoy!

Remember, too, that Explorer lets you customize your Windows desktop with Web pages. Here is a truly practical application for FrontPad. You can use its editing features to create custom desktop objects. Technical Editor Niels Jonker designed a simple example to show you how this can work. Figure 10.18 shows you the modified desktop designed in FrontPad.

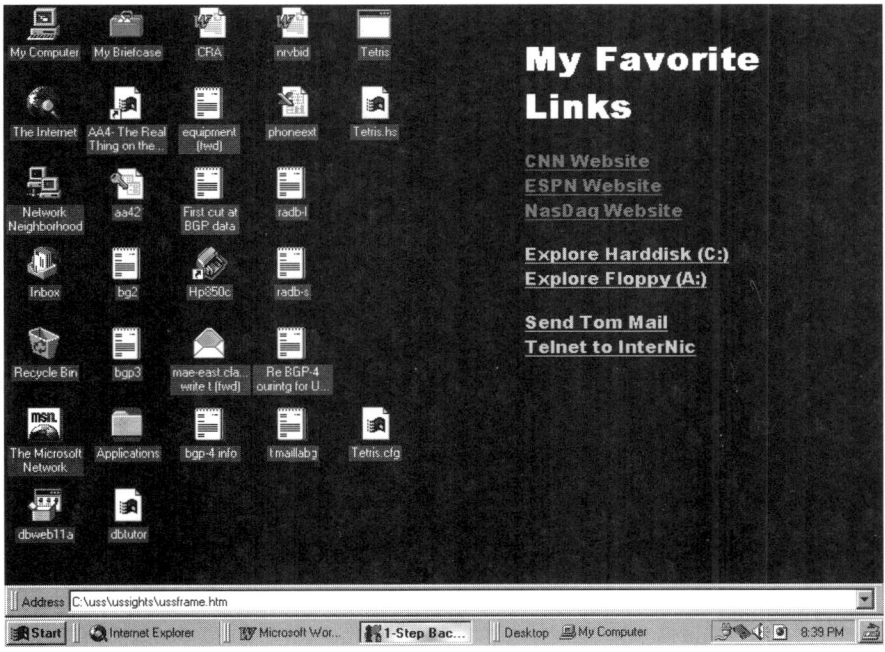

Figure 10.18 A Modified Windows Desktop created in FrontPad.

The goal is to use some of the wasted space on the big empty desktop. Notice the list on the right side of the desktop. It uses HTML to put some of your favorite activities right at your fingertips, one easy click away.

To create the page shown in Figure 10.18, do the following:

1. Launch FrontPad.

2. Use the Page Properties dialog box, available from the File menu, to set the background color of your new page to black. This will match the default Explorer Desktop color. In addition, this design changes the default text color to White, and changes the color of various types of Hyperlinks.

3. Type a title, such as My Favorite Links, and press **Enter**. Note that the cursor skips two lines. This is normal behavior in HTML. To make the cursor skip just one line, hold down **Shift** while pressing **Enter**.

4. On the next few lines, make a list of things you do often, pressing **Enter** or **Shift+Enter** after each line. Don't be concerned with formatting yet

NOTE

You can choose HTML from the View menu to get an idea of what your page looks like so far in HTML format. You will see something similar to Figure 10.19. So far, this is just a page with text on it. Next, you will add links and other action properties.

```
View or Edit HTML

<!DOCTYPE HTML PUBLIC "-//IETF//DTD HTML//EN">
<html>

<head>
<meta http-equiv="Content-Type"
content="text/html; charset=iso-8859-1">
<meta name="GENERATOR" content="Microsoft FrontPad 2.0">
<title>Untitled Normal Page</title>
</head>

<body bgcolor="#000000" text="#FFFFFF" link="#FFFF00"
vlink="#00FF00" alink="#00FFFF">

<p>My Favorite Links</p>

<p>CNN Website<br>
ESPN Website<br>
NasDaq Website</p>

<p>Explore Harddisk (C:)<br>
Explore Floppy (A:)</p>

<p>Send Tom Mail<br>
Telnet to InterNic</p>
</body>
</html>
```

Figure 10.19 The start of a custom Web Page in View HTML window.

5. Add links to any Web sites you have included. Highlight the text you want to link and choose **Hyperlink** from the Edit menu (**Ctrl+K**) on the main FrontPad screen.

6. Type the URL to the hyperlinked site in the URL field of the Create Hyperlink dialog box. You have to fill in the complete address for the site. If you are using the CNN site, for example, enter

7. Enter a name in the Target Frame field of this dialog box. This sample used the name Web, which tells Explorer to display the linked HTML document in a window separate from the one that contains the link. If you leave this field blank, the linked page appears inside the same page as your code

8. Click on **OK** to create the HyperLink. The hyperlinked text changes color.

9. Repeat the HyperLink steps for any other Web sites you have entered on your page.

10. Create HyperLinks for any disk drives or other local resources you want to view. Do this with the Create Hyperlink dialog box, as before, except enter the path to the disk drive, preceded by **file**:// and enter **File** in the Target Frame field.

11. Enter the HyperLink for the Mail line, using the **mailto** URL type (see Figure 10.20). Just type an e-mail address after **mailto**:. No Target frame is required

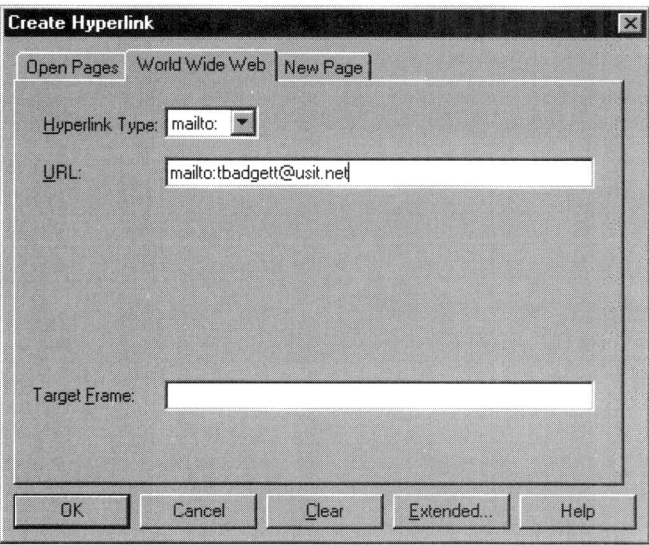

Figure 10.20 Create HyperLink dialog box with mailto Hyperlink Type.

12. Select any text you want to reformat and use the **Styles** pull-down list on the Format bar to change font, text size, or colors.

13. Click on **File** and choose **Save As…** from the File menu.

14. Click the **As file…** button on the Save As dialog box. You will now see the regular Windows Save As dialog box, opened in the Windows or Winnt directory. One of the subdirectories will be called Web—double-click to open it.

15. Name the file you are saving. **My.htm** would be a good name.

16. Exit FrontPad.

17. Right-click on the **Desktop** and choose **Properties** from the Options menu.

18. Click on the **Desktop** tab.

19. Click the **New** button on the Desktop tab and then click **Browse**.

20. Navigate to the Web subdirectory of the Windows or Winnt directory on your hard disk.

21. Select the document you just created and double-click. You will be returned to the Desktop tab of the Display Properties window (see Figure 10.21).

22. Click **OK** to install the new object on your desktop background.

23. Hover the mouse over the new desktop object to display two vertical bars in the top left corner.

24. Grab this symbol to move the object to where you want it. You can change the object size by dragging the triangle in the bottom-right corner.

Any of the functions on this object are activated by simply clicking on the HyperLink.

NOTE

For your convenience, this completed page is available on the World Wide Web. You can simply download and modify it to suit your needs by visiting *http://www.myhome.org/ie40/*.

There's much more in this product that you can discover on your own. A full discussion of Web page design is beyond the scope of this book. However, I recommend FrontPad to you as a way to learn about Web page design so you will understand how the pages you use operate. In fact, you should try to do at least some of your own Web page development, even if you have little or no experience in the process. And, of course, the fact that this utility is bundled with a generally available product such as Explorer 4.0 makes the whole prospect rather exciting.

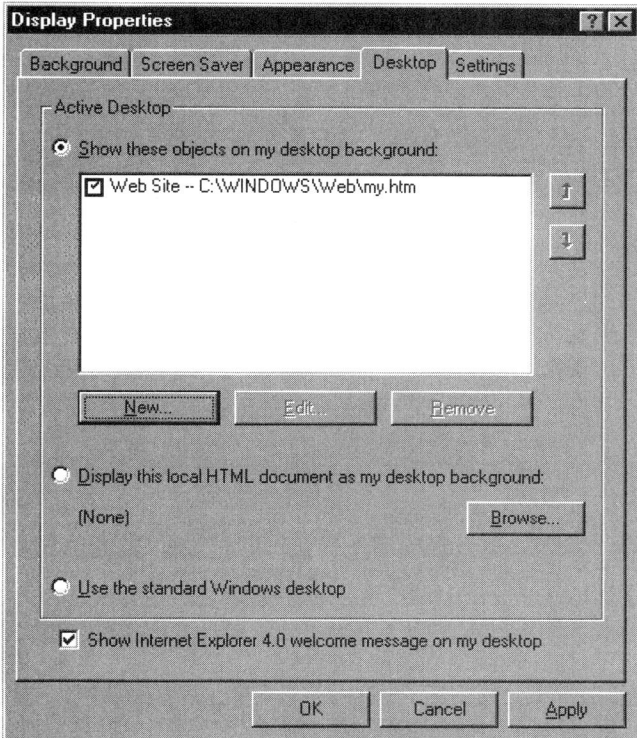

Figure 10.21 A completed Desktop tab of the Display Properties dialog box.

In the next chapter I'll give you a menu and toolbar reference to use as you learn you way around the Explorer 4.0 software suite.

CHAPTER ELEVEN

Menu Reference

As with all Windows-compliant programs, the Microsoft Explorer 4.0 suite uses a fairly logical menu structure that lets you navigate to the task or tasks you want to accomplish. I've introduced you to many of the available menu choices available in this suite during earlier portions of this book. However, I find that it is sometimes useful to have a reference to menu structures of Windows programs.

In this chapter I'll provide a fairly brief reference that may help you find your way around these programs so you can find easily the exact function you want. In the following sections you will see drawings of each individual menu and submenu. Menu items that end in an ellipsis display a dialog box that is the final step in the menu sequence.

Many of the menu commands shown in the charts also are duplicated in the toolbars. Simply hover over any toolbar icon to view tool tips and find out what the icon does. Some application include a customized option for the toolbar, usually located on the Tools menu. This lets you place the commands you want on the toolbar.

EXPLORER INTERNET BROWSER

The Internet Browser component of the Explorer 4.0 suite has six main menu items, each with several submenu options. Remember that the various components of the Explorer 4.0 suite are well integrated, so that a menu selection within one product may actually launch another component or another section of Explorer 4.0. These options are shown in Figures 11.1–11.6.

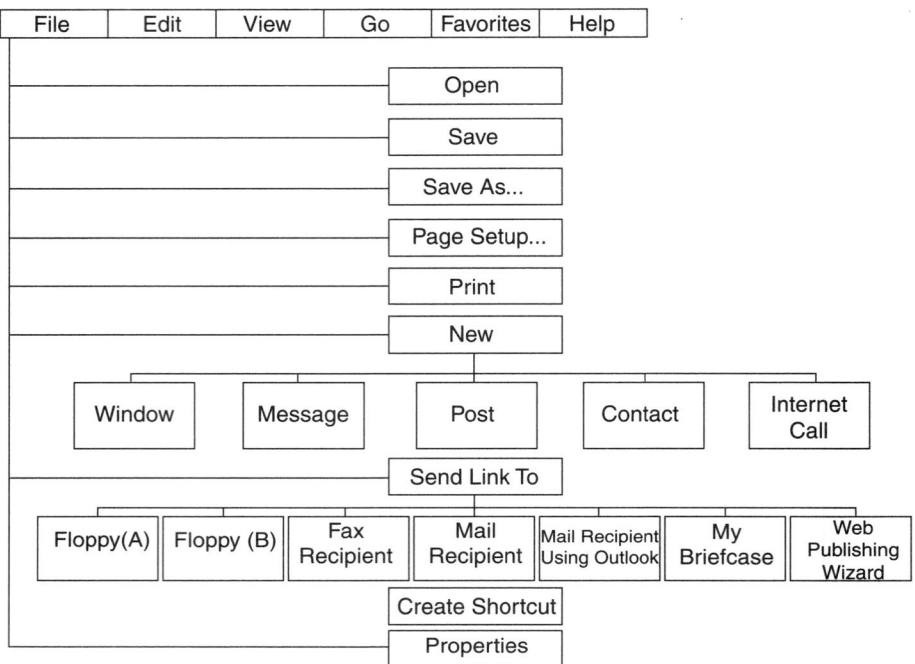

Figure 11.1 Internet Explorer File Menu..

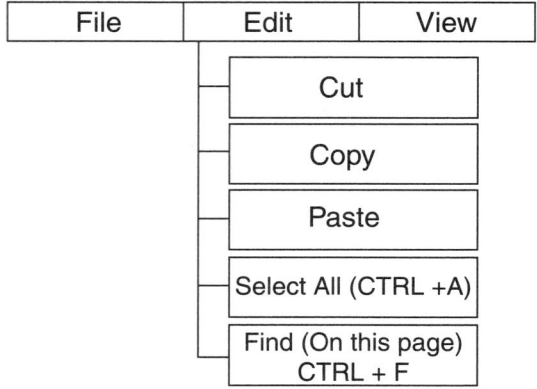

Figure 11.2 Internet Explorer Edit Menu..

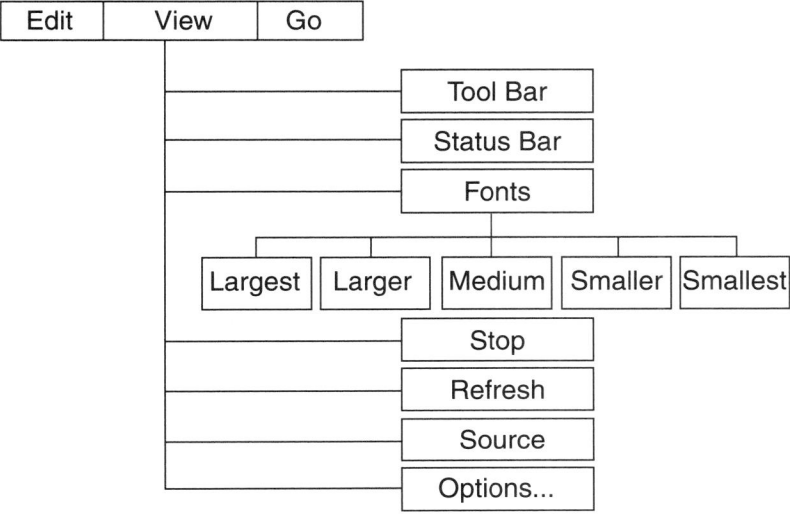

Figure 11.3 Internet Explorer View Menu..

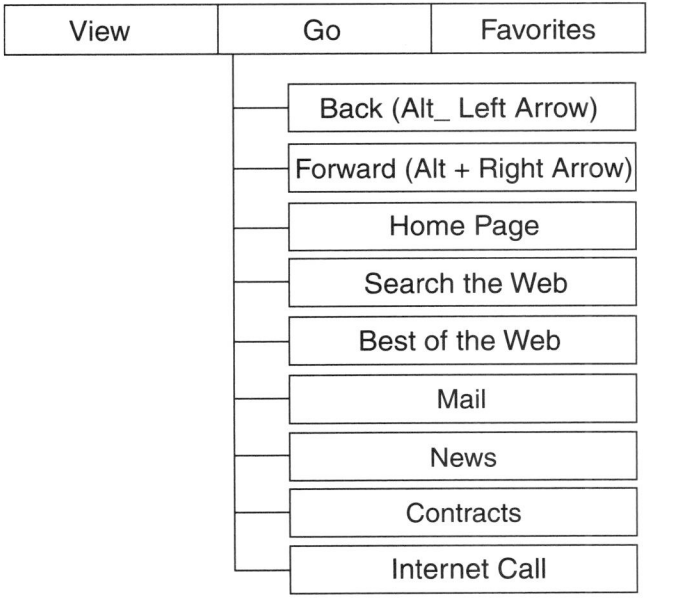

Figure 11.4 Internet Explorer Go Menu..

Figure 11.5 Internet Explorer Favorites Menu..

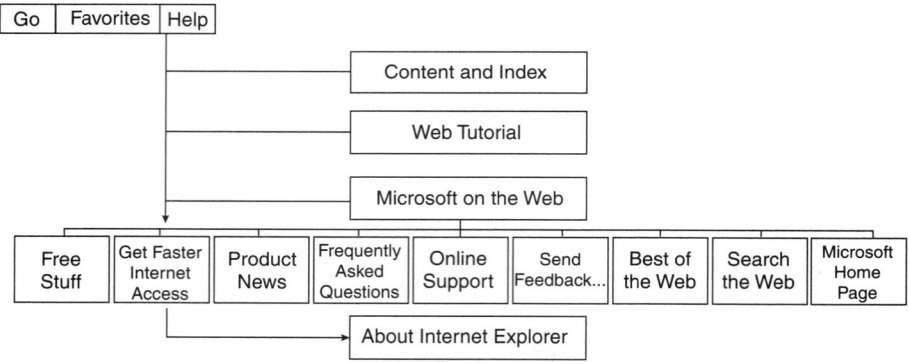

Figure 11.6 Internet Explorer Help Menu..

WINDOWS EXPLORER

The Windows Explorer utility is really Internet Explorer with some different menu options and a slightly different user interface. Again, Explorer is an integrated product that ties your desktop computer tightly to the Internet and the World Wide Web. Through Windows Explorer you can use Web-like techniques to browse your local and network drives. These options are shown in Figures 11.7–11.13.

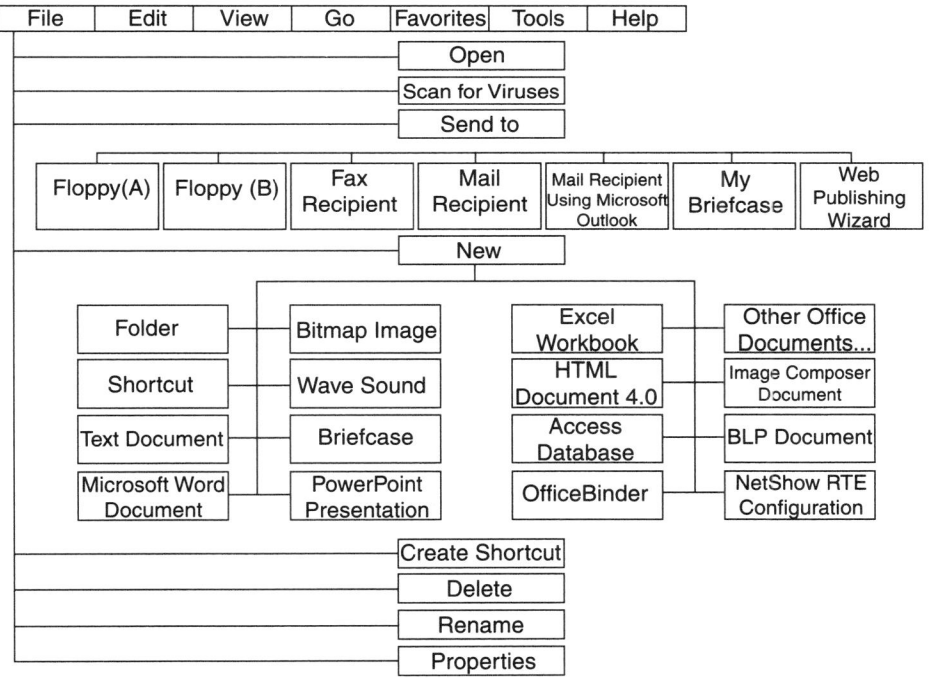

Figure 11.7 Windows Explorer File Menu.

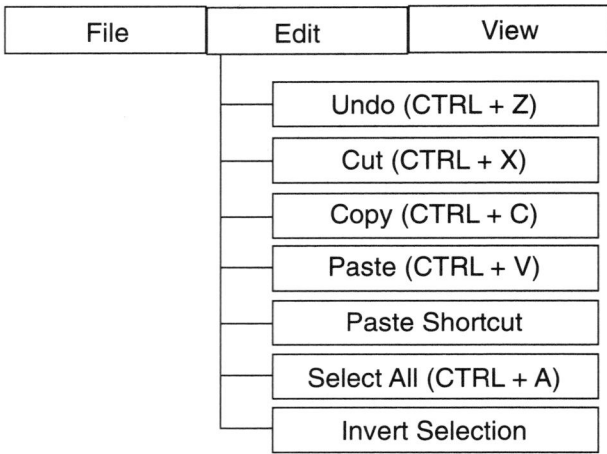

Figure 11.8 Windows Explorer Edit Menu.

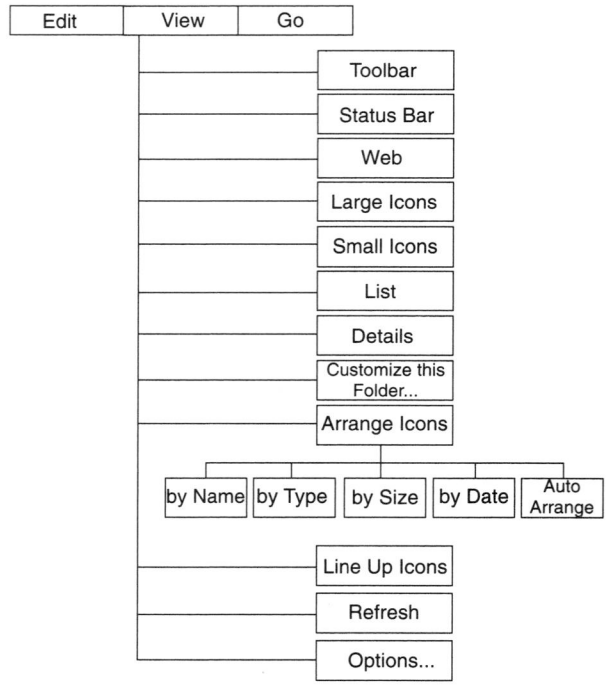

Figure 11.9 Windows Explorer View Menu.

Figure 11.10 Windows Explorer Go Menu.

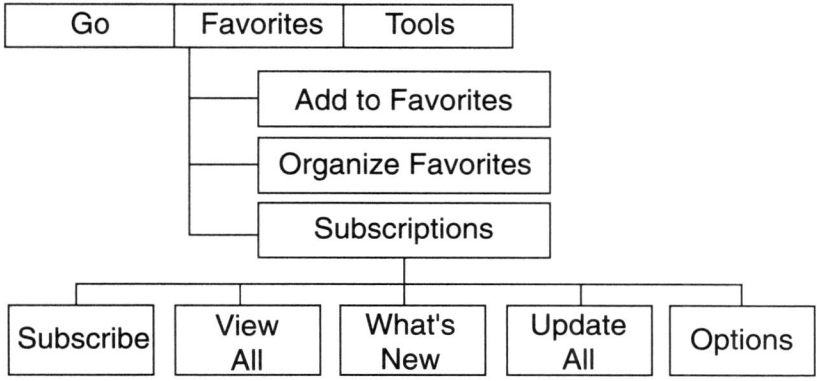

Figure 11.11 Windows Explorer Favorites Menu.

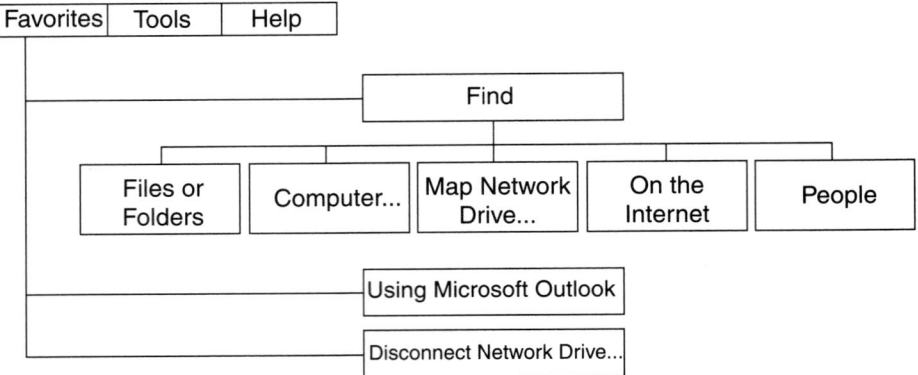

Figure 11.12 Windows Explorer Tools Menu.

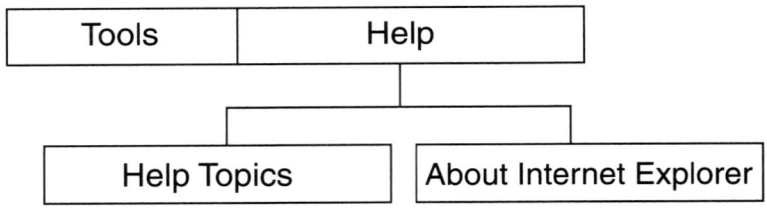

Figure 11.13 Windows Explorer Help Menu.

OUTLOOK EXPRESS

Outlook Express is Explorer 4.0's e-mail communications package. You can use it to communicate with other users over the Internet, a local area network, and via FAX. Outlook Express also includes access to an Address Manager that helps you track names, telephone numbers, e-mail addresses, and more. These options are shown in Figures 11.14–11.21.

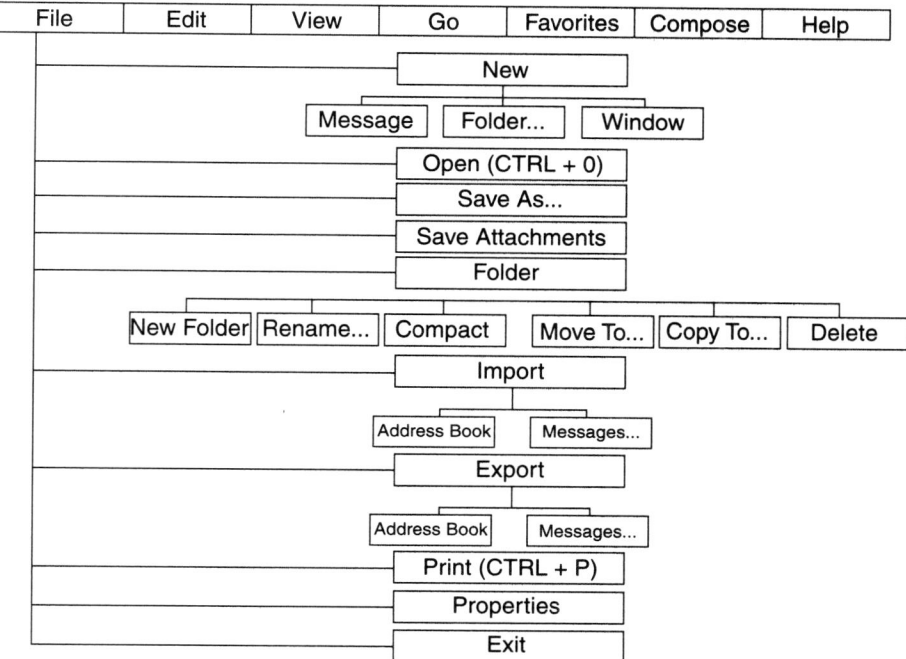

Figure 11.14 Outlook Express Mail File Menu.

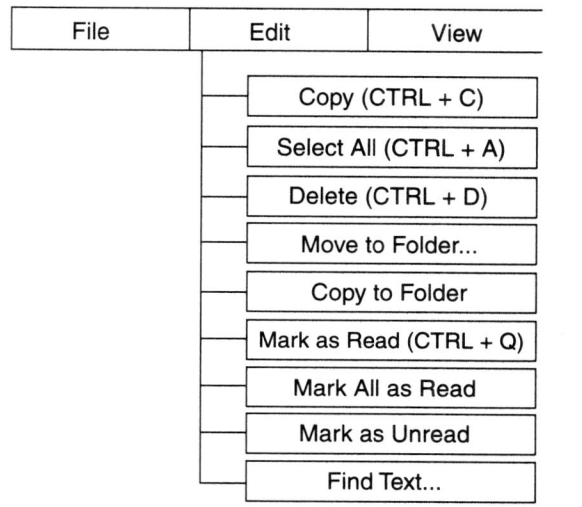

Figure 11.15 Outlook Express Mail Edit Menu.

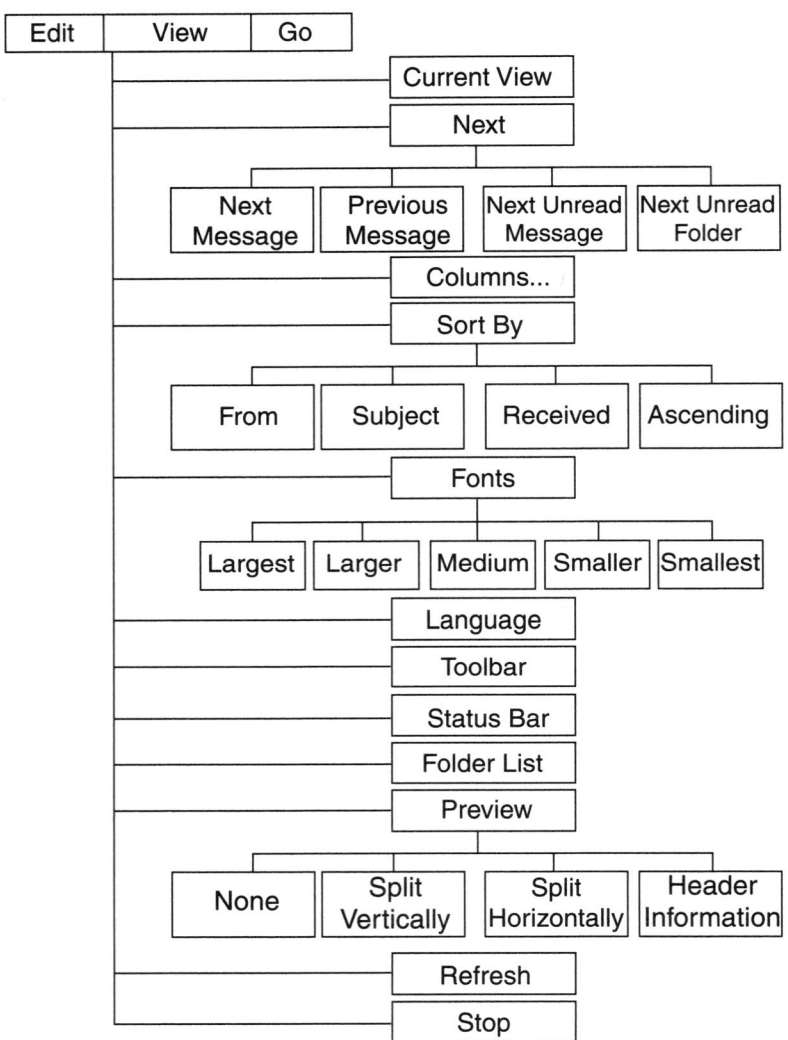

Figure 11.16 Outlook Express Mail View Menu.

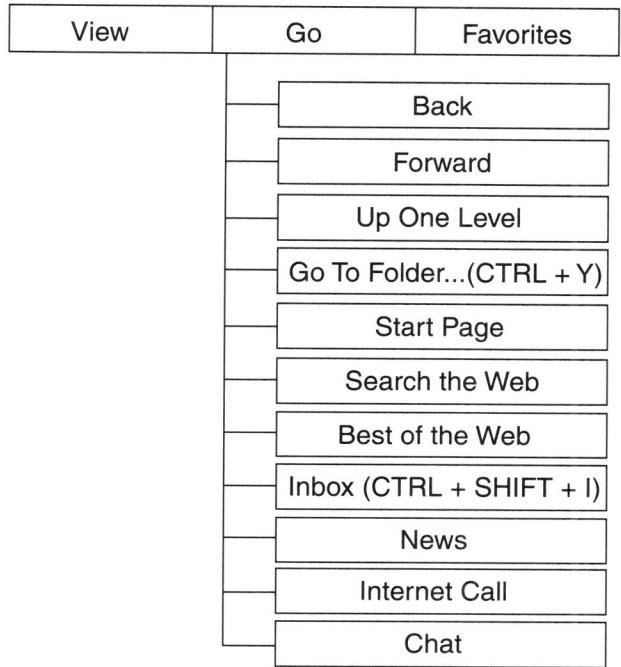

Figure 11.17 Outlook Express Mail Go Menu.

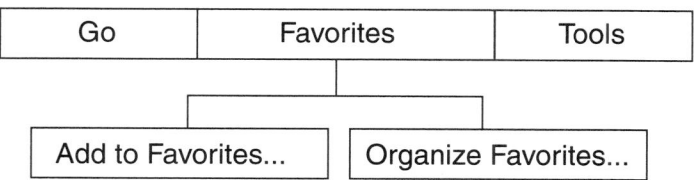

Figure 11.18 Outlook Express Mail Favorites Menu.

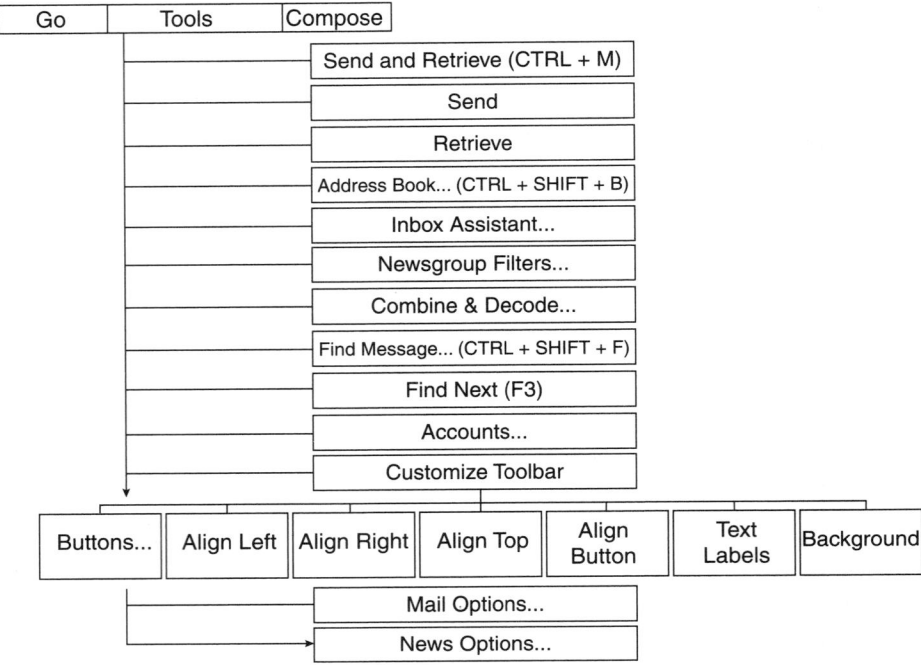

Figure 11.19 Outlook Express Mail Tools Menu.

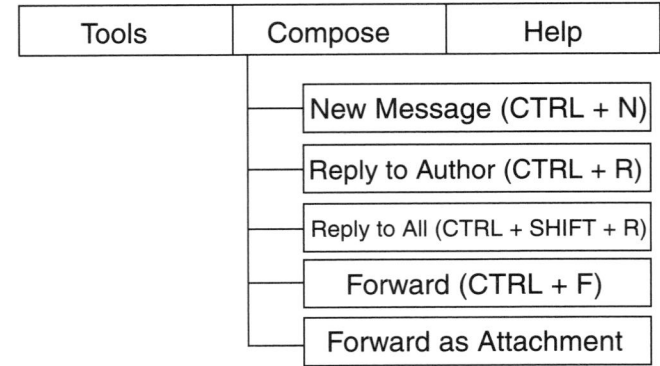

Figure 11.20 Outlook Express Mail Compose Menu.

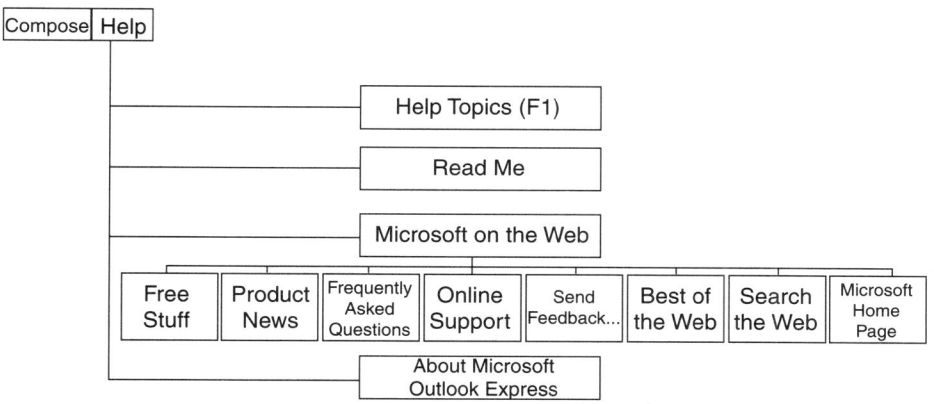

Figure 11.21 Outlook Express Mail Help Menu.

NETMEETING

NetMeeting is Microsoft's multiplatform communications utility that lets you see and talk to other NetMeeting users anywhere in the world. More than a video conferencing program, NetMeeting lets you share programs, exchange files, and more. These options are shown in Figures 11.22–11.28.

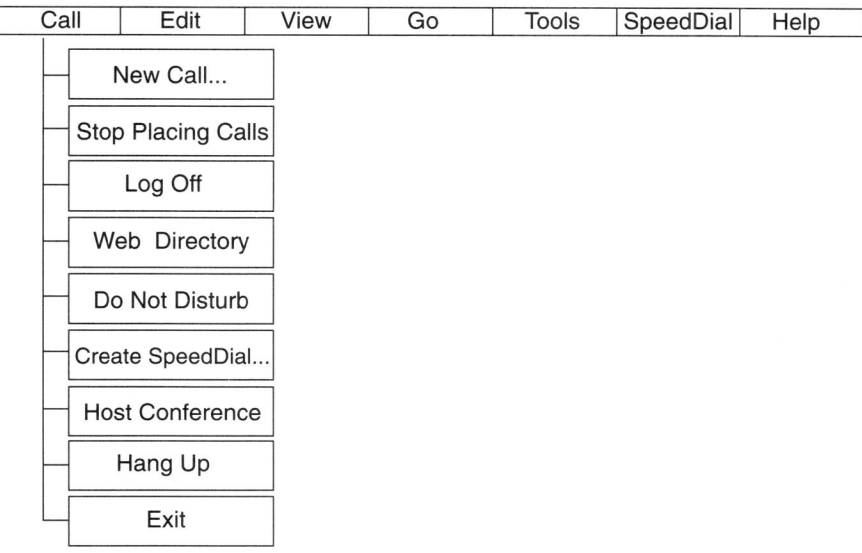

Figure 11.22 NetMeeting Call Menu.

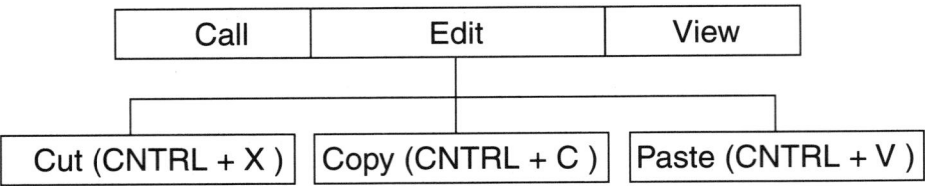

Figure 11.23 NetMeeting Edit Menu.

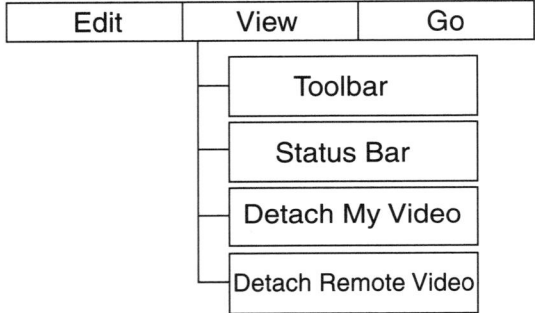

Figure 11.24 NetMeeting View Menu.

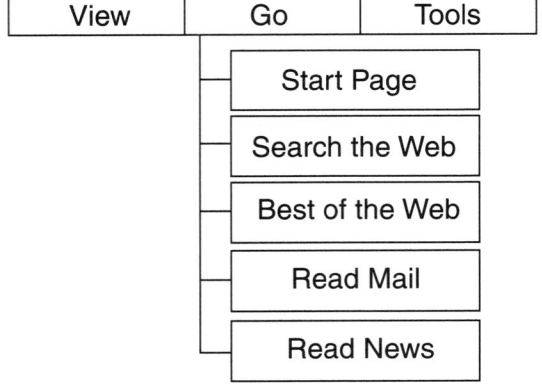

Figure 11.25 NetMeeting Go Menu.

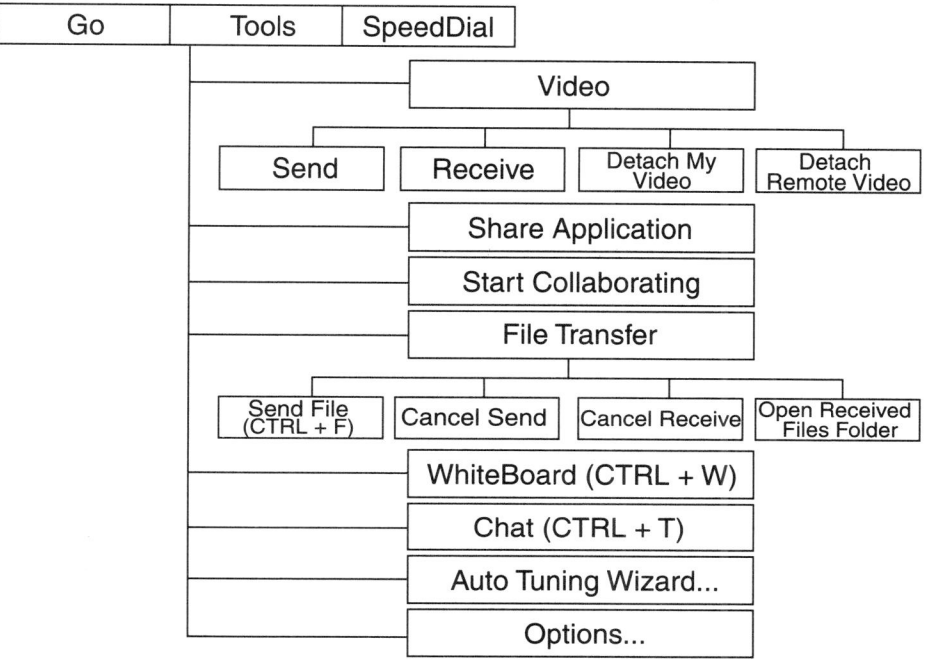

Figure 11.26 NetMeeting Tools Menu.

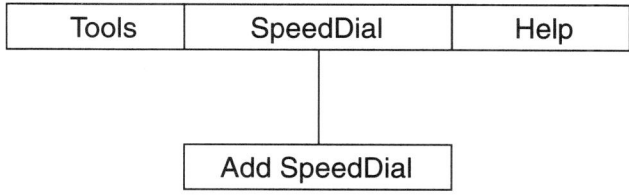

Figure 11.27 NetMeeting SpeedDial Menu.

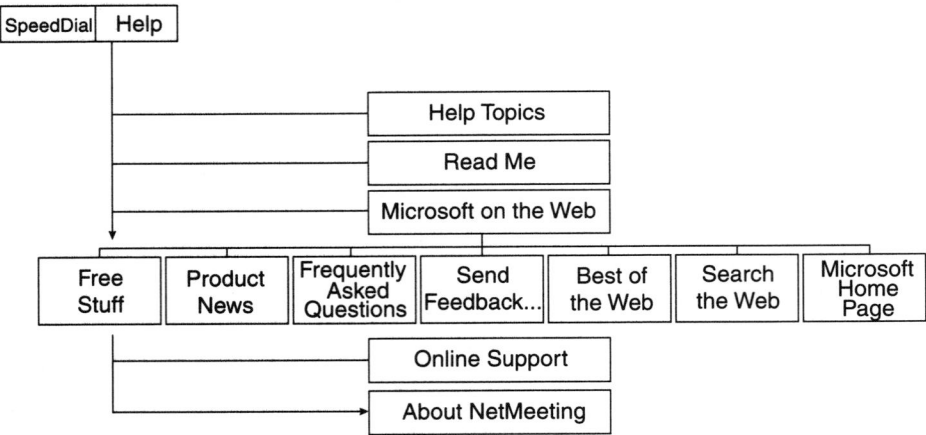

Figure 11.28 NetMeeting Help Menu.

NETSHOW

NetShow doesn't stand alone. You need to access a NetShow server to make use of the NetShow player that is included in the Explorer 4.0 package. As the popularity of this broadcast medium grows, you'll find more and more use for this useful utility. These options are shown in Figures 11.29–11.32.

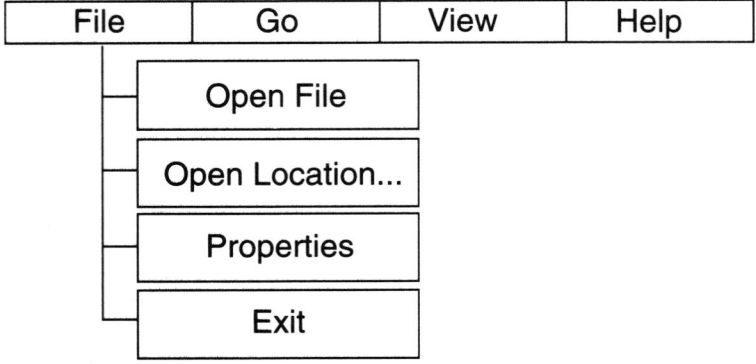

Figure 11.29 NetShow File Menu.

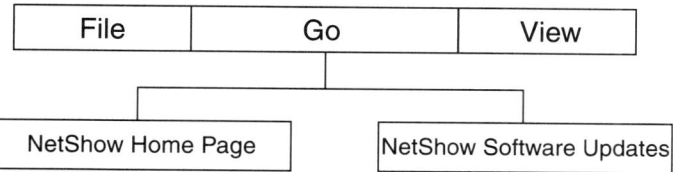

Figure 11.30 NetShow Go Menu.

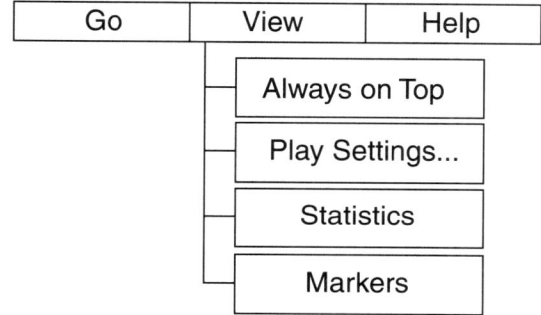

Figure 11.31 NetShow View Menu.

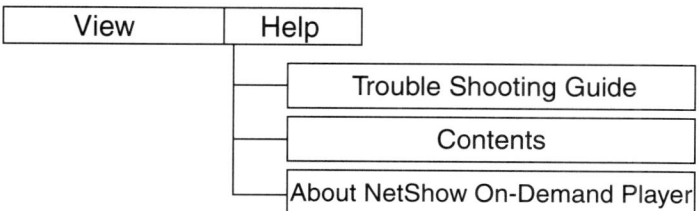

Figure 11.32 NetShow Help Menu.

FRONTPAD

The FrontPad editor gives you another level of control over your desktop and puts you in the driver seat when it comes to creating your own HTML documents. These options are shown in Figures 11.33–11.40.

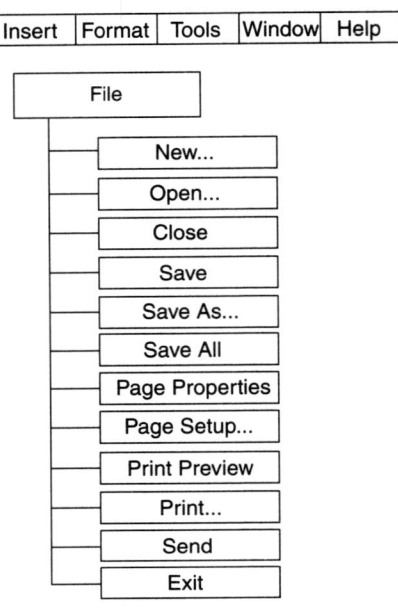

Figure 11.33 FrontPad File Menu.

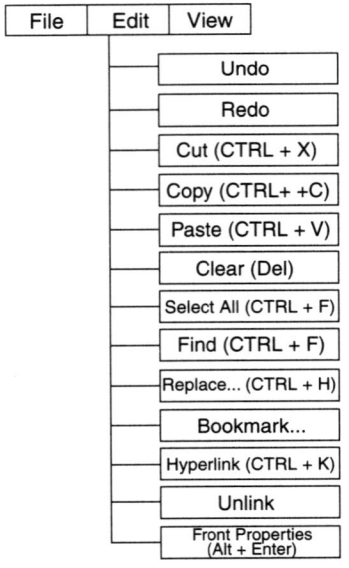

Figure 11.34 FrontPad Edit Menu.

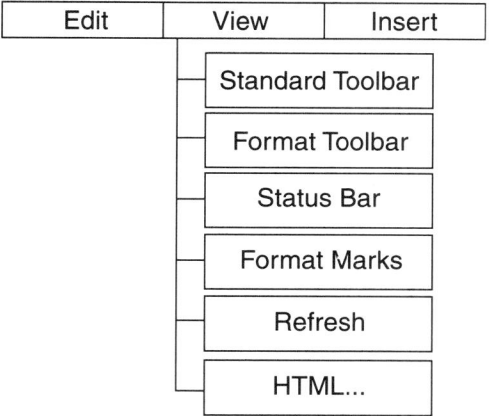

Figure 11.35 FrontPad View Menu.

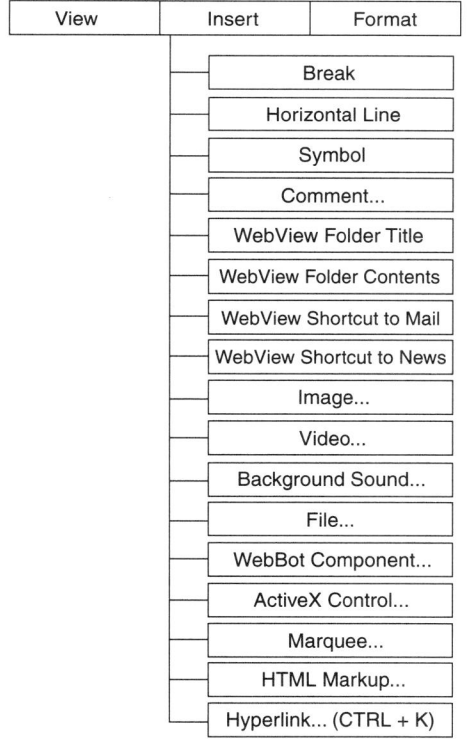

Figure 11.36 FrontPad Insert Menu.

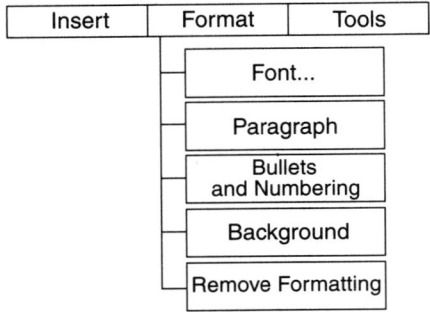

Figure 11.37 FrontPad Format Menus.

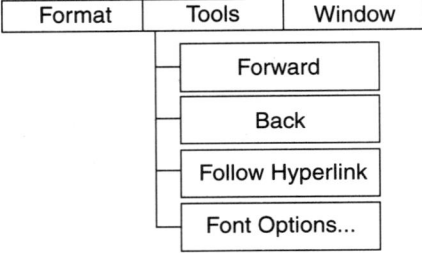

Figure 11.38 FrontPad Tools Menu.

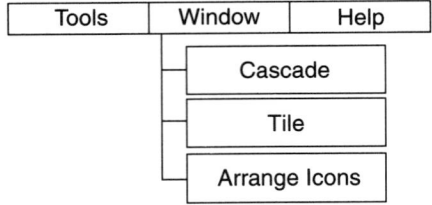

Figure 11.39 FrontPad Window Menu.

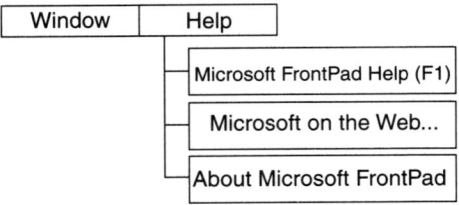

Figure 11.40 FrontPad Help Menu.

CHAPTER TWELVE

Getting Help

The Explorer suite of software applications is powerful and, for the most part, easy to use. If you know Windows and Windows software conventions, you should have no problems with the basic operation of any Explorer components. And, if you are moderately familiar with World Wide Web conventions, then you shoul d be able to adopt the Web-centric approach to these packages quickly and easily.

Nevertheless, there are times when you could use a little help with using some software features. Most Windows programs do a pretty good job of providing Help text that you access directly from the menu. Explorer is no exception, and this collection of software also offers some innovative online help features. Help is as easy to use as the software itself. I would like to point out a few possibilities in this chapter.

THE EXPLORER HELP SYSTEM

The Explorer software suit includes conventional Windows Help—separate Help files for each program—as well as online (Internet-based) help.

USING STANDARD WINDOWS EXPLORER HELP

The Windows Help system for all Explorer products operates just as you would expect it to. From anywhere in an Explorer application, click on **Help** on the Main menu and choose **Content** and **Index** to display the dialog box in Figure 12.1.

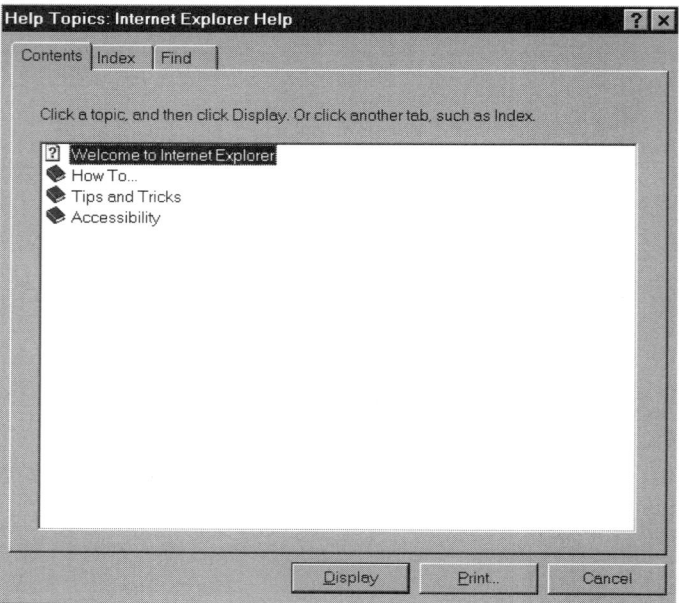

Figure 12.1 Help Topics: Internet Explorer dialog box.

From here, the Help system operates as you would expect from a Windows application.

N O T E Different Explorer components have different options on the Help menu. When you load Windows Explorer—a modified version of Internet Explorer, remember—you have only two choices, Help Topics (the same as Content and Index) and About Internet Explorer. From Internet Explorer, however, there are four choices: Content and Index, Web Tutorial, Microsoft Online, and About Internet Explorer. Outlook express has four help topics, but they're different from Internet Explorer.

USING THE INTERNET TUTORIAL

To find you way around Internet Explorer, choose the Web Tutorial from the Help menu with the Browser displayed. You will see the opening screen shown in Figure 12.2.

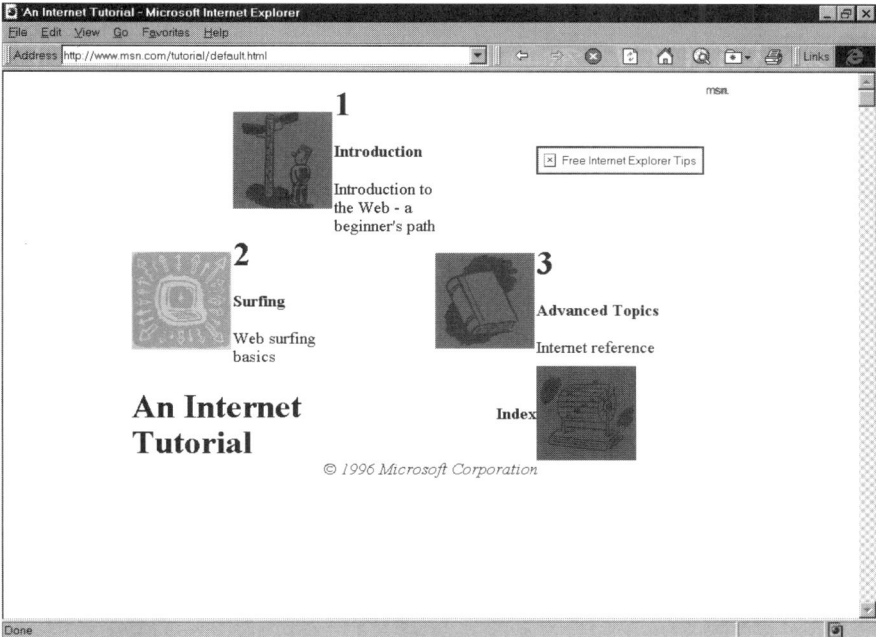

Figure 12.2 The opening screen from the Internet Explorer Web tutorial.

This is actually a World Wide Web site maintained as part of the Microsoft Web site. This is another example of the integration of your local desktop with the Web under Explorer 4.0. This type of Help facility can provide current, easily updated tutorial information. Of course, you will need access to the Internet for this facility to work. Remember, too, that the Web is a dynamic medium, so the pages shown in this book may not look like the pages you find live on the Web.

USING MICROSOFT ON THE WEB

The Microsoft on the Web choice from the Help menu is another example of Web and Desktop integration (see Figure 12.3).

- Free Stuff
- Get Faster Internet Access
- Product News

- Frequently Asked Questions
- Online Support
- Send Feedback
- Best of the Web
- Search the Web
- Microsoft Home Page

When you choose this option from the Help menu you will see another menu that contains nine choices.

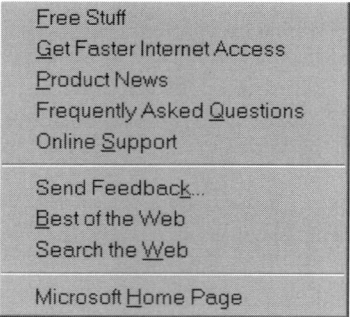

Figure 12.3 Microsoft Online Help menu.

These are all links to Microsoft Web sites. Access any of them by clicking on the menu choice. The Explorer Browser opens the Web site associated with the menu selection.

OTHER HELP OPTIONS

If you need more help, you can use the telephone and fax services. Choose the **Online Support** option from Microsoft on the Web Help topic. From the opening page of this site, click on **Support Options** and **Phone Numbers** on the list at the left of this screen. You will see the Web page shown in Figure 12.4.

Choose the support option you want from this page to display a list of telephone numbers and procedures you can use.

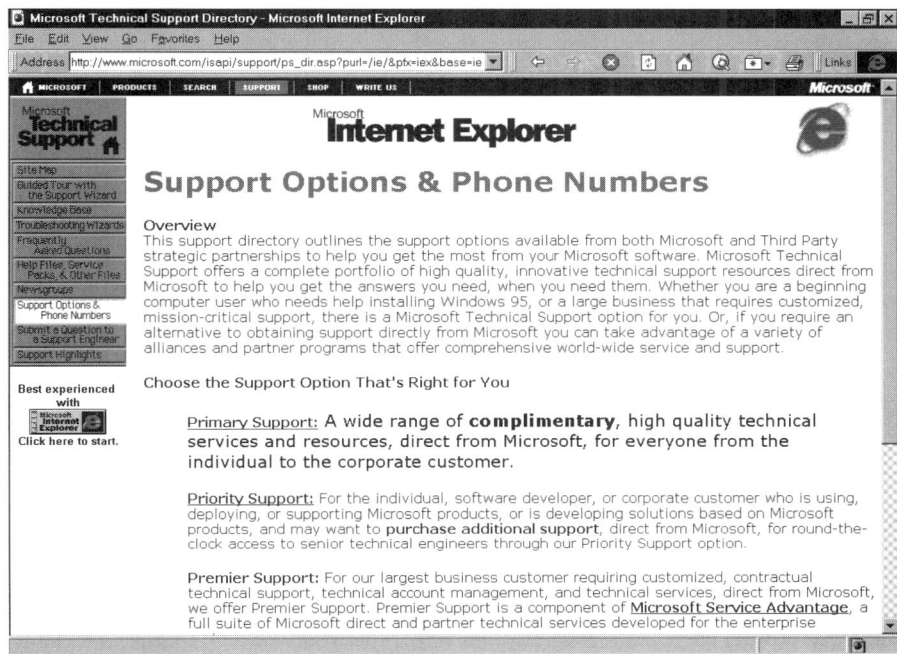

Figure 12.4 The Support Options and Phone Numbers Web page.

As this book is written, Explorer 4.0 is a beta product. As such, no telephone support is offered. You should be able to get full telephone technical support as this product comes into the mainstream.

NOTE

E-mail Security: Using Digital Signatures and Encryption

One of the problems inherent to Internet mail is that it can be easy to forge. It is possible with special software to send fake e-mail messages. For example, a co-worker could send a message that appears to be sent by you. This could have some potentially serious consequences. When you get a message, you are also not sure who sent it. After all, the person sending the message may not be who they appear to be!

As a solution to this problem, digital certificates were introduced. Using a digital certificate, you can sign an electronic message with a digital signature. The recipient can now verify that the message originated from you, and has not been tampered with.

Similarly, you can use digital certificates to send and receive encrypted e-mail. Without copies of the certificates used to encrypt or sign e-mail, it is practically impossible to tamper with it. Outlook Express supports both of these functions using Digital Certificates.

THE CERTIFICATE: PUBLIC AND PRIVATE SECTIONS

Every certificate has two sections: the Public and the Private section. The public section is what other people will use to verify messages signed by you, and to encrypt messages they want to send to you. This section can be made available to whoever wants it. As a matter of fact, you will send it to most of the people you deal with.

The private section is what you use to sign your messages, and to decrypt messages encrypted with your public key. This section is kept privately on your computer. It is the key to your identity. In the following sections, technical editor Niels Jonker explains how digital signatures work and shows you how to obtain your own digital certificates.

How Digitally Signed E-mail Works

At a strictly functional level, digitally signing an e-mail message isn't complicated. The actual, physical process, however is quite complex. It is a little like comparing the process of driving a car to the engineering and physical processes that occur while you do it. I won't discuss the underlying physical process here, but you might be interested in the high-level steps involved.

There are two basic steps to digitally signing a message when it is sent. The process must then be reversed on the other end to verify the message. To sign a message, the software creates a so-called hash value from the message text. Then the hash value is signed, using the private key of the signer.

The hash value is generated by a software algorithm that extracts a random number of bits of data from the original message. Depending on the algorithm used, the hash value consists of 128 to 160 data bits. The certificate or sign is created with this information and the private key. The resulting certificate is sent along with the original e-mail message.

When a signed message is received, the process is repeated. A software algorithm extracts a hash value from the original message. The signature is then verified using the public key of the signer. If the hash value and the signature match on the received end, you can be sure the message is authentic.

 This discussion is about signing electronic mail. similar techniques are being used to validate other types of online transactions, including credit card purchases, offering items for sale, and so on.

NOTE

Obtaining a Digital ID

Digital IDs exist on your computer in the form of certificates, which are granted by Certificate Authorities, or CAs. These CAs verify to a degree of certainty that you are who you say you are. The first step you need to take is to obtain a certificate from a CA. A good place to go is VeriSign. For a while, they will be giving away certain digital certificates for free to let the public get used to using them. We will describe how you can obtain one of these free "Class 1" certificates. You will need about 15 minutes of time to finish this process. It is important that you have a stable, uninterrupted Internet connection while you do this, since the process will almost certainly fail if you get disconnected in the middle. Even more important, while performing these steps you should be using the computer that will be using the digital certificate.

To start the process of obtaining your digital ID, go to VeriSign's Website at *http://digitalid.verisign.com/*.

Figure A.1 VeriSign Home Page.

You will want to request a digital ID. Click on Request a Digital ID to display the screen shown in Figure A.2.

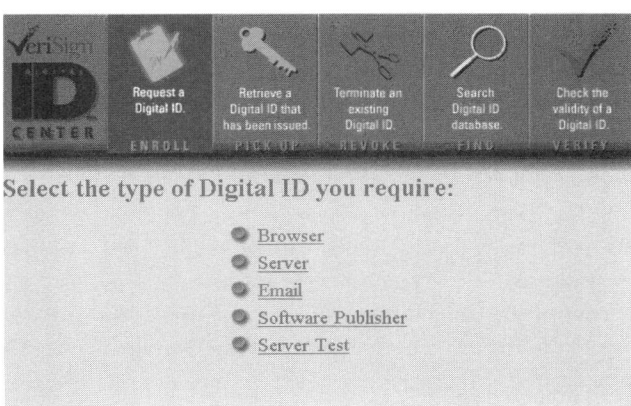

Figure A.2 Select Digital ID Type on VeriSign Web site.

Choose the ID for your Browser, even though the main purpose is for Electronic Mail. Select Browser on the ID type screen and the screen in Figure A.3 will appear, asking you what type of browser you use.

Since you are using Internet Explorer, select the **Explorer** Icon. You will now be given the choice of the type of certificate you want.

For starters, choose a **Type 1**. When you are more familiar with the operation of digital ID's, you can follow the same process described here and obtain a Class 2 Certificate. The screen shown in Figure A.4 appears after you select Class 1.

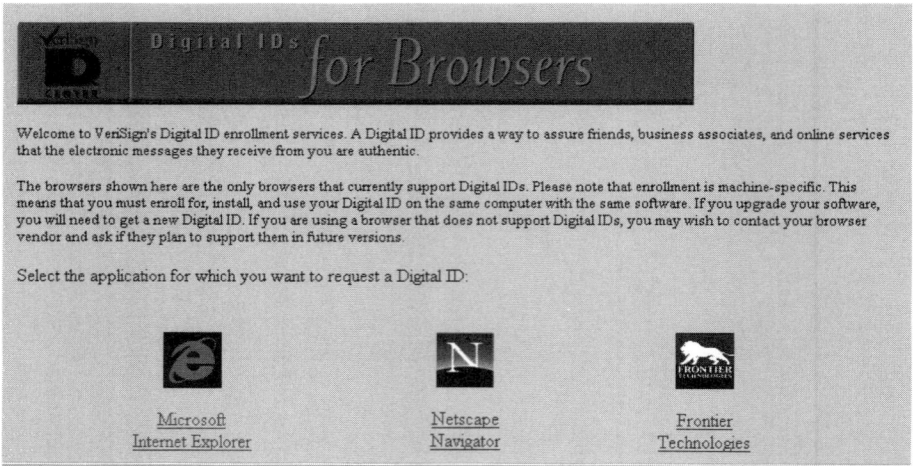

Figure A.3 Browser Type Query Web page.

You should fill in the blanks to suit your needs. It is not necessary to use your real name; however, it is essential to use your real e-mail account. In addition, make sure that you select Yes at the Include E-mail Address in Digital ID selection. Finally, you must make sure your Challenge phrase presents a real "challenge." Your security stands or falls with this phrase.

Note that the information for a Type 1 key is not very detailed, and no actual verification takes place to make sure you are who you say you are. A Class 1 ID will, however, show you all relevant principals. It will also assure you that a person claiming to be "Don Jonsen with e-mail don@miami.org" will be the same person every time he e-mails you. When you are more familiar with this form of identification, you will probably want to obtain a Class 2 ID, which also assures to a certain degree you are in real life who you claim to be.

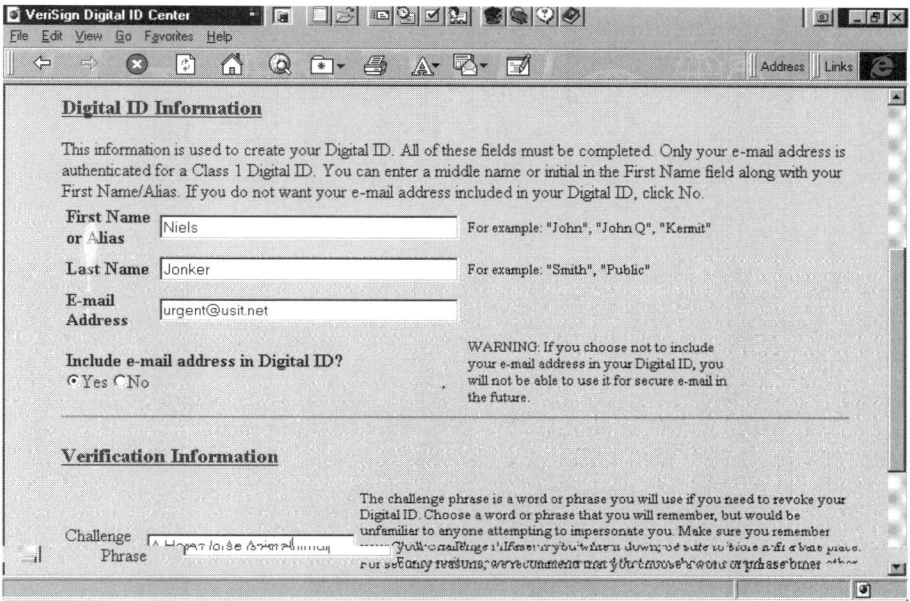

Figure A.4 Class I Details screen.

Next, press the **Continue** button at the bottom of the page. If all is well on this page, click **Continue**. The subscriber agreement appears. Read it and if you agree to the terms and conditions, click **Accept Now**. The actual Key Generation and Installation process starts.

At this point, make sure the CA is a legitimate operation. This is also done through the use of Digital ID Certificates. You will be asked to accept that the software used to install your "Digital ID" is indeed what you expect it is. You can click the HyperLinks to verify all this, and when you are satisfied the software is OK to run, you simply click **Yes** (see Figure A.5).

The Enrollment process will now continue as the new software is installed. This may take a few minutes depending on the speed of your network connection. When the installation is complete, you will see the Web page prompting you for the next Installation step. Click **Submit**, and the Credentials Enrollment Wizard Starts with the dialog shown in Figure A.6.

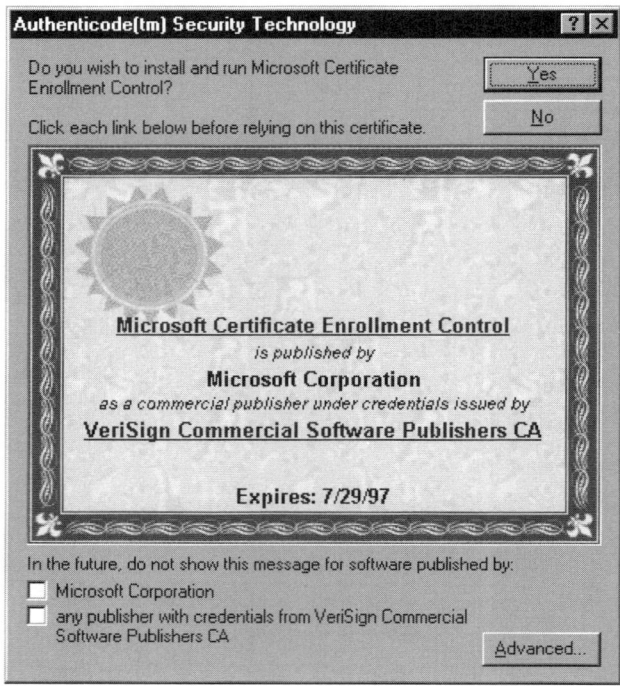

Figure A.5 Authenticode Security Technology screen.

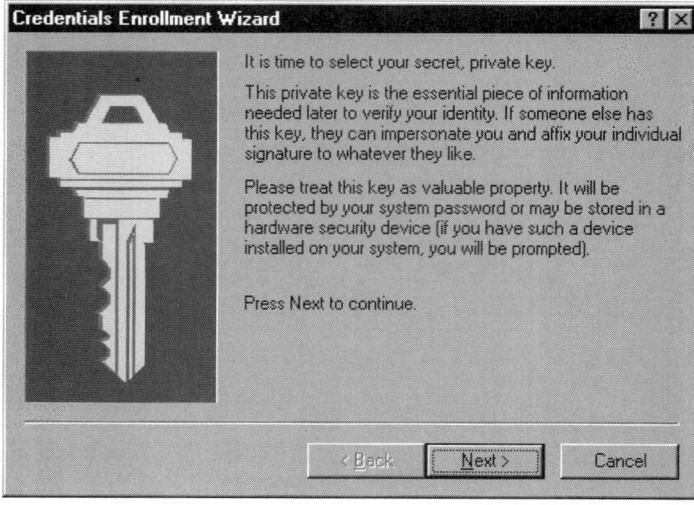

Figure A.6 Beginning Credentials Enrollment Wizard dialog box.

Click **Next**, and give your key a name with the dialog box shown in Figure A.7.

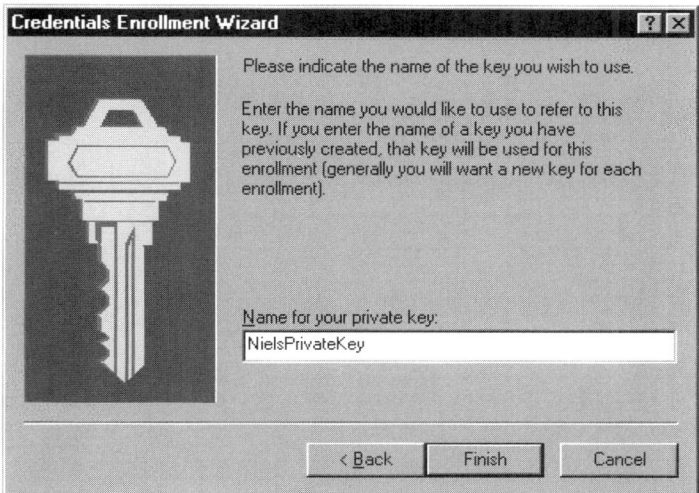

Figure A.7 Credentials Enrollment Wizard key name dialog box.

Now click **Finish**. It is time to leave the Web browser for a while. However, do not disconnect from the internet! Open Outlook Express to check your E-mail. You may have to click the Send and Receive button to make sure you get your newest mail. After a few minutes you will find a message from VeriSign. Double-click on the message in your Inbox to produce the display shown in Figure A.8.

Note your Pin number, or even better, highlight it with your Mouse, and then select **Copy** from the Edit menu. Now click on the URL to open the Web page, which will bring you to the next step of the application process.

Click on the **Digital ID Pin**: box. If you Copied the Pin from the e-mail, select **Paste** from the Edit menu to paste it in. Next, click the **Submit** button and be patient! It is important that you do NOT push any buttons on your browser while you wait; interrupting your connection at this point could cause the entire process to fail. After a while, the page shown in Figure A.9 appears:

Now it is time to click the **Install** button. After a few seconds, you will get confirmation that your digital ID was successfully installed. You will then be returned to the VeriSign main screen. At this point, your Digital ID certificate is installed and ready to use!

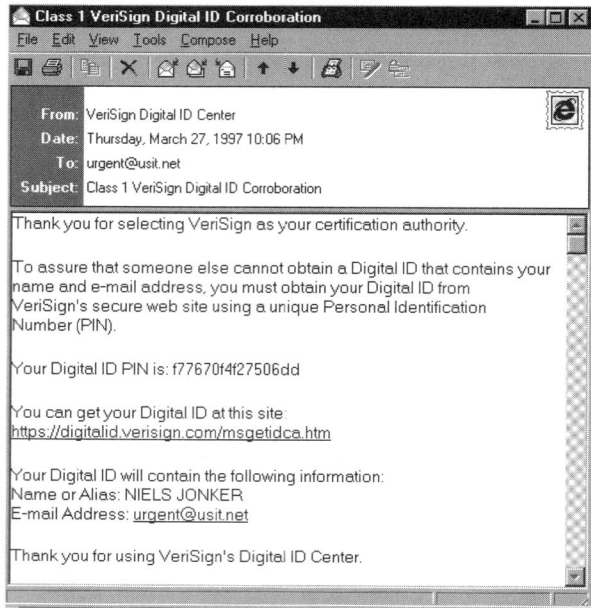

Figure A.8 The Initial VeriSign e-mail message.

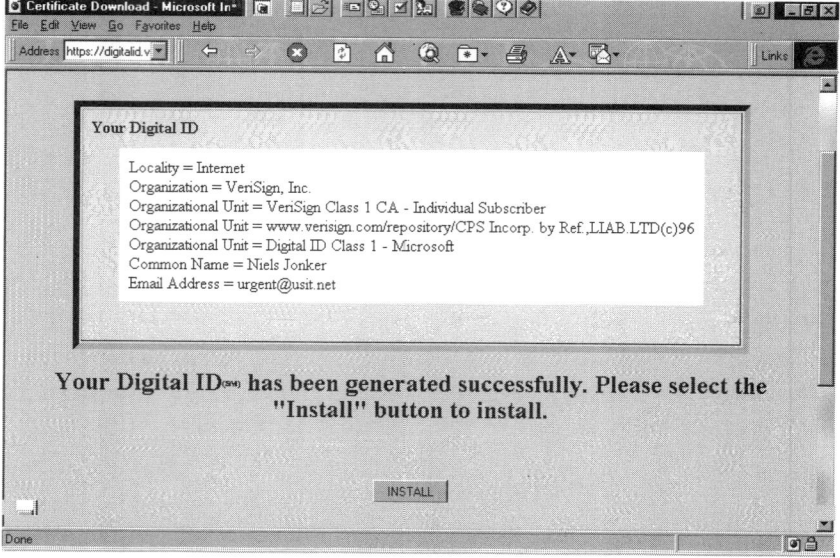

Figure A.9 Certificate Download: A Successful ID generation page.

Telling Outlook Express to Use Your Certificate

Creating the certificate is only part of the process required to make it work for you. Once your personal certificate is installed, you need to tell Outlook Express to make use of it. Here's how:

1. Click **Tools** and choose **Mail Options...** to display the tabbed Mail Options dialog box.
2. Click on the **Security** tab to bring it to the front of the display.
3. Click on the **Advanced Settings** button.
4. In pull-down lists for using digital signing and digital encryption, select the certificate you just created.

WARNING

Early preview versions of Explorer may not generate the desired certificate at this point due to a software bug.

5. Click the **Include my certificate with signed messages** button to enable it.
6. Click **OK** twice to close the Mail Options dialog box.

Sending Signed Messages

With a certificate created and registered and Outlook Express configured to use the new certificate, you are ready to send a signed message. Here's how:

1. As usual use **Compose** to create a new message.
2. Select **Tools** menu in message editor.
3. Check **Digitally sign**. Notice the gray Pen icon in Subject line. The message will be signed when you send it.

Sending Encrypted Messages

You can also use your new certificate to send encrypted messages. Here are the steps:

1. As usual, use **Compose** to create a new message.

2. Select **Tools** menu in message editor.

3. Check **Encrypt**. Notice the lock icon in the Subject line. The message will be encrypted when you send it.

GLOSSARY

ActiveDesktop—An Explorer 4.0 feature that lets you use the World Wide Web browser motif to navigate disk drives and other objects that are part of your desktop computer or Local Area Network.

Active Server Pages—An HTML technology in which code embedded in Web pages is executed by the server when the page is requested to generate custom Web pages.

AOL—America Online. A commercial network that provides e-mail, games, discussion, research, and other services. AOL users can link to the Internet via various services.

Applet—A very small software program that performs a specialized function within the context of a larger application, such as a Web site.

ASP— See *Active Server Pages*.

BRI—Basic Rate Interface. A type of ISDN telephone service that permits use of two simultaneous calls on one telephone line.

Browser—A software application that facilitates user access to information from a database or, more commonly, from the World Wide Web component of the Internet.

BTW—By the Way. Used as an abbreviation on e-mail and real-time conversation links.

CA—Certificate Authority. An entity that assigns Digital IDs.

Certificate —See *Digital ID Certificate*.

Channel—On IRC and other communications applications, a named area where users gather to discuss specific topics. In technologies such as audio delivery or video conferencing, the pathway over which content is delivered or sent.

Client—A software application that preprocesses information before sending it to a server and postprocesses the results. Internet clients link to Archie, Gopher, IRC, and other facilities.

CompuServe (CIS)—CompuServe Information Service. A commercial network that provides e-mail, games, discussion, research, and other services. CompuServe users can link to Internet via various services.

CompuServe Packet Network (CPN)—An international network provided and maintained by CompuServe. It was designed primarily to service CompuServe Information Service users, but also carries traffic for other networked services, including Internet providers such as U.S. Internet.

Cookie—A digital code issued by a server and stored on a client for later retrieval. Typically, servers use cookies to keep track of users and their visits to a site.

Decoding—The process of converting encoded data after transport, used in Mail, News, Web, etc. See *MIME*.

Digital ID Certificate—A set of codes that uniquely identifies a person or company. It can also be used to encrypt and decrypt messages for secure transmission.

Digital Signature—A technology used to sign e-mail using a Digital ID that enables the receiver to confirm that an e-mail was indeed sent by the actual owner of the Digital ID, which has not been changed.

Distributed Application—A software application that runs on multiple machines in different locations. One component may be the user interface, which is run on a local machine, while another computer executes the database searching component.

Domain—A method of identifying Internet nodes with words or abbreviations instead of numbers. The domain name system (DNS) is divided into groups for ease of management and name assignment.

Download—The process of copying a file or files from a remote computer to a local one.

DNS—Domain Name System. See *Domain*.

E-mail—Electronic mail. Text, graphics, sound, and photographs transmitted from one computer system to a specific user or group of users at a remote system or systems.

Electronic Mail —See *E-mail*.

Encoding—The process of converting data to make it suitable for transport, used in Mail, News, Web, etc. See *MIME*.

Exchange—A groupware product made by Microsoft.

DOS—Disk Operating System. Computer system software that handles disk drive reads and writes, keyboard input, monitor display, file management, and other duties. Early PC users interacted directly with DOS, a command-driven interface.

FAQ—Frequently Asked Questions. An abbreviation used on news groups, conversation links, and file structures. When researching a new topic, look for files labeled FAQ for quick, beginning-user information.

Fiber Optic—An optical technology to carry high-speed communications. Optic cable is being used increasingly for network backbone links.

File Transfer Protocol—A set of communication rules that provides for error-free transfer of files across a computer-to-computer link.

FrontPad—A Web development software tool built into Explorer 4.0. This editing and development facility is a subset of Microsoft Front Page.

Front Page—Microsoft's full-featured World Wide Web development and editor software. Front Page provides a logical upgrade path from FrontPad for users who require a stronger development environment.

FTP—See *File Transfer Protocol*.

FYI—For Your Information. An e-mail and real-time link abbreviation.

GUI—Graphical User Interface. A computer program interface that lets users select operations by clicking on icons or other objects with a mouse. Microsoft Windows and the World Wide Web are graphical user interfaces to computer operations.

Graphical User Interface—*GUI*.

Hit—In database terminology, a found record. If you search a database for files on games, for example, and you locate 23 files, your search resulted in 23 "hits."

Host—A computer system that accepts local and remote log-ins to provide some type of computer service, such as running programs, conducting database searches, communications, and network access.

Home Page—An opening or beginning location for a World Wide Web site. Sometimes the term refers to the entire site, but more properly the term is used to refer only to the opening or starting location, the entry point for a Web site.

Hover—A mouse movement term. To *hover* means to move the mouse pointer over an on-screen object without pressing any mouse buttons. With the Explorer Active Desktop features, a hover operation can initiate actions, such as displaying the amount of available disk space on a selected drive or popping up a supplemental menu.

HTML—Hypertext Markup Language. The interpretive programming language used to develop World Wide Web sites.

HyperLink—A logical connection between two computer objects. HyperLinks are used to navigate among documents and hosts on the World Wide Web and, with Internet Explorer 4.0, among logical objects. HyperLinks within a word processing or database file, for example, can cause linked data to be displayed within the current application.

HTTP—Hypertext Transfer Protocol. The protocol used to deliver Web content from the server to the client.

HTTPS HTTP with encryption features. Prevents the reading of an intercepted transmission.

IMHO—In My Humble Opinion. An abbreviation used on e-mail and real-time computer links.

Interchange Points—A network-to-network link. Provides a set of services, such as e-mail, commonly to users of the linked networks.

Interoperability—The ability of computer hardware and software systems from different manufacturers to work together. Interoperability takes on different forms, from complete software and hardware compatibility, to the ability simply to exchange data from specific applications.

IRC—Internet Relay Chat. A real-time, channelized Internet service that allows multiple users to talk among themselves.

IMAP—Internet Mail Access Protocol. A standard for a client to get mail and send mail using a Mail server.

ISDN—Integrated Services Digital Network. A digital telephone standard that offers simultaneous use of two channels of digital data and voice. Data transport over ISDN is significantly faster and more reliable than analog phone lines.

ISP—Internet Service Provider. A company that provides Internet access via dial-up and dedicated lines for a fee.

Java—An object-oriented, interpreted programming language used in World Wide Web site development and other visual programming tasks.

Kermit—A file transfer protocol.

Listserv—An automated application that maintains mailing lists and other data.

Local Area Networks (LAN)—A grouping of local PCs and other computers that connects the machines via Ethernet or another networking protocol. A LAN lets the linked machines share files and printers, exchange e-mail, and the like. Many LANs include a communications gateway that allow users to communicate with dial-up services or other networks.

Log File—A form or capture file generated and managed by your communications software. A log file captures all characters and keystrokes during a communications session.

Metropolitan Area Networks—A form of local network that connects users across a metropolitan area.

MIME—An encoding protocol used for e-mail and World Wide Web content encoding for transport.

Modem—Modulator/demodulator. An electronic device that converts a computer's digital information into analog data for transmission across a dedicated line or dial-up link. A modem also converts the transmitted analog data back into digital information for use by the computer.

Multimedia—A general term that describes a graphical user interface that includes sound, animation, motion video, graphics, or other objects. Multimedia objects form an important part of today's online data environment.

NNTP—Network News Transport Protocol. The method for sending and receiving UseNet news, between your news client and the News servers, as well as between multiple News servers.

NT-1—Network Terminator Type 1. A converter required on ISDN lines, often built onto the TA or router being used.

Object—Generally, anything displayed on your computer desktop. A window, an Icon, a graphical image, even a menu, can be considered an object. In today's graphical desktop environment, many objects are considered "intelligent" (intelligent objects), since they contain attached program code that causes them to operate in a particular way.

Packets—Groups of data for transmission over a network. Packets include information for error correction in addition to the actual data being transmitted.

Peer-to-Peer—A computer-to-computer network relationship that makes each computer equal in power. Peer-to-peer networks allow all computers to share resources equally rather than having a single server through which all computers on the network must work.

Plug-in—A small applet that will become part of, and work with, a Web browser to provide functionality such as streaming audio or streaming video.

POP3—Post Office Protocol version 3. A standard for a client to get mail messages from a mail server.

PPP—Point to Point Protocol, a software application that lets a personal computer or very small network become a full-featured node on the Internet. The PPP protocol is frequently used instead of SLIP.

Protocol—See *File Transfer Protocol*.

Router—A network facility that manages communications links.

Server—A software application that manages the major part of the application in conjunction with a remote client application. Also, a portion of a distributed application.

Service Provider—A company or other entity that provides Internet or other computer services for third parties. An ISP.

Shell—A user interface that provides access to an operating system or other application.

SLIP—Serial Line Internet Protocol. Similar to PPP.

SPID—Service Profile Identifier. An ISDN telephone number.

SMTP—Simple Mail Transfer Protocol. The standard used for a client to send mail to a server, and for servers to deliver mail to other servers.

Streaming Audio/Video—A technology that uses a channel to deliver real-time audio and/or video broadcasts over networks.

Subscription—A technology that will download updates to Web pages to the local computer so that they are available for quick viewing when desired. In addition, it is possible to be notified of updates.

TA—Terminal Adapter. A device for use with an ISDN line that performs functions similar to the modem on an analog phone line.

Terminal Adapter—*TA*.

Tag—A formatting command in HTML. Easily recognizable because it is enclosed in pointed brackets (<>).

Tar—A UNIX-based application that groups multiple files into a single file for transmission over a network or between two computers through a dial-up link. This enables the transfer of a single file when multiple files are required for an application. Tar files are frequently compressed before they are transmitted.

TCP/IP—Transmission Control Protocol/Internet Protocol. Networking data transmission protocols used on the Internet.

Telnet—A local software tool that lets you log into remote computers, using a standard protocol. Telnet software can convert domain names to Internet addresses and use those addresses to locate the target computer. Once your system is attached to the target, a normal log-on sequence is initiated.

Text File—A computer file that contains only text characters and no graphics or special symbols. A text file can be edited with most UNIX or PC editors and can be displayed on a computer screen without using a special application.

Upload—The process of transmitting a local computer file up the network link to a remote computer system.

USENET—A bulletin board network system used to exchange special interest information. USENET was in existence before the Internet, but now a lot of USENET traffic is carried over the Internet.

User Interface—A software system that presents the personality of a given operating system or application. User interfaces can be either graphics-based or text-based. Most Internet user interfaces are text-based systems.

UUCP—UNIX-to-UNIX Copy. A built-in feature of UNIX that also can be used to provide users with e-mail and file transfer access to the Internet.

Virus—A software application designed to infect existing software with the aim of causing damage. Viruses are sometimes injected into networks and computer systems to harass the users and to damage data.

VBScript—A trimmed-down version of Microsoft's Visual basic that can be used in Web pages to perform simple programming tasks.

WAIS—Wide Area Information Servers. An Internet facility for managing and distributing a variety of data across the Internet.

WebView—An Internet Explorer 4.0 intrinsic feature that lets users view local or remote information as a Web page. WebView is used to configure the desktop display.

Whois—A UNIX command that displays the owner ID and other information about the domain or entity specified. The Whois command is followed by a domain argument: **whois microsoft.com**.

Wide Area Networks (WAN)—A network that connects users from many areas that transcend cities or other geographical boundaries.

Windows—A series of Microsoft operating systems that provide a graphical user interface.

Windows for Workgroups—A Microsoft Windows operating system that supports peer-to-peer networking.

World Wide Web—A software and hardware protocol used to distribute multimedia information across the Internet or an intranet. The Internet or an intranet is the physical connection of computers and other components. In contrast, the World Wide Web is a logical component, the information and information delivery systems that use the physical connection.

WWW—World Wide Web.

WYSIWYG—What You See Is What You Get. A description of a software application that allows the user to view on the screen a document as it will appear on a printer, Web page, or other output format.

XMODEM —A file transfer protocol.

Xywrite—A popular word processor among early PC users. Xywrite used embedded text commands to control document appearance and attributes in much the same way as HTML documents do today.

Z—A file designator in UNIX that shows the file with which it is associated compressed with the COMPRESS command. You must use UNCOMPRESS to expand the file before using it.

ZMODEM—A file transfer protocol.

I N D E X

8086, 9
86-DOS, 9

A

Accepting a call
    in NetMeeting, 183
Active Desktop, 2, 43, 93
ActiveX, 34
Address
    new, in Wallet, 117
Address Book
    components of, 166
    configuring, 166
    using, 166
Address Manager, 115
    importing and exporting data with, 170
    in Wallet, 115
Answering e-mail, 158
Applet, 34
Applications sharing
    in NetMeeting, 191
Attachments
    with e-mail, 154
Audio
    using tuning wizard in NetMeeting, 189
    using, in NetMeeting, 188
Audio communication
    in NetMeeting, 174
Audio tuning wizard, 189

B

Background
    custom, in browser, 103
Best of the Web, 95
Browser
    address manager in, 115
    content advisor in, 122
    customizing, 103
    edit menu, 226
    file menu, 226
    options dialog box in, 109
    security settings in, 122
    setting options, 108
    using, 97
    using certificates in, 125
    Wallet in, 115
Browser extensions, 34

C

Call
    new, in NetMeeting, 181
Call menu
    in NetMeeting, 237
Certificates
    how they work, 252
    in browser, 125
    obtaining a digital ID, 252

storing with e-mail, 169
using with e-mail, 259
Chat
   in NetMeeting, 173
   setting format in NetMeeting, 185
   using, in NetMeeting, 184
Client software
   World Wide Web, 18
Collaborating
   in NetMeeting, 192
Collaboration, 22
Command line interface, 10
Communications features, 22
Compose menu
   in Outlook Express, 236
Configuration options
   with Explorer 4.0, 44
Connecting
   with NetMeeting, 180
Contacts Manager, 165
Content Advisor, 122
   settings in, 123
Control Program for Microcomputers, 9
Cookies
   in FrontPad, 207
CP/M, 9
CPU, 9
Credit Card
   settings, in Wallet, 120

D

Desktop
   creating toolbar from, 129
   features, 93
   inserting HTML documents on, 102
   removing shortcuts from, 98
   using hyperlinks with, 99
Desktop images
   moving and sizing, 46
Desktop interface, 92
Desktop tab
   changing settings on, 46

Directory
   HTML display of, 99
Display properties dialog, 45
   desktop tab with, 46
DOS, 8
Downloading
   custom HTML page for desktop, 221
Draft folder
   using with e-mail, 160
Drag and Drop
   with Explorer 4.0, 96

E

Edit menu
   in FrontPad, 242
   in Internet Explorer, 226
   in NetMeeting, 238
   in Outlook Express, 233
   in Windows Explorer, 230
E-Mail
   account properties dialog box, 142
   addressing messages in, 153
   components, 140
   configuring in Outlook Express, 141
   creating new folders in, 161
   creating new messages in, 152
   HTML format with, 156
   leaving on host, 146
   reading, 157
   replying to, 158
   security with, 251
   send options for, 148
   sending & receiving messages, 156
   setting format for, 148
   setting read frequency for, 149
   setting security options in, 152
   setting servers for, 143
   setting signature for, 151
   setting spelling options for, 150
   settings for, 113
   specifying connections for, 144
   using attachments with, 154

using certificates with, 251
using draft folder with, 160
using hyperlinks with, 155
using personal certificates with, 169
using with Outlook Express, 140
viewing folder list in, 160
E-Mail address
    definition, 65
    with Outlook Express, 65
E-Mail Settings
    changing, with Outlook Express, 72
Encrypted messages, 259
Explorer 4.0
    browser features, 55
    browser options dialog box in, 109
    browser screen, 54
    changing color scheme with, 43
    components, 53
    configuration options, 44
    content advisor in, 122
    customizing browser in, 103
    desktop changes with, 41
    desktop enhancements with, 43
    desktop interface with, 92
    drag and drop with, 96
    exploring World Wide Web with, 136
    menu reference in, 225
    modifying task bar in, 126
    options, 59
    restoring taskbar icon for, 136
    security settings in, 122
    setting browser options in, 108
    Start menu with, 96
    subscriptions with, 57
    text labels with, 56
    tooltips with, 56
    using certificates in, 125
    using the browser, 97
    viewing local drives with, 130
    Web site subscriptions in, 104
    welcome message with, 45
    windows explorer in, 131
    Windows Explorer with, 94
    World Wide Web browser with, 54

Exporting data
    with address manager, 170

F

Favorites menu
    in Internet Explorer, 228
    in Outlook Express, 235
    in Windows Explorer, 231
Features
    Internet Explorer, 55
Features and settings
    in NetMeeting, 86
    Outlook Express, 71
File menu
    in FrontPad, 242
    in Internet Explorer, 226
    in NetShow, 240
    in Outlook Express, 233
    in Windows Explorer, 229
File properties
    in NetShow, 200
File Properties
    in Windows Explorer, 134
File sharing
    in NetMeeting, 191
File Types
    setting in browser, 115
Files
    attaching to e-mail, 154
Folder
    HTML display of, 99
Folder list
    viewing in e-mail, 160
Folders
    creating in e-mail, 161
Format menu
    in FrontPad, 244
FrontPad, 22, 203
    compared to Word, 82
    components in, 204
    configuring, 204
    cookies in, 207

creating desktop document with, 219
creating hyperlinks in, 222
description of, 80
editing HTML documents with, 102
features of, 81
launching, 80
menus in, 241
opening screen, 81
page properties in, 210
saving files in, 208
setting colors in, 212
setting margins in, 213
using components in, 205
using Marquee with, 216
using watermarks in, 212
using WebBots in, 215
viewing HTML in, 214, 220

G

Go menu
    in Internet Explorer, 227
    in NetMeeting, 238
    in NetShow, 241
    in Outlook Express, 235
    in Windows Explorer, 231
Graphical User Interface, 7, 11, 27
GUI, *See* Graphical User
    Interface

H

Help, 245
    options, 248
Help menu
    in FrontPad, 244
    in Internet Explorer, 228
    in NetMeeting, 240
    in NetShow, 241
    in Outlook Express, 237
    in Windows Explorer, 232
Host session
    limitations in, 194
Host Session

startring, in NetMeeting, 193
Hovering, 42
HTML, 2
    background & evolution, 28
    code example, 30
    code explained, 31
    definition, 27
    directory display with, 99
    documents on desktop, 102
    downloading custom page, 221
    editing with FrontPad, 102
    using, on desktop, 219
    viewing in FrontPad, 214, 220
    viewing source code, 30
HTML document
    views for, 32
HTML documents
    creating toolbars with, 130
Hyperlinks, 15, 16, 42
    creating, in FrontPad, 222
    on World Wide Web, 16
HyperLinks
    using with e-mail, 155
    with desktop, 99
Hypertext Markup Language
    definition, 27

I

IAYF, 19
IMAP
    e-mail servers, 144
Importing data
    with address manager, 170
Inbox Assistant
    configuring, 75
    with Outlook Express, 73
Information at your fingertips, 19
Information delivery features, 23
Insert menu
    in FrontPad, 243
Installation options, 25
    Explorer 4.0, 38
IntelliMouse, 50
    actions with, 50, 51

Internet Explorer
  communications features, 22
  definition, 1
  features, 20, 55
  install directory, 39
  installation options, 25, 38
  installing, 37
  links toolbar with, 55
  Microsoft definition, 19
  origins, 19
  system requirements, 37
  user-focused improvements, 20
  versions, 19
Internet Explorer screen, 54
Internet tutorial, 246
Interoperability, 8

J

Javascript
  definition, 33

L

Launching programs, 98
Leaving e-mail on host, 146

M

Mail Options
  setting in Outlook Express, 147
Margins
  setting, in FrontPad, 213
Markers
  displaying, in NetShow, 202
Marquee
  inserting, in FrontPad, 216
  properties, in FrontPad, 217
Menu reference, 225
Messages
  creating new, in e-mail, 152
Microsoft on the Web, 247

Multimedia, 15
My Computer
  changes with Explorer 4.0, 41
My Info
  entering, in NetMeeting, 178

N

NetMeeting, 83, 173
  accepting a call in, 183
  applications & file sharing in, 191
  audio communication in, 174
  audio tuning wizard in, 189
  collaborating in, 192
  components in, 173
  configuration wizard in, 84
  configuring, 174
  configuring video in, 177
  establishing a connection with, 180
  features and settings in, 86
  host sessions in, 193
  menus in, 237
  new call in, 181
  properties in, 87
  setting chat format in, 185
  setting My Info in, 178
  setting protocols in, 176
  sharinig applications in, 174
  speeddial with, 88
  troubleshooting Web site, 189
  using audio in, 188
  using Chat in, 184
  using speeddial in, 178
  using video in, 190
  using whiteboard in, 186
  video communication in, 174
Netscape
  plugins for, 34
NetShow, 89, 195
  components, 195
  configuring player, 196
  features of, 89
  file properties in, 200
  menus in, 240
  on-demand player in, 197

opening screen, 89
properties of, 91
system requirements for, 90
using components of, 199
Networked drive
displaying contents of, 135
New Technology (NT), 12
News
configuring, 162
in Outlook Express, 77, 162
News groups
downloading lists, 79
Newsgroup
subscribing to, 164

O

Object Oriented Programming, 33
On-demand player
properties in, 198
starting, 197
OOP, 33
Outlook Express, 22, 61, 139
address book in, 166
changing configuration of, 75
changing e-mail settings with, 72
changing News settings in, 77
components of, 139
configuration wizard with, 63
configuring e-mail in, 141
configuring News in, 162
contacts manager in, 165
desktop shortcuts for, 62
downloading News groups in, 79
e-mail address with, 65
e-mail components in, 140
e-mail connections in, 144
e-mail send options in, 148
e-mail spell check in, 150
features and settings, 71
inbox assistant with, 73
initial configuration, 62
main screen, 70
menus in, 232

reading e-mail in, 157
setting e-mail options in, 113
setting e-mail read frequency in, 149
setting mail options in, 147
subscribe to newsgroup in, 164
using e-mail with, 140
using News client in, 162

P

Page properties
in FrontPad, 210
Payment Manager, 118
Personalized Information Delivery, 23
Plugins
for Netscape, 34
POP3
e-mail servers, 144
Premium chanels, 24
Properties
file, in NetShow, 200
in on-demand player, 198
Protocols
setting in NetMeeting, 176

R

Reading e-mail, 157
Remote pointer
in whiteboard, 187
Removing shortcuts, 98
Restore desktop, 41
RISC Workstations, 18

S

Saving files
in FrontPad, 208
ScreenScan, 44
changing settings for, 47
with Explorer 4.0, 47

Security
    settings, in browser, 122
    with content advisor, 122
Sharing applications
    in NetMeeting, 174
Signature
    setting, for e-mail, 151
Site diagram
    World Wide Web, 17
Source code
    viewing on Web pages, 30
Source view
    in HTML, 32
SpeedDial
    in NetMeeting, 88, 178
SpeedDial menu
    in NetMeeting, 239
Spell Check
    in e-mail, 150
SQL, 18
Start Menu
    with Explorer 4.0, 96
Streaming audio, 34
Structured Query Language, 18
Subscribe
    options dialog box, 108
    to newsgroup, 164
    Web site in Explorer 4.0, 104
Subscription
    configuring, 107
    deleting, 107
    properties of, 105
    view all, 107
Subscriptions, 23, 57
    properties for, 58
System requirements
    Explorer 4.0, 37
    for NetShow, 90

T

Task Bar
    modifying, 126
Taskbar
    restoring Explorer icon on, 136

TCP/IP, 14
    using in NetMeeting, 176
Text Labels, 56
Thumbnail images
    in Windows Explorer, 133
Today's Links, 95
Toolbars
    adding to desktop, 129
    adding to task bar, 127
    expanding display of, 58, 59
Toolbars menu, 127
Tools menu
    in FrontPad, 244
    in NetMeeting, 239
    in Outlook Express, 236
ToolTips
    with Explorer 4.0, 56
Transfer Control Protocol/Internet
        Protocol, 14. *See* TCP/IP.

V

Verisign, 253
Video
    configuring in NetMeeting, 177
    using in NetMeeting, 190
Video communication
    in NetMeeting, 174
View
    subscriptions, 107
View menu
    in FrontPad, 243
    in Internet Explorer, 227
    in NetMeeting, 238
    in NetShow, 241
    in Outlook Express, 234
    in Windows Explorer, 230
Virtual Machine, 33
VM, *See* Virtual Machine

W

Wallet
    add address in, 117

address manager in, 115
credit card settings in, 120
payment manager in, 118
Watermark
in FrontPad, 212
Web browsers, 17
Web Gallery, 95
Web integration, 24
Web view
in HTML, 32
WebBots
using in FrontPad, 215
WFW, 11
What You See Is What You Get, 32
Whiteboard
in NetMeeting, 173
setting display screen size, 187
using remote pointer in, 187
using, in NetMeeting, 186
Window menu
in FrontPad, 244
Windows
background & history, 11
Windows 95, 13
Windows Address Manager, 117
Windows Explorer
menus in, 229
Windows Explorer, 94, 131
file properties display in, 134
thumbnail images in, 133
using, 132
Windows for Workgroups, 11
Windows NT, 12
Windows NT 4.0, 13
World Wide Web, 14
site diagram of, 17
WYSIWYG, 32